Transforming Learning

Also available in the Institute of Education series:

TRANSFORMING LEARNING: Individual and Global Change

Susan Askew and Eileen Carnell

CASSELL

London and Washington

Cassell

Wellington House
125 Strand
London WC2R 0BB

PO Box 605
Herndon
VA 20172

First published 1998

British Library Cataloguing-in-Publication Data
A catalogue record for this book is available from the British Library.

ISBN 0-304-33989-X (hardback)
0-304-33990-3 (paperback)

Typeset by York House Typographic Ltd, London
Printed and bound in Great Britain by Redwood Books, Trowbridge, Wiltshire

Contents

Figures and Tables

Preface

Tony Blair was only half right when he proclaimed that the nation's priority is 'Education, Education, Education'. We suggest that, rather, the emphasis should be on 'Learning, Learning, Learning'. At last the country at large, and the establishment, have reconnected with the importance of education and change, and our book is a modest contribution to what has become an urgent and impassioned debate, not just about education and schools, but about learning for life.

Our focus throughout the book is about learning and change. Change at individual, group, organization and societal levels. Change is urgent if we are to build a different society based on cooperation and peace. As Singh, former minister for education in India and member of the International Commission on Education for the Twenty-first Century, writes in the UNESCO report:

> We must have the courage to think globally, to break away from traditional paradigms and plunge boldly into the unknown. We must so mobilize our inner and outer resources that we begin consciously to build a new world based on mutually assured welfare rather than mutually assured destruction. As global citizens committed to human survival and welfare, we must use the latest array of innovative and interactive pedagogic methodologies to structure a world-wide programme of education – for children and adults alike – that would open their eyes to the reality of the dawning global age and their heart to the cry of the oppressed and the suffering. And there is no time to be lost for, along with the emergence of the global society, the sinister forces of fundamentalism and fanaticism, of exploitation and intimidation are also active. Let us, then, with utmost speed, pioneer and propagate a holistic educational philosophy for the twenty first century. . . . (Singh, 1996, p. 226)

This book suggests such a philosophy for the twenty-first century: the Transformatory Approach to Learning. *Transforming Learning* is timely. It coincides with major changes in educational and political reform. For example, in 1997 the government rejoined the United Nations Educational, Scientific and Cultural Organisation (UNESCO) after a twelve-year absence.

There is a dearth of theoretical understanding about the interconnection of the affective, social and cognitive dimensions of learning. Our goal in writing this book is to fill this gap. We believe our book will provide a much-needed theoretical approach, within which teachers can identify, understand, critique and develop their practice. We have drawn on our experience and research, to support our vision of what a developing effective learning society would look like.

Our conversations with teachers provide evidence to support our view of a shift away from content and outcomes within boundaried subjects, to a concern about learning, and the ways in which teachers can engage and support others in learning. Teachers we work with tell us that this was not addressed in their initial training.

Teachers also tell us that there is a need to focus on understanding their own professional development and their own personal-social learning. Teachers who have considered their own learning will be more able to implement the Transformatory Approach to Learning with other learners.

This work grew out of 46 years of our combined teaching experience and research into learning. We both work in the 'Assessment, Guidance and Effective Learning' academic group at the Institute of Education, University of London. We began our careers in the same school – a large mixed comprehensive in Central London – 23 years ago. Since this time we have worked in a variety of roles including Advisory Teachers, Inspectors and Lecturers in Higher Education, with teachers across all phases of education.

We have also worked with parents, governors and other professionals, supporting learning organizations. We have worked with children in the classroom and worked on action research projects. We have been involved with equal opportunities work. We have worked in units for young people with emotional and behavioural disturbance, and as support teachers for children who are learning English as a second language. We have worked in the areas of personal and social education, health education and sexuality education. We have been responsible for pastoral programmes, tutoring and counselling in educational organizations. We have been concerned with the management of pastoral systems, relationships between school and home, and professional networks, tutoring and achievement. Our experiences in different settings, and with different groups, have led us to the belief that learning at deep rather than surface levels leads to lasting change, and that it comes about through a holistic approach encompassing the emotional, social and cognitive dimensions. We take a positive stance, believing that individual change can lead to organizational and societal change.

The book presents a controversial argument. This argument is a culmination of our own ideas, our own teaching experience and our own action research. Where appropriate we draw on the writing and research of others, to support our central argument. Some chapters present our ideas and theories; some chapters focus on our assumptions, and are supported by evidence from others; other chapters have a more practical base. Within some chapters there is a combination of these writing approaches. Our approach reflects our varied roles as classroom teachers, researchers and academics, and our experience of working in schools, education authorities, and higher educational establishments. We hope this combination will appeal to practitioners who have a scholarly interest in these issues.

The book is written for all who are concerned with learning and particularly with learning in formal educational organizations. It is relevant to teachers in all phases of education including higher education.

Susan Askew
Eileen Carnell
March 1998

Acknowledgements

We would like to thank the many people who gave us their support and encouragement. We would especially like to thank the teachers with whom we worked for giving so generously of their time. We appreciate the help of the young people we met in schools who inspired us to write this book. Our thanks are also due to Isobel Larkin, who proofread and gave us invaluable feedback on draft work; and our colleagues in the Assessment, Guidance and Effective Learning academic group at the Institute of Education for discussion about issues in learning. Finally we would like to thank each other for all we have learned about working collaboratively and the value of joint writing.

Introduction

Transforming Learning: Individual and Global Change introduces a new approach to learning: 'The Transformatory Approach'. We call our approach transformatory because we believe that effective learning involves change in the way we perceive ourselves and our experiences. Following this change in perception will be change in behaviour which will ultimately change our relationships and society.

This book has two main foci:

1. An emphasis on learning leading to change, highlighting the importance of the individual in bringing about change. Change in society is not enduring unless people change.
2. An emphasis on a holistic approach to learning which gives equal value to the emotional and social as well as the cognitive dimensions of learning. This is explored in relation to the learner, the learning context and the learning process. We challenge traditional views of learning which stress only the cognitive dimension.

The Transformatory Approach is fundamentally concerned with change at a societal level, and we believe that group, organizational and societal change comes about from individual change. We recognize that all change is difficult; it involves a long process, and there are external pressures which militate against change and impose changes we do not want. For example, in our experience of education we have seen many innovations, the most striking being the 30-year revolving debate from the instructional model of education, passing through child-centred enquiry and back again to the newly fashionable instructional model. This reflects political change over the same period. We argue that these innovations are at a 'surface' level because they are (a) imposed externally rather than being congruent with the values of those affected by the innovation, and (b) not based on the personal understanding and meaning of the learners. These 'surface' innovations can be implemented because they are linked to external resourcing and inspection and support the belief that change is happening. We argue that this is 'innovation without change' (Hoyle, 1986a). 'Surface' innovations do not have lasting impact.

In the Transformatory Approach, learning brings about change, and change is an opportunity for learning. Change in the Transformatory Approach involves understanding and a commitment to change in the practice of learners. In other words it is a 'deep' rather than 'surface' approach to change and is related to 'changing the meaning of experience' (Novak and Gowin, 1984). Deep change comes about when values inherent in the change are congruent with personal values. In the Transformatory Approach to Learning, change is not imposed externally, but is initiated by the individual, as a part of their commitment to growth and development. Deep change is a necessary part of self-actualization.

Our approach to learning stresses the transformatory power of being constantly engaged in a process of reflecting, learning and actions for change. The Transformatory Approach to Learning assumes that this process becomes part of the learner's way of being.

Part 1 outlines the Transformatory Approach and relates it to key theories of learning, of learners, of contexts and learning processes. We examine underlying assumptions in relation to all these aspects of the approach.

Part 2 is concerned with learning in formal educational settings. It explores the relation between the Transformatory Approach to Learning and models of education, and shows how the Transformatory Approach can be practically applied in classrooms and in learning organizations.

Part 3 takes the argument for a holistic approach to learning further, by showing how professional development for teachers in all phases of education is based on the Transformatory Approach.

PART 1: THE TRANSFORMATORY APPROACH TO LEARNING

In Chapter 1, 'Transforming Learning: Beyond the Cognitive Dimension', we introduce the Transformatory Approach to Learning and emphasize the learner, the learning context and the learning process, as interrelated aspects of our approach. We show how our approach to learning is aligned with some of the central theories of learning, including behaviourist, cognitive and humanist theories. The chapter explores two central questions: What are the problems associated with traditional theories of learning? and What is unique about our approach to learning?

In the next four chapters we focus on the learner, the group context, the social context and the learning process. While the learner, context and process are, in fact, indivisible, we are nevertheless attempting to explore them separately in order to analyse them fully.

Chapter 2, 'Inspiring Change: The Learner', outlines and makes a case for our assumptions and perceptions of 'learners' within the Transformatory Approach, which we introduced in Chapter 1. Among other questions, it asks: What is the relationship between the emotional, social and cognitive dimensions of learning? Is capacity for learning fixed? Do individual learners approach learning differently? In what sense is learning a subjective activity?

Chapter 3, 'Evolving through Collaboration: The Group Context', argues that learning is more effective when undertaken in groups. Collaborative learning engages learners actively in the learning process through enquiry and discussion with peers in small groups. This chapter asks such questions as: Do groups learn? How can a group context help individual learning? How do relationships in the group affect learning? How can we foster learning in the group?

Chapter 4, 'Moving Mountains: The Social Context' explores the social context within which learning occurs. This chapter discusses the Transformatory Approach to Learning, having in mind the dilemma between focusing on change in the individual and focusing on changing the social order. It explores the way stereotypes and expectations affect learning and how identity as learners is constructed and deconstructed, and considers how diversity can be recognized within social groups.

Chapter 5, 'Cycles of Change: The Action Learning Process', is the next stage of exploring the Transformatory Approach to Learning. We move the focus from the learner and learning context discussed in the previous chapters, and concentrate on process. We discuss important questions such as: What is the action learning process? How are cycles of learning understood? How does engagement in the action learning process help people learn about learning?

'Cycles of Change' demonstrates how change comes about through the action learning process. This process is key in transforming the individual and the learning context.

PART 2: EDUCATIONAL METAMORPHOSIS

Chapter 6, 'Developing Educational Frameworks', provides a typology of different models of education and explores the goals and concepts which underpin them: the Functionalist; the Client-centred; the Liberatory and the Social Justice models. It examines the ways in which the Transformatory Approach to Learning, discussed in Part 1, embodies the practical application of the Liberatory model of education. This chapter analyses educational frameworks within which the Transformatory Approach can be understood and applied.

Chapter 7, 'Facilitating Change in Classrooms', examines the practical implications of the Transformatory Approach. The chapter relates this to the values underpinning the Liberatory model of education discussed in Chapter 6. The chapter asks: What is the teacher's role in relation to the learner? What is the role of the learner? Collaborative group work is explored as essential to the process of implementing the Transformatory Approach in the classroom. Two case studies are presented which illustrate the principles in practice.

Chapter 8, 'Transforming Organizations', explores the concept of organization and the possibility of change and learning within it. The Transformatory Approach to Learning will flourish where there is congruence throughout the organization. This chapter explores perspectives on change, change strategies, and the role of action research.

PART 3: REFRAMING PROFESSIONAL DEVELOPMENT

Chapter 9, 'Learning on the Job: Action Research', considers action research as a form of teachers' professional development. It makes important links between the Transformatory Approach to Learning and action research. We argue that action research is more effective than many other forms of professional development because its *raison d'être* is change in practice. The chapter explores the purposes, advantages and limitations of action research and compares this approach to other research. This chapter makes key distinctions between action learning and action research and highlights the similarities in the process.

The final chapter, Chapter 10, 'Time for Change: Conceptualizing Teachers' Learning', focuses on planned professional experiences for teachers. It is argued that the approach to learning outlined in the Transformatory Approach is equally applicable to teachers' learning: the personal and professional development of teachers go hand in hand. The affective and social dimensions of learning are as important as the cognitive dimension. This chapter draws on action research into teachers' professional development.

We conclude by summarizing the central argument of the book; change is necessary at the levels of the individual, group and organization in order to bring about changes in society. We believe our approach makes a major contribution to the priorities defined by the Report to UNESCO (1996) of the International Commission on Education for the Twenty-first Century:

> It is the view of the Commission that, while education is an ongoing process of improving knowledge and skills, it is also – perhaps primarily – an exceptional means of bringing about personal development and building relationships among individuals, groups and nations. (UNESCO, 1996)

A Transformatory Approach to Learning can contribute to the development of an equitable and peaceful global society.

Part 1

The Transformatory Approach to Learning

ONE

Transforming Learning: Beyond the Cognitive Dimension

This chapter introduces a new approach to learning: The Transformatory Approach. In this chapter we challenge views about learning which stress individual cognitive development. We argue that a holistic approach to learning is necessary, which emphasizes the interconnection between the emotional, social, spiritual, physical and cognitive dimensions.

The Transformatory Approach integrates a focus on the learner, the group, social context and the action learning process (see Figure 1.1). While other models of learning pay attention to learners, contexts and processes, the Transformatory Approach presents a new way of perceiving them because it explores their interconnection, and subsequently argues that effective learning includes explicit discourse on this. Our approach is concerned with learning as a social event, taking place in social situations. From an individualistic view of learning, the Transformatory Approach shifts to a view of learning as multi-dimensional and complex.

The Transformatory Approach defines effective learning as learning that leads to change at the level of the individual, the group, the organization and, ultimately, society. Unlike the behaviourist model, we see change in behaviour as consequent upon change in 'the meaning of experience' (Novak and Gowin, 1984). Positive change is most likely to occur when the learning process is used to make connections between learners and contexts (see Chapter 5).

The Transformatory Approach presents a new approach to learning. It involves understanding that:

- the self is central in the learning process
- the learner has an impact on the context and the context impacts on the learner
- the action learning process involves learning about learning

The chapter continues by exploring the assumptions on which the Transformatory Approach to Learning is based.

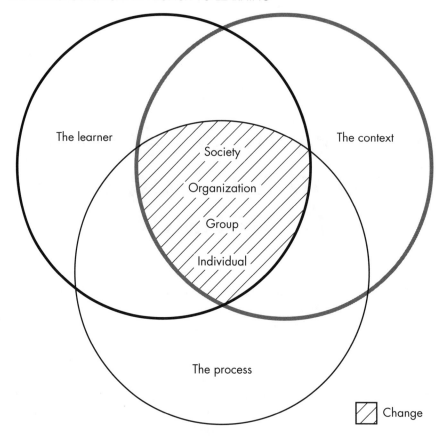

Figure 1.1 The Transformatory Approach to Learning

THE LEARNER

- the self is central in the learning process
- learners are striving towards self-actualization
- everyone wants to learn
- learners have an equal potential for learning
- learners have control over what they are learning
- learners progress through stages of either dependence or independence towards interdependence
- learners are prepared to take risks
- the whole person, including emotional, social, spiritual, physical and cognitive aspects, is involved in learning
- the emotional state of the learner affects the capacity to learn
- capacity for learning is not fixed and can be increased
- capacity for learning increases as learning increases
- capacity for learning increases when learners understand themselves as learners
- learners' past experiences influence their learning in the present
- learners experience situations differently and therefore learn different things from the same situation

- learners make decisions about whether to learn or not in particular contexts
- only the learner is in the position to identify and tell others what they have learned
- only the learners can evaluate what they have learned
- learners may approach the same task differently
- learners of the same social group may approach learning differently from learners of another social group

CONTEXT
Group

- groups are more effective in bringing about change than individuals
- individual change is facilitated by the support of the group
- learning is more effective in a collaborative group
- in a social situation, the group is a catalyst for learning as well as a source of learning
- feedback from others is a valuable part of the learning process
- different points of view, perspectives and experiences enrich learning
- learners have support and encouragement to take risks and make changes; be dependent, independent and interdependent
- learners learn about relationships by being in relationships
- conflict and controversy are essential aspects of learning
- learning in a group leads to a feeling of social identity and belonging
- the facilitator is instrumental in establishing the group culture
- the group takes responsibility for ensuring that structures are in place to facilitate learning
- individuals need to learn how to learn in a group in order for learning in the group to be effective
- in order for learning in a group to be effective, the group needs to address the different roles taken by different individuals at different times
- the group is affected by individuals and also develops independently of individuals in the group

Social

- effective change encompasses change at both the individual and social levels
- social change follows from learning and change at the individual level
- expectations and stereotypes about people affect learning
- learning is affected by sex, ethnicity and socio-economic position
- learning roles and styles are gendered
- our individual identity is socially constructed
- through the learning process of self-reflection, reflection on experiences, abstraction and generalization we are capable of deconstructing our identity
- the learning discourse affects what we understand and value
- the dominant learning discourse is determined by powerful groups in society

- there are conflicting learning discourses in society
- discussion of inequality in education and society must be part of the learning process
- discussion about how the social context affects learning must be part of the learning process
- the interrelationship between personal and social is valid discourse in the classroom
- diversity needs to be recognized within social groups

THE LEARNING PROCESS

- the action learning process transforms individuals and groups
- action learning changes the meaning of experience
- the process involves understanding, constructing knowledge, making connections, taking control and taking action
- learning never stops; all experiences contribute to learning throughout life
- reflection on experience is an essential part of action learning
- reflection on self as learner and context of learning is essential in the action learning process
- making the learning explicit is an essential part of action learning
- action is an essential stage in learning
- applying the learning is an essential stage of action learning
- feedback is an important aspect of reviewing, learning and taking action
- learning about learning is essential for effective learning
- the effect of the emotions on learning is valid discourse
- the effect of the learning context, and the interconnection of the context, learner and process, is valid discourse

The assumptions underpinning the Transformatory Approach are discussed in detail in the following chapters: Chapter 2 explores the learner, Chapter 3 focuses on the group context, Chapter 4 considers the social context and Chapter 5 examines the learning process.

This chapter continues by outlining some of the theories of learning which have been influential in the twentieth century so that the Transformatory Approach can be placed in its historical context. We think it is important to include this to enable an understanding of how the Transformatory Approach has built on, and developed from, previous ideas and thinking about learning. The Transformatory Approach transcends learning theory in that it is concerned with:

- a holistic and organismic model;
- the interconnection between all the dimensions of learning;
- learning leading to change in individuals, groups, organizations and society.

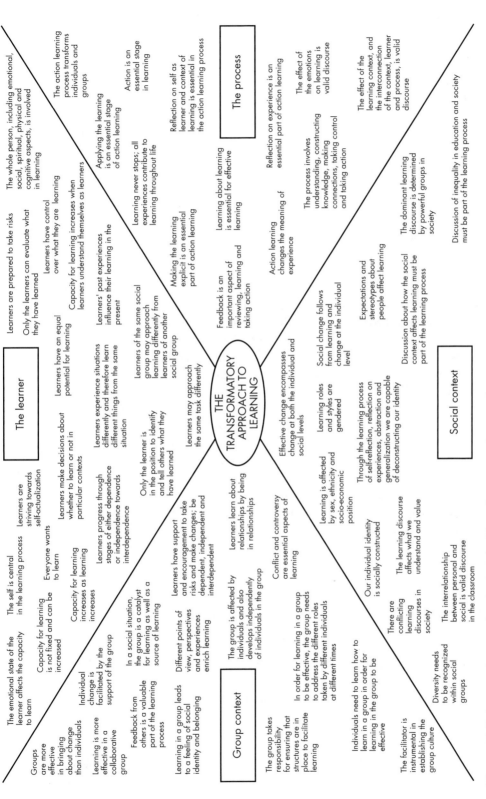

Figure 1.2 Assumptions underpinning the Transformatory Approach

MECHANISTIC AND ORGANISMIC MODELS OF THE UNIVERSE

Traditional approaches to learning and teaching stress behaviourist and cognitive aspects of development and learning, rather than emotional and social aspects. For almost a century education was influenced by psychologists working within a behaviourist tradition. In the 1920s the cognitive theories developed by Piaget gained prominence. His work is related to understanding differences in cognitive functioning at various ages rather than with learning *per se*.

Theories of learning are based on models of the universe, the person and their view of reality. In social science, a model is generally seen as a recreation of aspects of society which helps us identify key relations or to relate causes to their effects. Models help construct explanations.

The two models of the universe explored in this chapter are the mechanistic world-view and the organismic world-view (Reese and Overton, 1970). The mechanistic view sees the universe and people as machine-like. From this perspective, the universe is a machine composed of discrete parts. Movement and change in one part of the machine causes a chain-like reaction in the others. In theory, the effects of change can be predicted and measured. Essentially this view represents people as reactive, passive, robot-like, and as empty organisms which are inherently at rest. Activity is viewed as a result of external forces. In this model, thinking, wanting and perceiving are all reactions to external cues rather than the result of internal changes within the organism.

The organismic model presents a more holistic view stressing interaction and development of the organism. The term holistic comes from the Greek *holos* – whole – the concept refers to an understanding of reality in terms of integrated wholes, whose properties cannot be reduced to those of smaller units. In education, the focus on cognition at the expense of emotion or intuition has produced a hierarchy of human attributes. This mechanistic view is challenged by developments in science. It is argued that a focus on division and separation does not accurately reflect the way the world is and how we experience it. For example, until recently memories were thought to reside in compact bands of neurons in the brain. Scientists now believe that memories are not found in any single molecule or neural group:

> Memory is a dynamic property of the brain as a whole rather than of any one specific region. Memory resides simultaneously everywhere and nowhere in the brain. (Rose, quoted in *Time* magazine, 5 May 1997, p. 44)

The scientist Capra (1983) suggests that the mechanistic world-view of Newton and Descartes has brought us perilously close to destruction. Capra advocates a new vision which is systems-based and holistic, and more consistent with the findings of modern physics:

> This theory of integration and wholeness stands in contrast to the traditional theory of reductionism which demonstrates a preoccupation with seeking explanations to phenomena through fragmentation into smaller and smaller constituent parts.

Human activity, like traditional scientific theorizing, is characterized by division and distinction. Human endeavour is circumscribed within concepts of nationhood, language, religion, race, gender, class and economic wherewithal. We are labelled and compartmentalized according to such criteria and, in order to protect our interests, we learn to be secretive, devious and manipulative. We frequently come to regard others, especially those who are in different circumstances, as enemies to be feared, resisted, shunned, discriminated against, and in extreme situations, to be fought against and killed. What is worse, we have come to believe that these behaviours are both inevitable and acceptable and so we teach them to our children. (Capra, 1983, p. 35)

In the organismic model, the universe is perceived as organic rather than mechanical in nature. In a mechanical view the universe is seen as the sum of its parts, whereas in the organismic view it is the 'whole which constitutes the condition of the meaning and existence of its parts' (Reese and Overton, 1970, p. 133).

The difference between the mechanistic and organismic views of people and the universe can be illustrated by differences in approaches to medicine. In Western medicine, for example, if a person visited the doctor with a knee problem, the knee would be treated. This is a traditional mechanistic view, but in an organismic view, for example in holistic medicine, the knee condition would be seen as an outcome of imbalance in the organism, and the whole person would be treated.

In the organismic view, substance in the universe is perceived as active rather than static.

From such a point of view, one element can never be like another, and as a consequence, the logic of discovering reality according to the analytical ideal of reducing the many qualitative differences to the one is repudiated. In its place is substituted a search for unity among the many; that is, a pluralistic universe is substituted for a monistic one, and it is the diversity which constitutes the unity ... thus, unity is found in multiplicity, being is found in becoming, and constancy is found in change. (Reese and Overton, 1970, p. 133)

This view sees the person as an inherently and spontaneously active organism rather than a reactive one. Action is not initiated by external forces, but the organism is the source of acts. The person is perceived as an organized entity. This view does not look for cause and effect but for the interrelationship between the parts:

Inquiry is directed toward the discovery of principles of organization, toward the explanation of the nature and relation of parts and wholes, structures and functions rather than toward the derivation of these from elementary processes. (Reese and Overton, 1970, pp. 133–4)

This view stresses the role of experience, rather than training, in bringing about change within the organism and, rather than measuring change, it emphasizes the quality and process of change:

> The individual who accepts this model will tend to emphasize the significance of processes over products and qualitative change over quantitative change ... in addition he [sic] will tend to emphasize the significance of the role of experience in facilitating or inhibiting the course of development, rather than the effect of training as the source of development. (Reese and Overton, 1970, p. 134)

An organismic approach looks at the interrelationship between personal and social dimensions for bringing about change. The mechanistic model focuses on one or the other for bringing about change, and polarizes the personal and social – it argues that these are separate and conflicting.

The mechanistic view has underpinned most theories of learning in the twentieth century. We propose that learning for the twenty-first century needs to be holistic and organismic. Boud, Cohen and Walker concur:

> Learning is normally experienced as a seamless whole; there is a large degree of continuity between all our experiences even while we label them as different. Much writing about learning has treated it as if it existed in different domains which are separated from each other. A common division is between the cognitive (concerned with thinking), the affective (concerned with values and feelings) and the conative or psychomotor (concerned with action and doing). Although it can at times be useful to think of the different aspects of learning, no one aspect is discrete and independent of the rest and no one aspect should generally be privileged over the rest. (Boud *et al.*, 1993, p. 12)

In the West the mechanistic view has dominated science, education, medicine and all other major disciplines. The way knowledge is organized into distinct disciplines is itself mechanistic. This is reflected in the subject-based curriculum in school. Models of education and their relation to these views are considered in Chapter 2.

This chapter continues by exploring theories of learning in relation to mechanistic and organismic models.

THEORIES OF LEARNING BASED ON THE MECHANISTIC MODEL

One of the most influential theories of learning is behaviourist theory. Behaviourist research investigates learning from a mechanistic perspective. The basic assumption of behaviourism is that behaviour is shaped by the environment. Social learning theories developed from behaviourist theory, but differ from it with regard to the actual mechanism used to explain social learning; for example reinforcement, identification or imitation.

John B. Watson (1876–1958) is credited as the founder of behaviourism. Watson rules out the content of a person's consciousness as valid data for investigation, since it is not open to direct inspection or measurement by others. (This was, in part, a reaction to the work of Freud.) To Watson a science of psychology comprises the study of the relationship between a stimulus and the response – both observable data and measurable events. Learning consists of a change to behaviour measured in terms of a change in the response to stimulus. Subsequent behaviourists proposed that learning involves more than just a response to a stimulus. For example, Skinner showed how a subject operates upon the environment.

Behaviourist theories of learning are problematic for a variety of reasons. They do not view the organism as creating, choosing between options, acting on the environment to control it or problem-solving. This theory is limited in the way in which learning is evaluated, as learning is measured by an external agent in terms of observable changes in behaviour rather than by, for example, personal reflection on the part of the learner.

Edward C. Tolman (1886–1959) links the mechanistic and organismic models. Tolman presents a cognitive model of learning which he called 'Purposive Behaviourism'. He argues that rather than being a stereotypical response to stimuli, behaviour is directed towards a goal. Rather than learning a response, the organism learns the route to the goal. In the cognitive account, for example, an organism learns facts (or cognitions) not responses. This cognitive model attempts to account for the relationship between input and output – it does not prescribe how learning is utilized but takes into account the organism's goal and its capacity for flexibility of behaviour in the face of varying environmental conditions. Tolman concludes that behaviour is purposive and depends upon what the organism has learned, the expectancy of what is at the goal and the prevailing circumstances. If behaviour is purposive, then an organism is able to predict and control its environment.

Tolman's theory of learning is behaviouristic in the sense that, like Watson, he rejects introspection as a scientific method and is concerned with observable and measurable outcomes. He shifts from the mechanistic view towards the organismic because he views learning as more than cause and effect, and views the organism as more than passive, responding to an external stimulus. His concept of behaviour as purposive is an organismic one. However, Tolman's Purposive Behaviourism theory does not recognize the enormous complexity of the interrelationship between input and output. The organismic theory would not see the organism as developing cognitive maps in response to separate stimuli. It suggests organisms perceive stimuli in organized wholes. In the organismic view, perceptions of stimuli differ from organism to organism depending on previous experience: emotional state; analysis of consequences resulting from previous response to stimuli; connections and patterns made in relation to present and previous similar stimuli. In the organismic view the organism makes judgements, thinks, feels, has choices, takes actions, reflects, learns from experiences, plans future learning and prioritizes goals.

THEORIES OF LEARNING BASED ON THE ORGANISMIC MODEL

1. Cognitive models

The cognitive model of intelligence sees behaviour as mediated by cognitions which are used to represent the environment. In humans, these mental representations are apparently unlimited because of the availability of language. Perhaps the best-known cognitive model of intelligence is Piaget's. Piaget saw his task as building a description of how intelligence develops. He proposed that children's mental abilities develop through a regular series of stages. Piaget thought that children's ideas are neither innate (because they are not present at birth and change as children get older) nor learned in the behaviourist sense, as they are not taught by adults nor are they a reaction to stimulus in the environment. Piaget's thesis is that children construct their view of the world by acting on it, internalizing what is learned from experience and developing new mental concepts which enable them to adapt intelligently to reality. The child is innately predisposed to develop into an intelligent being, but this can only come about through interaction with the environment. Piaget based his work on observation of children's behaviour.

Two major ideas in Piaget's theory are centration and egocentrism. Centration refers to the ability to deal only with a single aspect of a situation. Ego-centricism means the absence of conscious awareness of the separate existence of others. Another key concept is representation – we internalize knowledge which is represented in the mind in some way; language is a key form of representation. Mental representations are not necessarily conscious, it is only later in development that an individual becomes conscious of them.

Piaget proposed four developmental stages. These are:

- the sensorimotor stage (approximately birth to age two). At this stage babies are concerned with mastering the links between their behaviour and its effects on the world. The young child learns that movement is not a random collection of unconnected actions, but a coordinated set of possibilities for manipulating the world. This stage sees the achievement of 'concrete operations'.
- the pre-operational stage (approximately between two and seven years). At this stage, the child's thinking is intuitive and egocentric. Things are as they seem to be. Children are unable to distinguish their perspective from that of others. They are unable to decentre and to empathize with different points of view.
- the concrete operational stage (approximately seven to thirteen years). The child develops an ability to employ logical thought-processes which involve making inferences. The child understands that objects may undergo transformation and yet remain the same. However, the child lacks the ability to conceptualize, abstract or consider hypothetical situations.
- the formal operational stage (from about thirteen years). At this stage the child can construct a formal logical theory of events, can construct hypthotheses and abstract concepts.

Piaget believed that children learn to think in an abstract way because they can adapt to their environment. They are self-regulating systems. The human organism constantly strives to achieve stability or equilibrium as imbalance or conflict is an unpleasant state.

Perhaps Piaget's most important contribution was his belief that children's cognitive development was a result of an interaction between the child and the environment. However, he did not include the social or cultural context as being part of the 'environment'. Piaget's saw children as 'little scientists' who make their own discoveries about the world. The teacher's role is to observe what stage the child has reached and to facilitate the making of these discoveries through appropriate nurture and stimuli. Piaget's work shifted opinion away from the view that child development is completely predetermined by biology and the view that children are essentially empty vessels to be filled with knowledge by adults, towards a more 'interactionist' approach looking at the interaction between child and environment.

Piaget's view of child development is congruent with the individualistic tradition of the Enlightenment with its emphasis on positivism, rationality and cognition. As such it fitted ideologies and the social organization developed during that period of industrial capitalism. In particular the rise of 'science' as a major form of legitimation happened at this time (Walkerdine, 1984, 1990). The cognitive view suggests that childhood is qualitatively different from adulthood. In modern Western industrial countries this notion is so obvious that it is generally regarded as 'common sense' rather than as socially constructed.

Piaget's work influenced the Plowden Report on primary education (Plowden Report, 1967). In practice many primary schools may not have organized learning through exploration, discovery and play (Galton *et al.*, 1980; Edwards and Mercer, 1989; Tizard *et al.*, 1988). Nevertheless, the ideas underpinning Plowden, including 'discovery learning' and 'stages of development' played an important part in shaping how we thought of primary education until the late 1980s.

While Piaget sees people as acting on their environment rather than reacting to the environment, nevertheless he neglects social aspects of the environment. For example, his theory does not take account of the different ways in which boys and girls may learn to act on the environment. Piaget also ignores emotional and motivational aspects of cognitive development. Piaget is not interested in how children become social people but in how they become thinking 'cognitive' people.

Other researchers seeking to explain cognitive processes have gone beyond Piaget to show how children come to understand the social world, the world of other people and their feelings, meanings and intentions. For example, Donaldson (1978) argued that contrary to Piaget's view, social and intellectual aspects of development are intimately connected, and that all the tasks which Piaget used with children had important social dimensions. She claimed that young children have an awareness of perspectives other than their own and that children must be able to make sense of any task socially before they can fully understand it.

Piaget's theory is individualistic because it stresses the child's individual adaptation to the physical world. However, other cognitive theorists stress the social role of adults in learning.

Vygotsky (1962), for example, sees children as having a zone of proximal development: a spectrum of achievement attainable only with the support of an adult. He is interested in what children can do with help, and with the ways in which adult–child interaction structures the development of children's thinking. The implications for teaching are that it involves a social exchange in which shared meanings are built through joint activity.

Criticisms of Piaget, Bruner and other cognitive theorists (Jones, 1968) include that they are unbalanced in their over-emphasis on cognitive skills at the expense of emotional development; that they are preoccupied with:

> the aggressive, agentic and autonomous motives to the exclusion of the homony-mous, libidinal, and communal motives and that they concern themselves with concept attainment to the exclusion of concept formation or invention. (Jones, 1968, p. 97)

Novak and Gowin challenge conventional behaviourist wisdom about learning as well as the neglect of feelings by cognitive scientists. They write:

> We reject this view, (that learning is synonymous with a change in behaviour) and observe instead that learning by humans leads to a change in the meaning of experience … Furthermore, behavioural psychology, and much of currently popular 'cognitive science', neglects the experience of feelings … Human experi-ence involves not only thinking and acting but also feeling, and it is only when all three are considered together that individuals can be empowered to enrich the meaning of their experience. (Novak and Gowin, 1984, p. xi)

2. Insight learning theories

A break with behaviourism also came with insight learning in the Gestalt theories of Wertheimer, Koffka and Köhler. They dispute that learning consists of the simple connection of responses to stimuli. They argue that experience is always structured and that we react to a complex pattern of stimuli, not to a mass of separate details. Stimuli need to be seen in organized wholes not in disconnected parts. Gestalt psychology is generally classified as within the family of field theories. These theories propose that the total pattern or field of forces, stimuli or events determines learning.

Lewin (1951) developed field theory. Lewin places more emphasis on motivation than any of the preceding theories. He conceptualizes each individual being in a life space in which many forces are operating. The life space includes environment features to which the individual reacts. This includes material objects which the person encounters and manipulates, people in the environment, goals, fantasies, tensions and thoughts. Behaviour is the outcome of an interplay between all these forces. Learning occurs as a result of changing cognitive structures which are in turn a result of two types of forces: change in the structure of the cognitive field itself or change in the internal needs or motivation of the individual. Lewin is interested in group and institutional dynamics because he believes the strongest forces affecting an individual's psychological field are other people.

3. Humanistic psychology

Humanistic psychology emerged in the 1950s. Founders included Kelly, Maslow and Rogers. Humanistic psychology was a reaction against the psychology of the time. This included both experimental psychology, which was influenced by behaviourism and tended to disregard consciousness as a legitimate study, and psychoanalysis, where the primary focus was interpreting consciousness and behaviour in terms of unconscious determinants. The humanistic view sees people as conscious agents. Humanism emphasizes individual experience and the attempt to understand personal motivation. It explores possibilities for action and the potential for change and personal growth.

Humanistic psychologists attempt to do justice to people's conscious experiences of themselves and their role in directing their lives. It stresses the sense of self-awareness and the capacity to reflect. Humanism is an orientation toward study of mental life rather than a 'school' of psychologists adopting common modes of research or a coherent set of ideas and theories. Instead of studying people as a natural scientist might, humanist psychology starts with the experience of being a person. Humanism stresses that for effective understanding in psychology we need to take into account:

- the significance of conscious awareness – this requires a focus on subjective awareness; an experiential approach (also known as a 'phenomenological' approach because it focuses on phenomena – things as they appear to us). An existential perspective stresses our awareness of the passing of time, of our mortality, of being distinct individuals who are inside ourselves and separate from others.
- the human capacity for personal agency – this stresses our power to choose. We can play a part in creating the kind of person we become. The best way to do this is to become as aware as possible of our feelings, motivations and what influences us. This process is called personal growth.
- each person as a whole – there are many aspects of our sense of self, and we need to consider them all (a holistic approach). These aspects include physical awareness, spiritual commitment, the social context, our feelings and thoughts.

Maslow's (1972) perspective, unlike psychoanalysis, did not focus on people with neuroses and problems, but on exploring the healthy personality. In his theory of motivation, Maslow argues that the needs of humans form a hierarchy which reflects their emergence both in terms of evolution and in the life of the individual (see Figure 1.3). These needs are physiological (food, drink, sex), safety (physical, emotional, economic), need for love and belonging (affection, intimacy, roots in family or group), need for esteem (competence, adequacy, self-respect and respect of others) and the need for self-actualization (becoming what one is capable of becoming).

Maslow studied public and historical figures whom he considered to be self-actualized. He argues that they are generally devoted to working at something crucial to them, are non-evaluative and accepting, creative, spontaneous, natural, capable of deep intimacy, but also enjoy being alone. According to Maslow (1972), the goal of learning is that of self-actualization. He sees growth towards this goal as being determined by two sets of forces operating within each individual:

One set clings to safety and defensiveness out of fear, tending to regress backward, hanging on to the past . . . the other set of forces impels him [sic] toward wholeness, to Self and uniqueness of Self, toward full functioning of all his [sic] capacities . . . we grow forward when the delights of growth and anxieties of safety are greater than the anxieties of growth and the delights of safety. (Maslow, 1972, pp. 44–5)

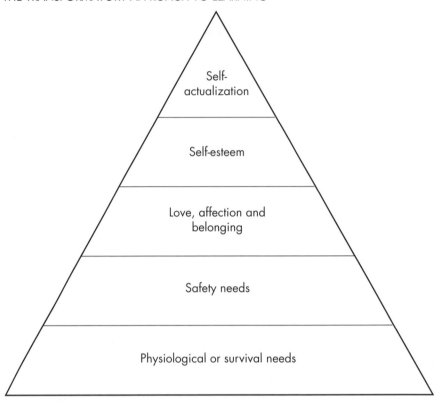

Figure 1.3 The hierarchy of need (Maslow, 1972)

Critics of humanism say that it gives insufficient concern to the social context and over-emphasizes personal agency. The Transformatory Approach adopts a humanistic stance while attempting to address the social context. We also argue that human agency is essential to social change.

DEVELOPING THE TRANSFORMATORY APPROACH TO LEARNING

The Transformatory Approach to Learning moves towards an organismic view of the person who is active in a change process. It recognizes the complexity of the interrelationship of the emotional, social, spiritual, physical and cognitive dimensions of learning. It has an affinity with humanism because it focuses on human experience and recognizes the ability to choose and the potential for change and growth. Our approach is humanistic to the extent that it recognizes the importance of self-awareness and self-reflection in learning and the importance of the emotions in this process. It sees self-actualization as one of the learning goals. Humanism emphasizes the importance of learning from experience. In *On Becoming a Person*, Rogers (1967) states that he writes about what he knows, and everything he knows comes from his experiences. He argues that nothing can be taught that is not already known. Learning is a matter of 'realizing' what is already there – people teach themselves. The Transformatory Approach stresses that teachers are primarily learners, and that learning is lifelong.

The Transformatory Approach also recognizes the importance of the group and social context in the learning process. In this respect it is influenced by Lewin's work on social and institutional dynamics and by his belief that the strongest forces affecting an individual's psychology are other people. However, unlike field theory, the Transformatory Approach also attempts to recognize that social inequalities and power imbalances affect learning.

Mezirow (1983) sees learning as a process of adjusting and acclimatizing to the world. For him, learning is 'the means by which people come to perceive, interpret, criticize and transform the worlds in which they live'.

While writing this book, we find that trying to construct an organismic approach to learning meets with difficulties. We live in a mechanistic society and are educated in a mechanistic system. We only have available the tools and concepts of that society. When teachers with whom we work attempt to write about an organismic approach to learning they have chosen metaphors, for example, the approach is like an aeroplane in flight, the approach is like a pond, the approach is like a tree, the approach is like a parachutist free-falling. We think, perhaps, the approach could best be represented in a three-dimensional form using new technology. However, in this book we are limited to a two-dimensional, static form, and to presenting the dynamic nature of learning in a linear fashion. When we begin to analyse an organismic approach we find ourselves using mechanistic tools and separating the component parts of learning. However, we are not surprised to find the boundaried format of academic writing comforting and familiar. We are curious, and continue to think about whether it is possible to write about the Transformatory Approach to Learning using an alternative approach.

We are aware that there are constraints when adopting this approach in educational organizations. We also believe that every teacher can adopt some of the premises and practices on which the approach is based. We accept that learning is complex and argue that our approach provides coherence and a comprehensive framework. We believe that the Transformatory Approach offers an exciting challenge to the dominant view of the individual learner, the learning context and learning process and raises important questions.

The remaining chapters in Part 1 are concerned with these three interrelated aspects of the Transformatory Approach to Learning. Many writers are currently focusing on the learner, the context and processes of learning and are basing their work on assumptions which are similar to those made by the Transformatory Approach. Where appropriate we draw on their research and writing to support our arguments. The assumptions we make about learners, contexts and processes are by no means unique, and it is exciting that so many people are on the cusp of change in learning and education. It seems to us that it is no coincidence that these changes in thinking about learning come at the dawn of a new millennium in the midst of many sweeping changes affecting a global society. We believe, however, that the Transformatory Approach *is* unique in its attempt to explore the interconnections between learners, contexts and processes and in its intention to emphasize and keep foremost the organismic and holistic nature of learning. It is also unique in its emphasis on learning leading to change at the level of individual, group, organization and society.

TWO

Inspiring Change: The Learner

This chapter outlines and makes a case for our assumptions and perceptions of 'learners' within the Transformatory Approach, which were introduced in Chapter 1. It asks such questions as: What is the relationship between the emotional, social and cognitive dimensions in learning? Is capacity for learning fixed? Do individual learners approach learning differently? In what sense is learning a subjective activity?

ASSUMPTIONS ABOUT LEARNERS IN THE TRANSFORMATORY APPROACH TO LEARNING

We start by exploring the assumptions we make about learners in more detail. These assumptions are again presented in the list below.

- the self is central in the learning process
- learners are striving towards self-actualization
- everyone wants to learn
- learners have an equal potential for learning
- learners have control over what they are learning
- learners progress through stages of either dependence or independence towards interdependence
- learners are prepared to take risks
- the whole person, including emotional, social, spiritual, physical and cognitive aspects, is involved in learning
- the emotional state of the learner affects the capacity to learn
- capacity for learning is not fixed and can be increased
- capacity for learning increases as learning increases
- capacity for learning increases when learners understand themselves as learners
- learners' past experiences influence their learning in the present
- learners experience situations differently and therefore learn different things from the same situation
- learners make decisions about whether to learn or not in particular contexts
- only the learner is in the position to identify and tell others what they have learned

- only the learners can evaluate what they have learned
- learners may approach the same task differently
- learners of the same social group may approach learning differently from learners of another social group

Rather than look at these assumptions individually we have grouped several assumptions together where there is logical connection.

Learning is essential for human development

- the self is central in the learning process
- learners are striving towards self-actualization
- everyone wants to learn
- learners have an equal potential for learning
- learners have control over what they are learning
- learners progress through stages of either dependence or independence towards interdependence
- learners are prepared to take risks

We argued in Chapter 1 that our Transformatory Approach to Learning is most closely aligned to humanism. A humanistic view incorporates the belief that self-actualization is the goal of human development. The self-actualized person is self-aware and self-reflective. Self-actualized people respond to any experience or situation from a position of high self-esteem which enables them to recognize the potential for learning within it, while at the same time recognizing and taking responsibility for the feelings which the situation may provoke, without blaming others or expecting them to 'fix' these feelings. Learners, therefore, take control over what is learned because they recognize that they have choice. This involves taking risks and interacting with others. Keane lists three learning processes which are important in the search for self-actualization:

- developing autonomy in searching
- trusting the harmony of the whole self
- learning how to learn more effectively
  (Keane, 1987)

In addition to stressing the centrality of self in this search for self-actualization, and the need to learn how to learn more effectively, the Transformatory Approach also stresses the need to learn *about* learning. Learning about learning includes learning to recognize our own particular style and approach to learning, whereas learning how to learn generally emphasizes learning techniques. Learning about learning is explored in Chapter 5, 'Cycles of Change: The Action Learning Process'.

Griffin also looks at the processes which are necessary in a search for self-actualization, including:

- maintaining self-esteem
- becoming increasingly responsible for own learning

- finding own direction for learning
- investing energy, involving and committing oneself
- dealing with personal energy ebb and flow
- relating to others
- finding personal meaning in content and experiences
- noticing, clarifying, consolidating, synthesizing new learning
- testing new ideas, skills, behaviour, ways of being
- asking for, getting feedback
- planning the uses of new learning in other situations
- finding and accepting satisfactions, joys, excitement in learning
  (Griffin, 1987)

In the Transformatory Approach people are seen as wanting to learn, and their potential for learning is massive. In the introduction to the UNESCO Report (1996) on Education for the Twenty-first Century, Delors stresses the importance of all societies moving toward 'a necessary Utopia' in which 'none of the talents which are hidden like buried treasure in every person must be left untapped' (Delors, 1996, p. 23).

When children of four or five enter the formal education system the amount they have already learned about the world is staggering. For example, they have all learned to speak at least one language fluently. They have all learned to group objects into conceptually complex categories (for example, small and large animals which bark and have four legs are recognized as dogs; objects with four legs or one leg, arms or no arms, a back rest or no back rest are recognized as seats). They have all learned that objects can be represented through symbols, the most important symbolic representation being language. All children have an infinite and equal capacity for learning. As Whitaker argues:

> One of the keys to understanding the learning process, and of being able to contribute to it successfully as an educator, is the appreciation that all the resources for learning are already within us; they are not acquired through teaching ... We need to appreciate that almost all of us are born as *going concerns* – with all the resources for successful growth and development available to us at birth. (Whitaker, 1995b, p. 2)

Holt described the natural curiosity and desire to learn which children of five come to school with:

> Almost every child, on the first day he [sic] sets foot in a school building, is smarter, more curious, less afraid of what he doesn't know, better at finding and figuring things out, more confident, resourceful, persistent and independent, than he will ever again be in his schooling or, unless he is very unusual and lucky, for the rest of his life. (Holt, 1971, cited in Whitaker, 1995a, p. 11)

The Transformatory Approach to Learning recognizes the potential of every human being to utilize their own resources:

We all bring into school a wholly unexplored, radically unpredictable identity. To educate is to unfold that identity – to unfold it with the utmost delicacy, recognizing that it is the most precious resource of our species, the true wealth of the human nation. (Roszak, 1981)

Papert (1980) also points out that children do not need teachers or curriculum to learn, and that by the time the child starts school they have exercised their huge learning potential in myriad ways to become sturdy individuals, with the skills of adaptation, self-management and communication already well established. It is the this capacity for self-development, intellectual growth and the desire to learn that humanistic psychologists have called the actualizing tendency – the basic directional force within all people to strive for understanding and fulfilment. It is also what Donaldson (1978) calls 'a fundamental urge to make sense of the world and bring it under deliberate control'.

The notions of dependence, independence and interdependence relate to the concept of self-actualization. In a dependent learning state the learner relies on someone telling them what to do or think. In an independent learning state the learner relies on themselves to find information and trusts their own ability to make sense of experiences.

Whitaker writes that:

> There has been a tendency to perceive learning as something that others do to us rather than as something we do for ourselves ... In the struggle to improve the quality of our educational system we need to adopt an altogether more life-enhancing and optimistic appreciation of the learning process. (Whitaker, 1995a, p. 1)

In the Transformatory Approach we emphasize that neither dependence nor independence leads to self-actualization. To become self-actualized a person needs to become an interdependent learner. That is, in order to develop our maximum potential we need a relationship with ourselves which requires the discipline and ability to reflect on our learning and thinking *and* a recognition that we also learn from others in relationship with them. We may become 'teachers' while understanding that we are the ones who learn most from our own teaching.

The Transformatory Approach also emphasizes the need to take risks if we are to become all we are capable of becoming. Unless we take risks we become stuck. Growth and change require that we take a risk to do things differently, to try something new. Zinker writes about learning as a creative process requiring risks:

> Creativity is an act of bravery. It states: I am willing to risk ridicule and failure so that I can experience this day with newness and freshness. The person who dares to create, to break boundaries, not only partakes of a miracle, but also comes to realize that in the process of being ... is a miracle. (Zinker, 1977)

The Transformatory Approach recognizes the potential for learning in every individual and argues that in order to become self-actualized all experiences can be perceived as opportunities for growth and reflection. Experiences will provoke a range of feelings in the learner which need to be considered when thinking about our search for self-actualization.

The whole person as learner

- the whole person, including emotional, social, spiritual, physical and cognitive aspects, is involved in learning
- the emotional state of the learner affects the capacity to learn

The Transformatory Approach to Learning is holistic; the central tenet is that every aspect of the individual is important in learning. To be a whole person we need to have connection to ourselves, connection to other people and connection to a spiritual source. This does not necessarily mean being religious, but does include a sense of purpose and meaning in life which may be obtained from various sources including nature. Connection to ourselves, other people and a spiritual source also connects us to society. Delors lists problems of the twenty-first century to be overcome through education, including the problem of spiritual development, which he describes as:

> The tension between the spiritual and the material: often without realizing it, the world has a longing, often unexpressed, for an ideal and for values that we shall term 'moral'. It is thus education's noble task to encourage each and everyone, acting in accordance with their traditions and convictions and paying full respect to pluralism, to lift their minds and spirits to the plane of the universal, and, in some measure, to transcend themselves. (Delors, 1996, p. 18)

The physical dimension also affects learning. For example, some psychotherapists (Kellerman, 1995) have become interested in the way in which our experiences are 'embodied' physically. We have learned particular postures and ways of using our body which trigger particular emotions or memories. By learning to recognize these, we can choose to change our posture and movement and subsequently experience ourselves differently.

It is significant to note that in modern and post-modern industrial societies and in their education systems, spiritual, emotional, physical and social attributes have traditionally been separated from the cognitive. Chapters 3 and 4 focus on the social dimensions of learning. This chapter continues by exploring the interconnection of the emotional and cognitive:

> Traditionally, educationalists talk of the cognitive and affective domains, implying that these are discrete areas of experience and learning. In fact the cognitive and affective are integrated . . . all cognitive learning will involve an affective dimension . . . On the other hand, learning which involves a high level of emotional involvement and exploration of feelings enables children (and adults) to make cognitive gains. (Epstein, 1993, pp. 145–6)

Whitaker points out that when attempting to develop a more holistic approach to learning it is important to consider the different dimensions of humanity that we bring to our growth and development.

> There has been a strong tendency in our society to prize the intellectual dimension above the emotional and intuitive and to denigrate and disparage those who introduce feelings and intuitions into organizational affairs . . . An effective learner is more likely to be one who brings all dimensions of being into the process of growth and development, thereby increasing the capacity to draw upon a full range of qualities and skills. For too long, the emotional and intuitive elements have been discounted in organizational learning, inhibiting the full expression of human potential. When people are only operating on two of their available cylinders, then serious under performance is the inevitable result. (Whitaker, 1995a, p. 21)

As we enter a new millennium, emotional literacy has become more important. In relationships the need for listening, being able to negotiate difference and resolve conflict, empathize and repair difficulties, is increasingly necessary. In industrial working situations there have been changes away from corporate hierarchies. This highlights the need for additional interpersonal skills such as improved feedback, intercultural competence and approaches to diversity and the building of networks and cooperative teams. On the other hand more people either are unemployed or have temporary work. This requires a shift in gaining our sense of self-worth from external sources to internal sources. In relation to health, Goleman suggests that there is an increasing need for 'emotional intelligence'; this highlights the connections between emotions, especially anxiety, and physical health as influential aspects of the healing processes. Goleman suggests that emotional intelligence consists of:

- knowing one's emotions: including improvement when recognizing and naming one's own emotions; being better able to understand the causes of feelings; recognizing the difference between feelings and actions
- managing emotions: including better frustration tolerance and anger management; fewer verbal put-downs and fights; less aggressive or self-destructive behaviour; more positive feelings about self, friends and family; better stress management; less loneliness and social anxiety
- motivating oneself: including being more responsible; being better able to focus on the task at hand and pay attention; being less impulsive and having more self-control
- recognizing emotions in others; being better able to take another's perspective; improving empathy and sensitivity to others' feelings; being better at listening to others
- handling relationships: starting to analyse and understand relationships; being better at conflict-resolution and negotiating disagreements; better at problem-solving in relationships; more assertive and skilled at communicating; more popular and outgoing, friendly and involved with others; more sought out by others; more concerned and considerate; more pro-social and harmonious in

groups; more sharing, cooperative and helpful; more democratic when dealing with others
(Goleman, 1996)

In the Transformatory Approach we agree that we need to be aware of our emotions, understand them and accept them. However, we argue that emotional literacy goes further and includes challenging our emotional reactions. Emotions affect learning and are themselves shaped by cultural ideas, practices and institutions. For example, particular behaviour or situations which we have come to associate with sadness may be associated with anger by others. This has class, race and gender dimensions – boys and girls may learn to experience different feelings in relation to the same situation. Emotions are, in part, socially constructed. Markus and Kitayama point out that

> the nature and function of emotional processes may depend crucially on the characteristics of the particular cultural reality in which these processes operate ... emotional processes ... will have to be described and analysed not only as constituted by more elementary component processes, but also as afforded, supported and held in place by a set of cultural practices and institutions in which these processes are embedded. (Markus and Kitayama, 1994)

Feminists have written about the ways in which feelings have been used as a source of knowledge about the world:

> As feminist pedagogy has developed, with a continued emphasis on the function of feelings as a guide to knowledge about the world, emotions have been seen as links between a kind of inner truth or inner self and the outer world – including ideology, culture, and other discourses of power. (Weiler, 1991, p. 141)

Hochschild discusses the social construction of emotions in contemporary society, arguing that emotion is a 'biologically given sense ... and a means by which we know about our relation to the world' (Hochschild, 1983, p. 219). At the same time she investigates the ways in which the emotions themselves are manipulated and constructed. Problems of using feeling or emotion as a source of knowledge include the notion that expression of strong emotion can be simply cathartic, and deflect the need for action to address the underlying causes of that emotion. The question of how we distinguish between a wide range of emotions as the source of political action is also important.

For the black feminist writer Lorde, feelings are a guide to analysis and action:

> As we come more into touch with our own ancient, non-European consciousness of living as a situation to be experienced and interacted with, we learn more and more to cherish our feelings, to respect those hidden sources of power from where true knowledge and, therefore, lasting action comes. (Lorde, 1984, p. 37)

In her explorations of feelings and rhetoric as a source of knowledge about the world, Lorde does not reject analysis and rationality. But she questions the depth of critical understanding of those forces that shape our lives that can be achieved using only the rational and abstract methods of analysis given to us by dominant ideology:

> Rationality is not unnecessary. It serves the chaos of knowledge. It serves feeling. It serves to get from this place to that place. But if you don't honour those places, then the road is meaningless. Too often that's what happens with the worship of rationality and that circular, academic analytic thinking. But ultimately, I don't see feel/think as a dichotomy. I see them as a choice of ways and combinations. (Lorde, 1984, p. 100)

Lorde's arguments are based on the assumption that people have the capacity to feel and know, and can engage in self-critique; people are not completely shaped by dominant discourse. The oppressor may be within us, but Lorde insists that we also have the capacity to challenge our own ways of feeling and knowing.

Emotional literacy, therefore, is not only about the ability to recognize our feelings and express them appropriately. It also involves questioning our attachment to a particular emotional experience and 're-framing' that experience in order to perceive it differently and, therefore, let go of our attachment to that emotion. Feelings are also a guide to action for change.

While our way of thinking affects our emotional reactions, our ability to think rationally is clearly affected by our emotions. If we are afraid, sad, upset or angry, we lose our ability to concentrate, we may become disoriented or our attention may be drawn to our bodily reactions rather than being fixed on a logical reaction or solution. For example, we may shake, feel sick, have palpitations or hyperventilate. Clearly, if we are experiencing strong emotions our capacity for learning may be diminished:

> The number of worries that people report while taking a test directly predicts how poorly they will do on it. (Hunsley, 1987)

Seipp's (1991) study of more than 36,000 people showed the same result:

> The more prone to worries a person is, the poorer their academic performance, no matter how measured – grades on test, grade-point average, or achievement tests. (Seipp, 1991)

Goleman (1996) reviews the connections between the rational and the emotional. He explains that on occasion emotions can overwhelm, giving a quick but inaccurate, impulsive rather than reflective, idiosyncratic rather than shared response which says more about the past than the future. He reviews recent research on brain functioning which explains why continued emotional distress can create deficits in a child's intellectual abilities and block the capacity to learn. However, decision-making that is devoid of the emotional component can lead to disastrous results.

This section has emphasized the importance of considering the whole person when thinking about learning and has outlined our view that unless we do this our understanding of learners will be deficient. Chapter 3 outlines ways in which the emotional aspects of learning together with all other aspects can become part of the learning discourse.

Capacity for learning

- capacity for learning is not fixed and can be increased
- capacity for learning increases as learning increases
- capacity for learning increases when learners understand themselves as learners

The Transformatory Approach challenges the prevalent view that learners have a fixed capacity for learning. We argue that capacity for learning can be increased, especially when learners have opportunities to understand themselves as learners.

The assumptions made about the learner in the Transformatory Approach present a view of the individual which is dynamic, changing and positive. This matches the view of Watkins *et al.* (1996) that learner characteristics are not fixed and that previous experiences and beliefs influence the learning in hand.

Holland (1959) showed that most teachers categorize their students along two dimensions: bright–dull and cooperative–nuisance. The bright–dull dimension presumes that something called 'ability' or 'intelligence' is present in individuals in different quantities and that its presence affects the quality of the learner.

Sternberg and Wagner (1986) show that almost all traditional theories of intelligence were developed in an academic context. 'Intelligence' or IQ tests were developed to predict performance in school in relation to more abstract performance in concrete-symbolic and formal tasks. The concept of a high IQ relating to a single 'super-ability' is comparatively recent and stems from the introduction of compulsory schooling at the beginning of the twentieth century. French psychologists Binet and Simon found that some children gained more from their education than others and were asked to suggest tasks that might sort out those likely to succeed in school from those who would not. Historically, the first IQ tests developed by Binet and Simon were designed to predict school performance rather than looking at 'intelligent behaviour' in other contexts. Critiques, of both the concept and the instruments developed for measuring it, focus on the context within which intelligence is measured. How well we perform on an IQ test may well relate to how motivated we are to do the test, whether the test questions are gender or culturally specific, etc. For example, Carraher *et al.* (1985) report some research with children of street vendors who help out their parents with the business. They found that the children could solve context-embedded problems more easily than mathematical tests with no context. Of the 63 problems presented in the informal context-embedded test, 98.2 per cent were correctly solved compared with 36.8 per cent of the problems presented out of context. Criticisms of IQ, therefore, focus on two issues – whether the instruments developed to measure IQ are accurate and, more fundamentally, whether there is such a thing as general intelligence which some people have more of than others.

Today, most education practitioners are sceptical about the value of IQ tests and the assumption that the outcome of schooling is dependent on a stable factor that is inherent in young people. Studies have also shown how much a labelling of a student as 'bright' or 'dull' will affect performance. For example, Beez (1970) randomly selected young people for individual tutoring by teachers on a simple symbol-learning task. The teachers were given false information about the IQ scores of the young people. For example, they were told that one child was dull and slow with an IQ of 94 and that another child was quick and promising academically with an IQ of 107. The results matched the teachers' expectations. One student, labelled bright, but with a real IQ of 74 was given 14 symbols to learn and learned 7. Another student, with a real IQ of 127, but labelled 'dull' was given only 5 symbols to learn and learned only 3. (Other studies support the self-fulfilling prophecy. For example, Finn, 1972; Meichenbaum *et al.*, 1969; and the original Rosenthal and Jacobson work of 1968.)

Whether or not we find the concept of intelligence useful, several theorists who accept this concept disagree with the notion of general intelligence and argue instead that there are several autonomous intelligences.

Gardner identified seven autonomous intelligences, or 'frames of mind'. These are:

- bodily-kinaesthetic (gymnasts and dancers)
- musical (composers, performers)
- linguistic (poets, writers)
- logico-mathematical (scientists, mathematicians)
- spatial (architects, artists)
- interpersonal (skilled negotiators)
- intrapersonal (mystics)
  (Gardner, 1993)

He identified these areas on the basis of studies of brain localization (for example, particular lesions resulting in specific behavioural impairments) and of exceptional attainment in specific areas (for example, child prodigies in language or music). Children who perform very well in one of these areas may not do so in others. Gardner, therefore, suggests that these intelligences are autonomous. Schools tend to focus on only two of these areas – logico-mathematical and linguistic. Gardner suggests that schools should address the other five because otherwise we develop in a lopsided way and ignore the potential that many children may have.

Goleman also suggests different kinds of intelligence. The three kinds of intelligence identified by him include reflective intelligence, neural intelligence and experiential intelligence.

- Reflective intelligence is learned. It includes strategies for memory, problem-solving, etc.; mental management (mental self-monitoring and management, sometimes called meta-learning or meta-cognition); positive attitudes toward investing mental effort, systematicity, imagination.
- Neural intelligence is largely genetically determined. It includes neurological speed and precision. Genes are a major influence. Goleman suggests different neural structures for different kinds of intelligence, including individual talents.

- Experiential intelligence is also learned. It involves extensive common knowledge and skill as well as specialized knowledge and skill.
  (Goleman, 1996)

We challenge the concept of general intelligence because it suggests that capacity for learning is rigid and fixed. Similarly we argue that the work of Gardner and Goleman, while recognizing the limitations of general IQ as a concept, nevertheless base their work around an acceptance of 'intelligence' which relates to content rather than process. We argue it is necessary to question our attachment to words such as 'intelligence' in order to construct a more holistic and dynamic view.

More recent theories of intelligence have taken a process-oriented view rather than a content-oriented view. The process-oriented view attempts to show how intelligent behaviour works. We agree this is a much more useful approach and one which fits more easily with the Transformatory Approach to Learning since it implies that intelligent behaviour can be learned. Additionally, rather than our intelligence being decided by an externally applied test, we can decide whether or not our behaviour is intelligent by deciding if the outcomes of our behaviour are working for us.

One process-oriented approach is to look at intelligence-in-context (e.g. Glaser, 1991). This approach sees intelligence as a way of behaving towards particular tasks rather than something residing in individuals; someone is not unintelligent – aspects of their behaviour are not intelligent in some of the tasks undertaken so far because their behaviour does not result in what they want. If they have plenty of experience, a knowledge base, structured teaching and the chance to interact differently, they will behave intelligently. This approach puts:

> the focus on the learner-in-context and on such factors as motivation, task difficulty and other contextual factors that can be controlled rather than on internal factors that cannot. (Biggs and Moore, 1993, p. 160)

Another model of intelligence which focuses on processes rather than content is the information integration theory (e.g. Das *et al.*, 1979). Das *et al.* propose that the key task in the process of task-completion is planning. Plans are analogous to computer programs. Poor planners use superstition (the colour green seemed to work for me yesterday so I'll use it today) and they tend to ignore feedback. Good planners use their prior knowledge to work out their strategy, they vary few variables at a time, they take a logical set of alternatives and exhaust that before trying a different set. High-level abstract planning seems to be related to what we mean by 'intelligent' behaviour. Traditional tests of IQ ignore the planning stage since they assess not how, but only how well the subject solves the task. The implication of this theory is that children need to be given experiences of planning different tasks and activities. This conforms with the learning cycle discussed in Chapter 5 which stresses the importance of conscious and rational planning as part of the learning process. If we accept a process view of learning, it follows that the capacity for learning increases as learning increases and when learners understand themselves as learners.

In Sternberg's triarchic theory of intelligence (1985, 1991) he takes into account the cultural side of intelligence as well as the mechanisms that underlie intelligent behaviour. He attempts to show how intelligent behaviour reflects a process of purposeful adaptation to the environment and the shaping of the environment in an attempt to make it fit one's skills, interests and values. In modern Western society, the contextual theory of intelligence focuses on problem-solving and academic skills, whereas in other cultures, hunting skills or navigational skills may be more intelligent behaviour. The cultural context of learning is discussed in Chapter 5.

If we accept that children differ according to general or specific abilities, it follows that we allow for these differences by grouping young people according to ability or achievement. Young people are generally put into homogeneous ability groups because they are thought easier to teach and because it is thought that 'bright' students are less likely to be bored, or the 'dull' to be left behind. However, there is evidence which contradicts these arguments. Rosenbaum (1976) showed that streaming by IQ does not reduce variability of particular classes and that there is considerable overlap in performance levels between classes. While students in the top stream may be more comfortable when streamed, all other students feel less comfortable and their perform-ance is worse (Biggs, 1966; Good and Marshall, 1984; Rosenbaum, 1980). Of course, the quality of teaching is likely to be worse in lower streams since newer, inexperienced teachers may be assigned to these classes, and they are likely to be taught lower-level content.

Subjectivity of learning

- learners' past experiences influence their learning in the present
- learners experience situations differently and therefore learn different things from the same situation
- learners make decisions about whether to learn or not in particular contexts
- only the learner is in the position to identify and tell others what they have learned
- only the learners can evaluate what they have learned

Several writers have emphasized the importance of recognizing that all learners have different experiences and that, therefore, they will experience the same learning experience differently (Boud et al., 1996; Gipps, 1992; Boud et al., 1993).

The meaning of experience is not a given, it is subject to interpretation. It may not be what at first sight it appears to be. When different learners are involved in the same event, their experience of it will vary and they will construct (and reconstruct) it differently. One person's stimulating explanation will be another's dreary lecture. What learners bring to an event – their expectations, knowledge, attitudes and emotions – will influence their interpretation of it and their own construction of what they experience. In general, if an event is not related in some fashion to what the learner brings to it, whether or not they are conscious of what this is, then it is not likely to be a productive opportunity. (Boud et al., 1993, p. 11)

Learning is subjective in the sense that only the learner can identify, and therefore evaluate, what they have learned from any particular experience. Personal change which results from effective learning can only be in the control of the learner. As teachers we may intend that students learn particular knowledge or ideas. For subject-specific skills and broader learning strategies external assessment is possible. We can test recall of knowledge or skills, but cannot know what effect our teaching has had on students' self-concept or self-knowledge, or whether teaching has 'changed the meaning of experience' for learners. Only the learner, through a process of reflection, new insight and understanding and, possibly, new behaviour, can know this. How meaningful any learning experience is will depend on previous experience and 'readiness to learn'. Teachers and peers can offer advice guidance and feedback, through action-planning and goal-setting. Rogers also comments on the evaluation of learning:

> Learning is evaluated by the learner. He [sic] knows whether it is meeting his need, whether it leads towards what he wants to know ... The locus of evaluation ... resides definitely in the learner. (Rogers, 1969, p. 5)

Kelly (1955) refers to the individual and unique perception of each person. He highlights the differences in individual perception and response to the one event, and stresses that teachers need to be aware that their perceptions are not necessarily the same as students' perceptions. Freire (1970) similarly emphasizes differences in perceptions, although he stresses cultural rather than psychological factors and argues that perceptions of the world are culturally induced and can only be understood in their unique social and political context.

To summarize, it is most important to remember that 'one must again and again return to the person before us' (Abbs, 1974). Students' experiences of learning will differ, just as their approach to learning will differ. We turn to this in the next section.

Differences in approach to learning

- learners may approach the same task differently
- learners of the same social group may approach learning differently from learners of another social group

In the Transformatory Approach we recognize that we may access the same task differently and that this will depend on our previous experiences, our individual characteristics and our beliefs about our strengths and weaknesses. Different learners may approach the same task differently and the same learners may approach different tasks differently at different times depending on their intentions. People in the same social group may have some similarities in how they approach a task, and this may be different from how people in another social group approach the task. For example, there may be differences in the ways in which two women learn to drive a car. However, there may also be some similarities in the ways in which women as a group approach learning to drive as compared to men. We argue it is important for learners to recognize how they approach a learning task so that they may understand themselves as learners, make decisions about whether they want to continue to learn in this way and increase their repertoire of approaches to learning.

Researchers (Marton, 1975; Säljö, 1981; Gibbs *et al.*, 1982; Entwistle and Ramsden, 1983) identify approaches to learning which they classify as either deep or surface approaches. Approaches to learning were initially conceptualized by Marton (1975) in the context of students reading a text. He found that students approached this task with one of two intentions: to remember the words used, or to try to discover the author's meaning. If remembering words, they would rote learn: Marton called this a 'surface' approach. When we adopt a surface approach we tend to memorize information. If discovering meaning, we attempt to understand the semantic content – a 'deep' approach, concerned with meaning. The deep approach is one in which students seek an understanding of the meaning of what they are studying, relate it to their previous knowledge and interact actively with the material at hand. This implies that people go about learning in different ways, some more effective than others. Teachers can optimize students' chances of learning in more desirable ways and decide which approach is required for a particular intention.

Entwistle and Ramsden (1983) describe the deep approach as an integration of formal learning with personal experience, the formation of relationships between parts of knowledge, and a search for meaning. They describe the surface approach as treatment of tasks as unrelated, an emphasis on memorization and an attitude of unreflectiveness.

Approaches to learning reflect the learners' intentions – a concept similar to motivation. Biggs and Moore suggest four broad categories of motivation:

- extrinsic motivation is central to surface learning; the person carries out the task due to positive or negative reinforcing consequences
- social motivation relates to the influence of those who formed the motive (parent, peer or teacher) and the nature of the process (modelling, conformity or cooperation)
- achievement motivation relates to learning for the purpose of passing a test or getting a job. For example, we are willing to carry out the work to pass the examination because life will be more unpleasant if we do not. We use the strategy of rote learning and try to reproduce the important facts accurately. Because of surface motivation we do not see interconnections between elements, or the meanings and implications of what is learned. We may deliberately rote learn facts which are not understood. We will not engage in the task in the way it should be engaged and will cut corners. This approach may, nevertheless, lead to a considerable degree of academic success.
- intrinsic motivation relates to deep learning
  (Biggs and Moore, 1993)

With the deep approach there is a personal commitment to learning, consequently the student relates the content to personally meaningful contexts or to existing prior knowledge. 'Deep learning changes the way the world appears and is understood'

(Biggs and Moore, 1993, p. 312). The deep approach will involve a high degree of meta-learning (learning about learning, see Chapter 5) including awareness of self, task and context. The achieving approach is like the surface approach in that it is focused on the product. In this case, the focus is the ego trip that comes from obtaining high grades and winning prizes. This approach may involve the deep approach if this means obtaining high grades. However, the deep approach adopted will be a means rather than an end in itself.

Whether or not we take a surface or deep approach may depend on a number of factors. There may be differences in our expectations that mean we have learned to handle a number of tasks at a 'surface' level or that we prefer to engage in a deep way with one task at a time. It may relate to the demands of the situation which require us to jump from one experience to another in a relatively short period of time (as children in school are asked to jump from English, to Science, to Art), or it may be that we choose to take a surface approach at times and a deep approach at others.

Approaches to learning and learning style are not the same. The former reflects the interaction between a learner's current motivation and the context and is generally accepted as modifiable. For example, we may be motivated to take a psychology degree because we are becoming unemployed and want to retrain. We are doing this purely for instrumental reasons and take a surface approach in order to pass the exam. We would choose to take a deep approach if our motivation was to understand and learn about psychology and our job was secure.

However, learning style is thought by some to be like a cognitive style, as a permanent characteristic or trait is displayed over a range of tasks and situations and develops independently of formal education. Several personality and background factors have been found to be related to students' approaches to learning (Biggs and Moore, 1993, p. 316). We challenge this view in the Transformatory Approach. We recognize that we may have a preferred learning style which is practised and, therefore, familiar, and also argue that just as it is possible to adopt a different learning approach, it is also possible to extend our repertoire of learning styles.

Kolb (1976) developed the 'Learning Style Inventory'; four styles of learning are examined:

- *Convergers*. The convergers' skill is to home in on one issue. They are practical thinkers and most comfortable with handling ideas that have a practical outcome, such as a problem requiring a single, specific solution. They are adept at abstract conceptualization and actively experimenting to work out a practical solution. Their way of working is methodical and focuses on one task at a time. Convergers are likely to describe their learning style as: present-oriented, doing, concrete, practical, experimenting, impartial and questioning.
- *Divergers*. These thinkers want to understand rather than solve problems. They are interested in exploring the broad context of a specific issue and to discover what it means, what values are implicit and what the implications might be. They broaden out from the original point. Their insights come from exploring the implications of individual cases and they enjoy discovering new aspects or ideas and fresh angles relating to the central issue. Divergers are likely to

describe their learning style as: reflecting, feeling, experiencing, being intuitive, being aware and discriminating.

- *Assimilators*. Assimilators work with abstract concepts and models. They use theories to produce order and symmetry underpinned by logic. They are called assimilators because they are skilled in organizing and manipulating unassimilated data into an integrated explanation. Their concern is that these theoretical models should be intellectually consistent rather than realistic or practicable. The models are conceived through hypotheses, reflection and speculation. Assimilators are likely to describe their learning style as: analytical, evaluative, logical, conceptualizing, rational, abstract and future-oriented.

- *Accommodators*. These thinkers direct their thinking toward achieving effective action. They are pragmatic in their thinking and look for new opportunities. They then devise strategies for exploiting these opportunities. Their goal is personal advance and success, and they want to make an impact and have something to show for their efforts. Their thinking is versatile and adaptive. If one strategy does not work they will design another. They accommodate to changing situations. They have specific goals and excel in devising strategies. Accommodators are likely to describe their learning style as: pragmatic, watching, active, involved, observing, productive and relevant.
(Kolb, 1976)

Value judgements are not attached to these learning styles; none is better than any other. In fact, each person's learning style will be a combination of the four learning modes. However, it may be that each of us prefers one mode over the others and uses one mode more frequently.

We argue that reflection on our approach to learning can lead us to decide to adopt an alternative approach. We also believe that understanding our preferred learning style can lead to other experiences which allow us to develop the skills needed for other learning styles.

We have shown in this section that our individual approaches to learning will differ. Approaches to learning may also differ in relationship to our membership of a particular social group or groups. We focus on this in more detail below.

Research shows that boys and girls may approach the same learning activity differently (Head, 1996; Askew and Ross, 1989). Learners from different social groups may also have different knowledge. For example, many of the differences in girls' and boys' responses to teaching and assessment activities indicate that the common knowledge invoked by the activities is not shared (Murphy, 1995). Boys and girls may also perceive different problems in similar circumstances because their view of what is relevant differs (Harding, 1996). Our approach to learning will also depend on how we perceive ourselves. For example, girls and women may have been taught that they have a responsibility to ensure that relationships between people are cooperative and positive. This will affect how girls and women learn in groups.

If we are brought up in the West we may expect a mechanistic approach to learning and have difficulty with a more organismic one. If brought up, for example, in the East, we may expect a more organismic approach. While membership of a particular social group(s) affects our approach to learning, perceptions of us by others – their expectations, stereotypes, prejudices and inequality at an institutional level – will also affect how we learn. This 'social context' will be discussed in Chapter 4.

The report to UNESCO (1996) on education in the twenty-first century is aptly called *Learning: The Treasure Within*. We have argued in this chapter that everyone is a learner. We have unimaginable potential and resources if we are only encouraged to see ourselves so. All too often we see ourselves as limited; we are fearful and avoid taking risks. We avoid confronting ourselves and others over the ways in which we constrain and stunt our growth. In the Transformatory Approach to Learning, major steps need to be taken in the way we perceive ourselves and facilitate others' perceptions of themselves. Only with these changes in perception can we make the changes in ourselves which are demanded in a changing society and which will themselves lead to positive changes in the world.

THREE

Evolving Through Collaboration: The Group Context

In this chapter we focus on learning in groups. In Chapter 2 we emphasized the importance of the emotional, social and cognitive dimensions of learning. These dimensions are equally important when we think about learning in groups. However, it is the interpersonal dimension that is highlighted when learning in a group context. In a group we learn more about ourselves, including such things as our preferred role, for example whether we prefer to let others take the lead or to take the lead ourselves; how we react to feedback; how we attempt to gain power and how we deal with conflict. We also have an opportunity to further our conceptual understanding and knowledge through discussion with others, and through hearing alternative perceptions.

This chapter asks such questions as: Do groups learn? How can a group context help individual learning? How do relationships in the group affect learning? How can we foster learning in the group?

In Chapter 1 we outlined our assumptions about the group context:

ASSUMPTIONS ABOUT THE GROUP CONTEXT IN THE TRANSFORMATORY APPROACH TO LEARNING

- groups are more effective in bringing about change than individuals
- individual change is facilitated by the support of the group
- learning is more effective in a collaborative group
- in a social situation, the group is a catalyst for learning as well as a source of learning
- feedback from others is a valuable part of the learning process
- different points of view, perspectives and experiences enrich learning
- learners have support and encouragement to take risks and make changes; be dependent, independent and interdependent
- learners learn about relationships by being in relationships
- conflict and controversy are essential aspects of learning
- learning in a group leads to a feeling of social identity and belonging
- the facilitator is instrumental in establishing the group culture

- the group takes responsibility for ensuring that structures are in place to facilitate learning
- individuals need to learn how to learn in a group in order for learning in the group to be effective
- in order for learning in a group to be effective, the group needs to address the different roles taken by different individuals at different times
- the group is affected by individuals and also develops independently of individuals in the group

This chapter explores these assumptions in more detail.

The effectiveness of learning in groups

- groups are more effective in bringing about change than individuals
- individual change is facilitated by the support of the group
- learning is more effective in a collaborative group

We have argued that effective learning leads to change. We believe that learning in collaborative groups is more effective in bringing about change than learning on our own. Collaborative groups contain the potential for support, challenge and feedback; for learners to cooperate and collaborate. The organismic world-view discussed in Chapter 1 also emphasizes collaboration over competition. Cognitive theorists such as Vygotsky (1962) emphasize dialogue as the important instrument in building new-found conceptions and the importance of learning in relationships. Lewin's (1952) field theory also favours collaboration over competitiveness. Knowles points out that field theories emphasize:

> encouragement of group loyalties, supportive inter-personal relations and a norm of interactive participation (Knowles, 1980, p. 123)

The Transformatory Approach challenges the idea that competition between individuals encourages people to struggle, to work harder and to achieve their goals. Instead, it is suggested that competition leads many individuals to give up, to feel failure and to evaluate their abilities negatively. The kind of learning encouraged by competition is also less likely to lead to a fundamental change of perception or behaviour. This is also suggested by Entwistle:

> If competition is over-emphasized, the increased emphasis on extrinsic rewards will increase effort, but towards reproductive learning. (Entwistle, 1987)

Hall and Oldroyd (1992) suggest that there is a continuum from conflict to collaboration. They discuss this in relation to collaboration between organizations, but it is equally useful when looking at collaboration between people working in collaborative groups in the classroom (see Figure 3.1).

This continuum reflects two dimensions. The first relates to how far success can be achieved for all those engaged in interaction (a win–win situation), or for one individual

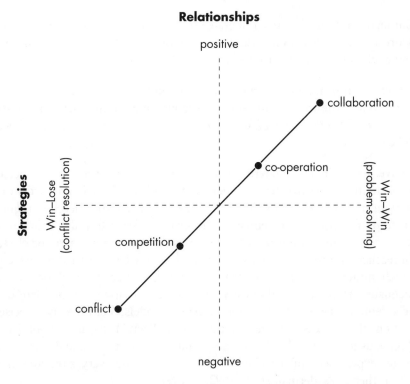

Figure 3.1 The conflict–collaboration continuum (Hall and Oldroyd, 1992)

or group to achieve success to the detriment of another (a win–lose situation). The second dimension looks at how far relationships are positive and mutually supportive, or negative, where one individual or group achieves success at the expense of others' feelings. Collaboration is similar to cooperation; it involves working together, but the latter involves less commitment to joint goals. Competition implies one individual or group striving to achieve goals at the expense of another. Conflict relates to overt struggle. Within this it is possible that collaboration within one group involves competing with another group. The learning that stems from competition is more akin to the 'surface' learning discussed in Chapter 1 rather than 'deep' learning which allows the learner to integrate new learning into their perceptions and understanding of the world and to make changes.

Many authors in recent years have challenged the premise that competition is the dominant explanation for evolution and instead proposed cooperation as a better explanation (Jantsch, 1980; Maturana and Varela, 1988; Lovelock, 1988; Sheldrake, 1991). Samples (1992) argues that nature taught us to cooperate to learn – society teaches us how to learn to cooperate. He points out that in education cooperation is usually a way of organizing experience to have students perform better at schoolwork. Samples believes that if this is the only goal, nothing of real consequence will change. Instead, he proposes, cooperation should become a life skill:

> Co-operation is a much larger idea than any of the current educational technologies ... We do have the privilege and responsibility to reintroduce this primal

evolutionary commitment to co-operate into our times . . . These new times require new dreams and new commitments to co-operate . . . Through a new co-operation a new world view can be born. (Samples, 1992, p. 40)

Cooperation, in this analysis, is not only important so that students achieve more highly, it is vital if the world is to evolve in the next millennium beyond self-seeking, struggle and war. Zelderman *et al.* describe the importance of what they call 'learning to think' cooperatively:

> Effective action in the modern world requires co-operation among persons of diverse abilities, expertise, temperament and background . . . There hardly exists an important modern problem that isn't multi-disciplinary and therefore requires for its solution a collective judgement . . . in order to learn to judge collectively, we must learn to think co-operatively . . . successful students prepare for class, learn from teachers, do well on tests, and apply what they have learned to new contexts . . . such students lack the skills that would enable them to think on the basis of inadequate information, without experts, where a solution to a problem does not have a definite shape or there are no previous models. Yet these are precisely the conditions that increasingly characterize our intellectual, social, and political world and force us to develop the skill we have called co-operative thought. Our students have no experience and practice in responding to the very situations that will confront them. (Zelderman *et al.*, 1992, p. 139)

Unfortunately, while cooperation has played a central role in evolution, competition is the linchpin of both the Western economy and its education system:

> Competition has characterized educational practice from its beginnings . . . This spirit of competition seems to go with our system of free enterprise and the American preoccupation with being number one. (Davidson and Worsham, 1992, p. xi)

The Transformatory Approach suggests that collaboration and learning with other people has the potential for enhancing the learning of both individuals and the group. Kasl *et al.* (1993) ask how group learning differs from descriptions of group process and development which are prevalent in group dynamics literature. Their answer is that group learning emerges when the group frames itself as a learning group. As a result, experience and effectiveness of the group changes qualitatively. Mezirow (1991) describes how individual learning is more potent when the learner becomes more conscious of self as a learner. Kasl *et al.* (1993) apply Mezirow's term 'meaning scheme' to understand group learning. A meaning scheme is the composite of knowledge, beliefs, value judgements and feelings that we use to interpret experience. Similarly the group has a meaning scheme. If it shifts from a task-oriented group to a 'learning' group, Kasl *et al.* argue that individuals can more easily dissociate themselves from their individual meaning schemes and can engage in 'generative learning'. This generative or transformative learning allows them to more easily reach quality solutions to group tasks.

Research on the effects of cooperative learning has been extensive. During the past 90 years, over 600 studies have been conducted on cooperative, competitive and individualistic work in different phases of education. This research indicates that cooperative learning promotes higher achievement than does competitive and individualistic learning. These studies compared the effects of cooperative learning with other methods including lectures or individual learning. For example, Johnson and Johnson (1989), Slavin (1990) and Sharan (1980, 1990).

> The superiority of co-operative over competitive and individualistic learning increases as the task is more conceptual, requires more problem solving, necessitates more higher-level reasoning and critical thinking, needs more creative answers, seeks long-term retention, and requires more application of what is learned. (Johnson and Johnson, 1989)

Cooperative learning has positive effects on academic achievement; development of higher-order thinking; inter-group relations, including friendships amongst people of different social groups; self-confidence and self-esteem of learners; development of social skills and the ability to take the perspective of another. Slavin (1990) argues that the most useful effects of cooperative learning occur when there is a combination of group goals and individual accountability.

Bligh (1986) surveys the research evidence on different forms of teaching and concludes that discussion methods are more effective than didactic methods (for example, the lecture) for stimulating thought, for personal and social adjustment, and for changes of attitude. Most surprisingly perhaps, discussion is as good as the lecture for effectively transmitting information.

Resnick (1987) observes that more effective programmes of thinking improvement in the USA have cooperative problem-solving components and advocates cooperative thinking for enhanced learning. Davidson and Worsham (1992) ask why, if thinking is a personal process which individuals use to create their own understanding, is cooperation beneficial? Their answer is that shared visions and understanding enlarge the scope for individual exploration, so making the enhancement of individual thought as boundless as the shared visions. Another possible answer is that thoughts become more concrete when they are shared. When we hear our own thoughts and the reaction to them we are given the opportunity to reconsider and reflect on our ideas and beliefs in a more dynamic and creative way.

Presselsen argues that learning in groups facilitates meta-cognition:

> Students must explain how they reach a conclusion or arrive at an answer. First and foremost, they find the need to examine their own thought processes. Students engaged in co-operative learning need to reflect on what they think about the particular tasks of instruction, but they must also consider how they arrived at such thoughts and what the significance of a particular act happens to be. Thus, initially, they are engaged in a metacognitive involvement, one of the first acts of constructive thinking. (Presselsen, 1992, p. 2)

This sub-section is concerned with the argument that collaborative group learning leads to more effective learning outcomes both for individuals within the group and for the group as a whole. Learning to work collaboratively is a skill which is only developed by practice in collaborative groups. We argue that the skills learned from working in groups, including negotiation, conflict-resolution, feedback, risk-taking and interdependence, are the skills which are necessary for bringing about changes in the group and in organizations. Clearly, change in organizations is more likely to occur when individuals within the organization work toward shared goals and a shared vision. At the same time learning with others gives the opportunity for feedback and challenge which can lead to individual change.

The group as a vehicle for learning

- in a social situation, the group is a catalyst for learning as well as a source of learning
- feedback from others is a valuable part of the learning process
- different points of view, perspectives and experiences enrich learning
- learners have support and encouragement to take risks and make changes, be dependent, independent and interdependent

In the 1960s and 1970s a variety of terms were used to describe collaborative group learning such as 'small group learning', 'group work'. The term 'cooperative learning' became more prevalent in the 1980s. We use the term 'collaborative group learning' to emphasize commitment to joint goals and learning.

Collaborative group learning may be used as part of a number of different learning activities including individual work, discussion in a large group or as part of input in the form of a talk or lecture from the teacher. There is no single universal method of collaborative group learning and no single 'expert' on collaborative group learning who can speak for the entire field. Johnson *et al.* (1984) define those aspects of cooperative learning that distinguish it from simple group work. These include positive interdependence, heterogeneity, shared responsibilities and social skills development.

Collaborative group learning procedures are designed to engage students actively in the learning process through discussion and enquiry with their peers in small groups. The group work is carefully organized and structured by the teacher to promote the participation and learning of all group members in a cooperative or collaborative undertaking.

> Co-operative learning is more than just tossing students into a group and telling them to talk together. (Davidson and Worsham, 1992, p. xii)

Davidson and Worsham point out that the diverse methodologies used in collaborative group learning have a common key:

- A task or learning activity suitable for group work
- Student-to-student interaction in small groups
- Interdependence structured to foster cooperation within groups

- Individual responsibility and accountability
  (Davidson and Worsham, 1992)

Davidson and Worsham identify attributes which are found in some but not all approaches to collaborative group learning:

- Heterogeneous or random grouping
- Explicit teaching of social skills
- Processing social skills: reflecting on the way social skills were employed and on how their use could be improved in a future lesson
- Means of structuring positive interdependence (goals, tasks, resources, role assignments, rewards)
- Team-building and class-building to foster a sense of inclusion, cohesion and common identity in the team or class
- Perspective-taking: learning to understand the perspectives of others, even when these differ from one's own
- Status treatments designed to recognize the competence of low status students and to enhance their status in the classroom
- Shared leadership within groups
- Use of structures to allow a focus on group processes
  (Davidson and Worsham, 1992)

Collaborative group learning gives many opportunities for learning social skills. Feedback from others in the group becomes a valuable part of the learning process. However, in the Transformatory Approach to Learning, the group dynamics are also a focus for discussion about learning. The cycle of learning, discussed in Chapter 5, includes reflection on such questions as: 'What role did you take in the group task?', 'Over a period of time, has your role remained the same?,' 'Is this a satisfactory role for you?', 'How can roles be alternated?', 'Was there any conflict in the group?', 'Was the conflict successfully resolved?', 'What strategies for conflict resolution are useful for future conflict?' In the Transformatory Approach to Learning the group becomes a catalyst for learning as well as a source of learning.

Clearly, learners must feel that they are in a safe environment in order for learning to be enhanced. Perhaps not so obviously, they must also perceive the learning organization as one in which risks are possible (Marzano, 1992). Covington (1983) points out that learners must believe that their ideas will be honoured and valued and their failures will not be met with ridicule. Combs (1982) argues that closely related to a sense of psychological safety is a sense on the part of learners that they are accepted by their teacher and peers. In a successful collaborative group, learners have support and encouragement to take risks and make changes, be dependent, independent and interdependent. University Teachers Method Unit (UTMU) makes this point in relation to collaborative group learning in higher education, but it is equally relevant to all phases of education:

It could be said therefore that an important function of group work in higher education is to enable students to know enough about themselves and about others to enable them to work independently and yet co-operatively within a team . . . The group experience can, in fact, be extremely important in achieving freedom from dependency if the students learn to play a variety of roles in the group and begin to develop a sense of responsibility for its success or failure. In the process of learning these roles they will need to develop more acute self-understanding, to become aware of their own inhibitions, defences and assumptions, and be able to recognize the difficulties which other students have and begin to help them to overcome them. (UTMU, 1978)

As discussed in Chapter 1, risk-taking is an important part of learning and of becoming 'self-actualized'. If we continue to do what feels safe, we will experience little growth and will eventually come to feel 'stuck' in our lives. Making a positive decision to take a risk is different from self-destructive risk-taking behaviour which is likely to lead to a deterioration in the quality of our lives. However taking a risk often feels frightening and the support and encouragement of others is often welcome. The collaborative learning group can be a place where we can take risks by practising new roles and behaviours. Perkins points out that creative people take risks – they 'live on the edge of their competence', testing their limits (Perkins, 1991). Costa and O'Leary also pay attention to the possibility of greater creativity in collaborative groups:

Working in groups causes greater stimulation of ideas and thus provides a setting in which to generate creative thought. Students will want to pay attention to how their ideas flow more freely when they listen to and 'bounce off' others' ideas in a freewheeling atmosphere. (Costa and O'Leary, 1992, p. 62)

Hilt is also concerned with the possibilities for change, growth and creativity which the group can bring:

Students learn how people see things differently, and how those differences can be a strength. A rich mixture of diverse views broadens one's perspective and is a vital ingredient for innovation . . . In order to avoid stagnant or lockstep thinking, difference stimulates fresh approaches to problems and thus becomes a valuable group asset. (Hilt, 1992)

The group can provide inspiration, spark off new ideas and provide challenge where individuals appear to be stuck. Learning in a collaborative group can be more enjoyable and an antidote to the sense of isolation that may accompany individualistic approaches to learning:

Four important words seem to be missing in most academic courses: support, commitment, enjoyment and imagination. The first three may be created in a group where a climate of open communication, involving trust, honesty and mutual respect, takes place. Imagination should blossom in this climate. It might also create it. (Jaques, 1995, p. 11)

We acknowledge that for some of us, collaborative group learning may be anathema. Group membership may bring up all kinds of painful and negative experiences from which we want to escape by escaping from the group. We may enjoy the sense of individual achievement and excitement which meeting our personal goals brings. We do not intend arguing in this chapter that collaborative group learning is necessarily always better or superior to learning alone. However, we are arguing that some aspects of learning which are vital as part of a self-actualizing process can *only* be learned in a collaborative group.

Relationships in the group

- learners learn about relationships by being in relationships
- conflict and controversy are essential aspects of learning
- learning in a group leads to a feeling of social identity and belonging

We have emphasized that learners learn social skills by participating in a collaborative group. In other words, we learn about relationships through being in relationships. Part of such a relationship involves learning to resolve conflict which is an inevitable aspect of relating to others. The Transformatory Approach emphasizes change. This is not about imposing our will on others, but about taking responsibility for self and deciding what changes we want to make in order for our lives to be more satisfactory. In this model the group does not impose change on individuals. Feedback from others in the group can be challenging and enable the individual to think of alternatives. Each individual in the group is viewed as an expert on themselves. Conflict and controversy are not in themselves negative experiences. On the contrary, they are learning experiences when (and if) they become the focus for reflection and a catalyst for new ways of behaving. Interestingly, educational experiences which revolve around competition encourage conflict, rather than the development of conflict resolution skills. Johnson and Johnson suggest that controversy is a necessary part of problem-solving and higher achievement:

> Controversy exists when one student's ideas, information, conclusions, theories, and opinions are incompatible with those of another, and the two seek to reach an agreement. Controversy, compared with concurrence-seeking, debate, and individualistic efforts, results in higher achievement, higher quality decisions and problem-solving, more creative thinking, higher level reasoning and critical thinking, greater perspective-taking accuracy; greater task involvement, more positive relationships among group members, and higher academic self-esteem. (Johnson and Johnson, 1992, p. 136)

However, they suggest that controversy will only produce its potential effects if students are taught conflict-negotiation skills. For example,

- Emphasise the mutuality of the situation and avoid win–lose dynamics. Focus on coming to the best possible decision, not on winning.
- Confirm others' competence while disagreeing with their positions and challenging their reasoning. Be critical of ideas, not people. Challenge and refute the ideas of others, but do not reject them personally.

- Separate your personal worth from criticism of your ideas.
- Listen to everyone's ideas even if you do not agree with them.
- First bring out all the ideas and facts supporting both sides and then try to put them together in a way that makes sense. Be able to differentiate the differences between positions before attempting to integrate ideas.
- Be able to take the opposing perspective in order to understand the opposing position. Try to understand both sides of the issue.
- Change your mind when the evidence clearly indicates that you should.
- Paraphrase what someone has said if it is not clear.
- Emphasize rationality when seeking the best possible answer, given the available data.
- Follow the golden rule of conflict – act towards your opponents as you would have them act towards you. If you want people to listen to you, then listen to them. If you want others to include your ideas in their thinking, then include their ideas in your thinking. If you want others to take your perspective, then take their perspective.
  (Johnson and Johnson, 1992)

Working in collaborative groups allows people to learn at different levels. They learn cognitive skills from participating in, and finding solutions to, tasks. They also learn socio-emotional skills. These are far less likely to be learned in traditional individualistic tasks. Jaques writes that:

> There is plenty of evidence both from research and experience that groups of all kinds operate at both a task and a socio-emotional level. If we look at groups in an academic context we can see that they can also be viewed as functioning within both intrinsic and extrinsic dimensions. (Jaques, 1995, p. 72)

He demonstrates the interrelationships between these four aspects in a matrix format (see Table 3.1).

Jaques believes that the intrinsic dimension is given least attention in education and that teaching is often solution-oriented rather than problem-oriented. It takes external requirements as its starting-point rather than the needs and interests of students. We would add that education rarely makes relationships the central focus of learning. Discussing learning in groups in higher education, Jaques also points to the importance of groups in contributing to the sense of belonging and social identity:

> some sort of small group experience would seem vital in the unit or modular system to give students the possibility of developing a sense of social identity and a feeling of belonging and commitment to the intellectual life of the institution. (Jaques, 1995, p. 148)

Many people in all phases of education feel isolated. We argued in Chapter 2 that emotional problems have a negative effect on cognitive gains. Collaborative group learning, when organized in a sensitive way, gives the opportunity for developing supportive and challenging relationships and to establish a sense of belonging. The

Table 3.1 Types of aims and purposes in group teaching (Jaques, 1995)

	Task	Socio-emotional
Intrinsic	Expressing selves in subject	Greater sensitivity to others
	Judging ideas in relation to others	Judging self in relation to others
	Examining assumptions	Encouraging self-confidence
	Listening attentively	Personal development
	Tolerating ambiguity	Tolerating ambiguity
	Learning about groups	Awareness of others' strengths and weaknesses
Extrinsic	Follow-up to lecture	Giving support
	Understanding texts	Stimulating further work
	Improving staff/student relations	Evaluating student feelings about course
	Gauging student progress	Giving students identifiable groups to belong to
	Giving guidance	

next section turns to issues in making the group work in the ways which we advocate.

Making the group work effectively

* the facilitator is instrumental in establishing the group culture
* the group takes responsibility for ensuring that structures are in place to facilitate learning
* individuals need to learn how to learn in a group in order for learning in the group to be effective
* in order for learning in a group to be effective, the group needs to address the different roles taken by different individuals at different times
* the group is affected by individuals and also develops independently of individuals in the group

A very large proportion of our time may be spent working in groups. There is a great potential for learning and skills development to take place whilst working in groups, and many important decisions that affect our lives are made in the groups to which we belong. However, working in groups may also be frustrating, time-wasting and counterproductive. Jaques points out:

> Group discussion, while potentially more democratic than lectures, does not of itself guarantee student participation in the choice, pacing and direction of study. (Jaques, 1995, p. 161)

Whether or not collaborative group learning achieves the goals we have outlined will depend very much on the skills of the facilitator. Lewin conducted a classic series of experiments in 1951 to see what effect different leadership styles had on group dynamics. He concludes that:

- Authoritarian-led groups produced a greater quantity of work over a short period of time, but experienced more hostility, competition and aggression – especially scapegoating, more discontent beneath the surface, more dependence and less originality.
- Democratically led groups were slower in getting into production, were more strongly motivated, became increasingly productive with time and learning, experienced more friendliness and teamwork, praised one another more frequently and expressed greater satisfaction.
- Laissez-faire groups did less and poorer work than either of the others, spent more time in horseplay, talked more about what they should be doing, experienced more aggression than the democratic group but less than the authoritarian, and expressed a preference for democratic leadership.
(Lewin, 1951)

Jaques writes that groups thrive best when the leadership functions are democratically shared among the members of the group. He also suggests that the 'teacher as helper' role may stifle individual growth and development of resources:

There is a feeling in groups where visible authority is present that the ultimate responsibility for each person's action and its consequences resides in the figure of authority . . . Many of us respond to a student's sense of helplessness by offering to meet it and without questioning its nature. The problem here is that the teacher who is an incurable helper, in satisfying one of his or her basic needs, may fail to develop the student's capacity for self-growth into greater autonomy and responsibility. (Jaques, 1995, p. 17)

In the Transformatory Approach to Learning the teacher's traditional authoritarian style of leadership is inappropriate. We adopt Abercrombie's (1979) suggestion that part of the role of the tutor is to help group members 'to see themselves as capable of change'. Additionally, the development of collaborative group learning requires that the teacher take on a different role:

If we look again at this question of authority in the group, it may now be apparent that some aspects of it are an unnecessary encumbrance to the creative tutor who may decide to devolve the leadership role among the members. (Jaques, 1995, p. 126)

Hill proposes the criteria below for gaining a common understanding of what effective discussion can be like. This involves a set of roles and functions which enables the devolution of the teacher's authoritarian role:

- a happy non-threatening atmosphere prevails
- learning is accepted as a co-operative exercise
- learning is accepted as the object of discussion
- everyone participates and helps others to take part
- leadership functions are distributed
- material is adequately covered
- members attend regularly and are prepared for the discussion
- evaluation and/or assessment is accepted as an integral part of the discussion group
(Hill, 1977)

Learning is maximized when the learning cycle described in Chapter 5 is employed. In addition to being a member of the group and carrying out the tasks, much is to be gained from:

- reviewing what happens in the group, including roles taken
- analysing the learning of the participants and the group
- applying learning to future work of the group or to other contexts; that is considering what would be done differently in the same or another situation

Campbell and Ryder (1989) distinguish between 'group work' and 'work in groups'. They argue that, given the widespread use of group strategies for learning, it is important that teachers are aware of the distinctions and clear about their aims and methods. They state that what is special about collaborative group learning is its deliberate use of the experience of participating in the group as a source of learning rather than group activity focusing only on the shared task. Collaborative group learning can, therefore, provide a valuable opportunity to reflect on individual and group learning, and participants can apply their learning to other situations.

Group behaviour can be fascinating, complex and subtle. We can better facilitate the learning of people with whom we work when we have more knowledge of our own behaviour and the behaviour of others in groups. Observing individuals in groups helps our understanding of the different roles people take. These may be either assumed or given roles. Group members can take on a number of roles within one group and can take on different roles according to the different groups they are in. Alternating roles provides opportunities for the development of different skills and can add to the dynamic nature of the group. Group members who stay in 'fixed' roles can lead to the group being 'stuck' and limit the potential for learning and development.

The roles taken in groups usually concentrate around two main areas: those concerned with the task and those concerned with the maintenance and welfare of the group. In other words, roles are concerned on the one hand with the content of the group's work and about getting the tasks completed, and on the other hand with the processes of work and the emotional life of the group. Both types of role are important. Without task roles the work would not be done and without maintenance roles the group would not function well. To maximize learning in the group, it is important that group members have the opportunity to increase their repertoire of skills by being encouraged to take turns in these different roles when appropriate.

Table 3.2 Identifying task and maintenance roles in groups

	Positive	Negative
Task roles	Helping participants achieve the task of the group, e.g. giving and seeking information and opinions, clarifying and summarizing	Blocking the task of the group, e.g. dominating, withdrawing, not sticking to the ground rules
Maintenance roles	Helping maintain the group, e.g. asking about feelings, helping others to contribute, encouragement	Undermining the group, e.g. ignoring participants, putting people down, making unhelpful comments

Maintenance roles are important in encouraging cooperation and a collaborative and friendly, relaxed culture where participants feel comfortable, contribute and feel valued by the group. Maintaining the group includes: supporting group members, reviewing group processes, adding personal experience and light relief. Task roles relate to completing the collaborative task successfully and include: starting the task, providing information, ensuring that the task is understood and that every group member is aware of their responsibility, keeping the group on task (see Table 3.2).

We have argued that collaborative group learning provides participants with the opportunity to develop important learning aspects. Exploring relationships, developing interpersonal and communication skills can be the focus of collaborative group learning. All skills need to be practised. Moreover, giving and receiving feedback in relation to skills development is a vital part of the learning process (see Chapter 5).

The Transformatory Approach to Learning emphasizes cooperation and collaboration in groups. It does so firstly because it is believed that people working in groups are more likely to bring about effective change in their environment than people working individually. Secondly, the collaborative group brings opportunities for learning involving the three dimensions which have been emphasized in all chapters in this section: the emotional, social and cognitive. We learn to relate socially by being in groups; we learn to negotiate, communicate, deal with conflict and empathize with the experience of others. In relating socially, we also learn more about ourselves. We learn to deal with our emotions, including anger and frustration. We have opportunities to see ourselves reflected in the behaviour of others and to become more tolerant of others and of ourselves because of this. Finally, we have provided evidence in this chapter that learning in collaborative groups brings cognitive gains, including more support for the development of conceptual understanding, problem-solving skills, complex reasoning and critical thinking skills, long-term retention of information and application of learning.

The next chapter explores the social context within which both individual learning and learning in the group takes place. Learning in groups provides opportunities for exploring inequalities, but there are also problems inherent in this. Chapter 4 explores some of the ways in which inequalities in society affect learning, and some of the ways this affects group processes.

FOUR

Moving Mountains: The Social Context

Our social position and membership of particular groups affects our individual approach to learning, but inequalities in the group, in the school and in society also affect the processes of learning. Watkins *et al.* argue that we learn how to learn within a specific social context:

> Approach to learning is learned, alongside and linked to other core aspects of the person: gender, race and so on and is partly shaped by messages of value about those aspects, by family dynamics, and cultural heritage. (Watkins *et al.*, 1996, p. 2)

While our social position and membership of particular groups will affect our individual approach to learning, inequalities in the group, in the school and in society will also affect the processes of learning. This raises a dilemma for those concerned with social justice. Do we focus on enabling change in the individual? In this case we will be accused of individualism; accused of failing to acknowledge that the individual is powerless in the face of institutionalized inequalities; of seeing the individual as at fault. Or do we focus on changing the social order? In this case we are in danger of ignoring difference in experience, of assuming that change in the structure can be brought about without a corresponding change in our assumptions, values and perceptions of ourselves and the world. This chapter highlights the importance of the personal dimension in bringing about change and argues that social change is not enduring unless people change. We discuss the Transformatory Approach to Learning with this dilemma in mind.

We make a number of assumptions about learning and the social context in the Transformatory Approach:

- effective change encompasses change at both the individual and social levels
- social change follows from learning and change at the individual level
- expectations and stereotypes about people affect learning
- learning is affected by sex, ethnicity and socio-economic position
- learning roles and styles are gendered
- our individual identity is socially constructed

- through the learning process of self-reflection, reflection on experiences, abstraction and generalization we are capable of deconstructing our identity
- the learning discourse affects what we understand and value
- the dominant learning discourse is determined by powerful groups in society
- there are conflicting learning discourses in society
- discussion of inequality in education and society must be part of the learning process
- discussion about how the social context affects learning must be part of the learning process
- the interrelationship between personal and social is valid discourse in the classroom
- diversity needs to be recognized within social groups

In this chapter we discuss these assumptions in detail.

Challenging social injustice and its effects on learning

- effective change encompasses change at both the individual and social levels
- social change follows from learning and change at the individual level

One position amongst social scientists maintains that there is a complex relationship between the individual and the social levels. An emphasis on the individual stresses the property of agency: that people are able to choose; to create different kinds of social relationships. An emphasis on the macro-social context emphasizes the constraints imposed by structures, institutions and social processes. The character of each level is changed by its interaction with the other level. However, each level has its own decisive impact as shown in Figure 4.1 by the two-way direction of the arrows.

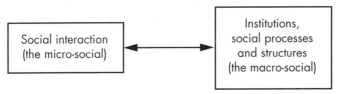

Figure 4.1 The two-way relationship between social interaction and social structures

Goffman (1959) was one of the first social scientists to study social interaction as a micro-reality in its own right. He believes that social structure or biology cannot explain order in social interaction. Goffman's work is concerned with the way individuals bring about interaction on the basis of their knowledge of social expectations. Their identity and understanding of themselves as individuals is structured by social interaction. Goffman's work has aspects in common with humanism in its stress on individuals as capable of reflecting on their experience and self-consciously applying their resources to change social interaction. In this approach individuals are viewed both as constructing social interaction and as dependent on pre-existing social resources. A study of social interaction can help us understand how power structures embedded in social relations are managed.

Social scientists have become increasingly concerned about the either/or nature of the debate about structure or agency. For example, Hearn discusses it in relation to masculinity:

> While it can be argued that a major sociological project is to find ways of providing for the interplay between such distinctions [between agency and structure], it may also be argued that the very setting up of the problem in these terms is problematic ... A critical examination of the distinction between agency and structure may be necessary in order to develop further the critical analysis of masculinities and of the diversities of men's responses, including the ways in which some men are themselves beginning to provide (for) a critique of the gender order of which they themselves are a part. (Hearn, 1987, p. 181)

Explanations of social inequality offered by the various social sciences over the last twenty years have tended to concentrate on either structural or individual explanations for inequality. For example, they have explained racism as the psychology of prejudice or they have focused on institutional racism and the racist structures of society. These explanations have assumed a split between the individual and society. Henriques *et al.* (1984) suggest that individuals cannot exist outside of society and society is composed of groups of individuals. This individual–society dualism is a false dichotomy. Henriques *et al.* explain that this

> allows even radical analyses to be pressed into the service of existing social relations, thereby reinforcing and perpetuating them. (Henriques *et al.*, 1984, p. 60)

If everything is determined by the structure of society, there is little possibility for change of any kind. Henriques points out that the liberal notion of prejudice as individual responsibility and the radical idea that responsibility lies with 'the system' are locked together, one on each side of the individual–society dichotomy 'in a mutually propelling antagonism' (p. 62).

Henriques *et al.* (1984) develop explanations of inequality through an analysis of Foucauldian ideas about discourse, on psychoanalysis and understanding of socio-economic and political factors. They emphasize that none of these factors operates on its own or can be said to be the primary cause of inequality.

We argue that effective learning involves a conscious and structured process of personal reflection on experiences, followed by an analysis of learning from the experience, and about ourselves, which leads to change in our approach to new experiences. It will also lead to a change in the meaning, and our perception, of those original experiences – a reframing process.

We argued in Chapter 1 that the Transformatory Approach was most closely aligned with a humanistic view of the person which stresses our ability to make choices and to change. However, we also recognize that individuals are socially constructed and that there are structural factors which limit our choices and our ability to change. Humanism generally has not focused on the ways in which racism, sexism, socio-economic circumstances and heterosexism affect our life chances.

We come from backgrounds which led us to favour fighting for social change above individual change and to see the struggle to bring about personal change as individual-istic and, sometimes, 'victim-blaming'. Our experiences, however, have led to a change in our position, and we now believe that personal change must accompany change at the social level or group level. We are committed to the ideal of a more equitable and just society following from individual change. This is a pragmatic conviction; it is impossible to change others and difficult enough to change ourselves. It also stems from the thought that external situations to some extent mirror and reflect our internal beliefs.

Power relationships affect perceptions of individuals as learners and affect how they learn

- expectations and stereotypes about people affect learning
- learning is affected by sex, ethnicity and socio-economic position
- learning roles and styles are gendered

We all are affected by stereotypes and expectations about us depending on our social class, ethnic group, sex, sexuality, physical ability and age. We may think people are naturally 'good' or 'bad' at particular subjects. In relation to individual learners these expectations are self-fulfilling (see Chapter 2). While they limit the potential of individuals, they also limit the potential of children in particular social groups. For example, girls are expected to be good at languages; they are told they are good at languages; they believe they are good at languages and, so, they become 'good' at languages. Goldenberg (1986) writes about his high expectations of children from a middle-class background. He admits that his identification of a child as 'middle-class' may rest solely on what that child looks and sounds like. As teachers, we may unconsciously gravitate toward children from a particular social group and relate to them in a different way. Their cultural background may be similar to our own and it may be that all of us feel more comfortable with the familiar in others. Children from particular social groups may 'mirror' back aspects of ourselves when young, and perhaps we will more easily identify with them because of this. The aspirations, dreams and hopes which we had as children may therefore be projected outward onto these young people.

Murphy writes about how power relations operate at different levels in educa-tion:

> Feminist research has revealed how particular relations are reflected and repro-duced in schooling at a number of levels. At the ideological level ideologies of 'race', 'ethnicism' and 'gender' act to socialize students for their future roles. At the structural and organizational level of institutions both in their overt and covert practices, messages are relayed to students about the relative power positions of different groups and individuals; and about the subjects and aspects of those subjects which are deemed appropriate for them to study. These subject divisions typically reflect the occupational structures in societies and the sources and selection of knowledge represented in curriculum subjects. (Murphy, 1996, p. 13)

In Chapter 2 we argued that individuals have different learning approaches and styles. From our observation and research we also argue that learning roles and style are socially constructed. For example, learning roles and styles may be gendered. Girls and boys approach collaborative tasks differently (Askew and Ross, 1989). Girls may be more likely to adopt maintenance roles in groups (see Chapter 3). Girls may possibly achieve more highly in groups than boys because of their socialization, which may stress the importance of relationship and cooperation; the socialization of boys may stress competition. There is evidence that girls respond better to the type of self-reflection suggested by the cycle of learning in Chapter 5 (HMSO, 1988). Competitive, individualistic learning styles which emphasize surface learning may favour white, middle-class boys; and because of the way girls are socialized, they may more easily adopt the self-reflective approach highlighted in the Transformatory Approach to Learning. In Chapter 3 we explain that cooperation and negotiation are vital lifeskills and necessary for everyone if they are to succeed in the changing world. Boys need to learn these skills too.

Some forms of organization and teaching in school favour children from a particular social group (Garvey, 1994; Connell, 1994). Garvey describes streaming itself as a 'masculinizing practice' and Connell makes a similar point about the competitive academic curriculum:

> Other school practices sub-divide and complicate gender blocks. Of these, none is more important than the competitive academic curriculum. The organization of learning in terms of individual competition in mastery of abstract, hierarchically organized bodies of knowledge, inevitably defines some groups as successful and others as failures. Combined with the organizational practices of tracking, stream-ing, or selective entry, this curriculum creates different social situations that call out responses in gender terms. (Connell, 1994, p. 10)

In the Transformatory Approach to Learning we recognize the constraints on learning imposed by ideology and social structures, and argue that these must be addressed within the organization. Learning is enhanced if there is congruence at different levels (see Chapter 8). The principles and processes outlined in the Transformatory Approach (see Chapter 5) need to be applied at the different levels of group, classroom, whole-organization and community. If the principles are applied at these different levels, the organization becomes a learning community adaptive to and promoting change.

The social construction and deconstruction of identity

- our individual identity is socially constructed
- through the learning process of self-reflection, reflection on experiences, abstraction and generalization we are capable of deconstructing our identity

Over the last two decades formal education in the UK has been influenced by Piaget's view of child development (see Chapter 1). Piaget emphasized the individual development of identity rather than its social construction. Piaget's view in particular influenced the Plowden Report on primary education, which emphasized discovery learning. The Transformatory Approach to Learning recognizes the importance of the social construction of identity while also paying attention to the construction of individual identity. Epstein comments:

> It is clearly possible to recognize both the individuality of children and the way they are situated within and constitute society. Nevertheless, political and ideological factors – which have tended to favour disregarding social aspects of education – and the individualism of the Plowden discourse have been combined. The outcome is that it is only with the advent of feminism in the 1970s and anti-racism in the 1980s that children have begun to be considered as members of society. (Epstein, 1993, p. 92)

Piaget's views reflect the positivist and individualistic tradition of the Enlightenment. Walkerdine (1984, 1990) argues that the view of the individual as rational, and the emphasis on the cognitive, is congruent with ideologies and forms of social organization which arose during the development of industrial capitalism, in particular the rise of 'science' as a form of legitimation. These notions are aligned with the stress on competitiveness rather than cooperation discussed in the previous chapter.

Piaget believes that children's cognitive development is a result of interaction between the child and the environment. However, he did not include the social or cultural context as part of the 'environment'. Piaget's view of children is that they are 'scientists' who make their own discoveries about the world – the role of the teacher is to observe the stage the child has reached and facilitate the making of discoveries.

Alongside the view of children as 'scientists' is the belief that children are unable to de-centre and to empathize with others' points of view. Piaget proposed that children go through definite and discrete stages in the development of cognition. These stages unfold automatically but can be encouraged by appropriate nurture and stimulus. The view that child development follows sequential paths and the notion that children cannot de-centre until they reach a 'mental age' of ten or eleven implies that primary age children cannot handle concepts of racism and sexism. The Transformatory Approach to Learning challenges this notion and argues that even young children can take part in discourse on sexism, racism and other inequalities.

The strength of Piaget's work is in the shift of opinion away from a mechanistic view of children's development, as completely predetermined by biology and as of empty vessels to be filled with knowledge, toward a more 'interactionist' approach concentrating on the interaction between child and environment. As such it is more in line with the organismic view of human nature than with the mechanistic.

Social identities are socially constructed, and it is also important to stress our ability to deconstruct these identities through the process of self-reflection, abstraction and learning discussed in Chapter 5. There is, therefore, a two-way process of social construction and deconstruction. Epstein also makes this point:

> I have stressed that children are active in the construction of their own identities and in making their own meanings from the experience of social relations. In so

doing, they construct and reconstruct dominant ideologies and discourses, but are also able – given the scaffolding in the form of counter-discourses – to deconstruct them and develop new, anti-oppressive meanings. The very complexity of identity and the contradictory nature of our positions within various discourses means that possibilities are always present for opposition. (Epstein, 1993, p. 146)

Social-constructionist approaches to child development and education derive from the work of Vygotsky (see Chapter 1). They stress culture and the social context as the basis for learning and recognize children as active in the construction of their own reality. Language is the medium through which children construct meaning. Sociologists and teachers have developed the discourse of social constructionism to facilitate dealing with social and controversial issues in the classroom. Social constructionism requires pedagogies based on active engagement of teacher and taught and changes in their relationship. Pollard (1987) points out that much interpretative sociology reveals that children's experience of school is one of vulnerability, of power relations and of 'trying to protect their dignity' (Pollard, 1987, p. 4). Making experiences explicit, and reflecting on them, is a crucial element of social-constructionist approaches to equality. Lee and Lee (1987), Epstein and Sealey (1990) and Grugeon and Woods (1990) use social-constructionist approaches as a basis for anti-racist intervention. All show a commitment to negotiation; shared decision-making; developing empathy; cooperative learning; rejecting the idea that young children cannot cope with controversy or with social issues; and a view that 'talking is learning' and that talk is not merely teacher-to-child but child-to-child and needs considerable time (Lee and Lee 1987; see also Chapter 3 and Chapter 5).

Child-centred education in the 1970s and 1980s tended to avoid issues of equality, particularly in primary schools, and to focus instead on equal opportunities and multi-culturalism. These approaches tend to regard sexism and racism as individual problems, to be dealt with on an individual basis. Alternative versions of anti-sexist and anti-racist education concentrate on teaching about racism and sexism in a didactic fashion. This approach focuses on the role of state and society. These divisions establish false debates.

> An approach is needed which combines understandings about 'society' with understandings of individual subjectivities . . . social constructionist interpretations of child development provide a more promising groundwork for developing effective anti-racist pedagogies. (Epstein, 1993, p. 107)

Such approaches to discussion of inequality as part of the cycle of learning are suggested by the Transformatory Approach to Learning.

Learning discourse is socially constructed

- the learning discourse affects what we understand and value
- the dominant learning discourse is determined by powerful groups in society
- there are conflicting learning discourses in society

We have already emphasized that knowledge and approaches to learning are socially constructed. The knowledge base which is thought important in any society will depend on the needs and values of that society. The dominant learning discourse and knowledge base is determined by powerful groups in society, and knowledge itself constitutes one kind of power in society. The knowledge base in the West will tend to reflect the values of middle-class, white, ethnocentric culture.

The National Curriculum reflects these dominant learning discourses. However, we have pointed out that counter-discourses are available, although in a limited form. Feminists have discussed how discourses and counter-discourses are formed in relation to the state. For example, Arnot (1992a) analyses the ways in which gender issues were part of the political context behind the recent reorganization of education in the United Kingdom. She argues that New Right educational discourses are contradictory. Arnot (1992b) writes that the New Right promoted an uneasy alliance between, on the one hand, authoritarian values and the wish to re-establish traditional family structures and 'remoralize' the nation's children and, on the other hand, neo-liberal notions of individual liberty, particularly economic freedom in the marketplace as consumers, and political freedom from coercion and excessive state control. The solution to this dilemma could not be found by expelling women from the marketplace, especially since capital still required female waged labour. Instead, the Conservative government of the late 1980s and early 1990s sustained the liberal strategies of the last two decades, depoliticizing and neutralizing the effects of feminist educational demands and restoring patriarchal relations. In the 1990s these relations take a different form and have had different consequences to those of the post-war period.

> Conservative political thinkers ... have manipulated concepts of competitive individualism and equal opportunities for their own purposes, thus hiding both their own ideological confusion, and also their continued support for patterns of male dominance. (Arnot, 1993, p. 188)

Watson (1990) also argues that feminist demands have been 'diluted' or even 'co-opted' through engagement with the institutions and discourses which constitute the state' (p. 6). Feminist educational campaigns lost their impact by assimilation into the National Curriculum, which appeared to offer equal entitlement. In reality it re-established a curriculum which highlighted male values, hierarchies of knowledge and priorities. Subjects which were traditionally the preserve of working-class girls, for example, home economics, were abolished (Arnot, 1989). The 'new vocationalism' resulted in changes in teaching, learning and assessment which favoured middle-class male students. The introduction of a compulsory common curriculum reduced concerns about curricular choices, but differentiated options and levels within subjects have re-emerged.

> Teacher autonomy has again been used to justify the refusal to offer political commitment to sex equality in the new reforms. (Arnot, 1993, p. 205)

Clearly a new agenda is being set and new discourses emphasized.

New sets of gender relations are being constructed through education which are likely to work in favour of white middle-class boys and to disadvantage working class, black and female students (Arnot, 1993, pp. 205–6)

Ball (1990a and 1990b) argues that the education market was established by the Education Reform Act (1988) through enshrining parental choice, competition in schools, diversity of provision and devolution of funding.

> The model of organization which the ERA implies is clear, it is that of governors as Board of Directors and head teacher as Chief Executive. Schools are to become businesses, run and managed like businesses with a primary focus on the profit and loss account. The parent is now the customer, the pupils in effect the product. Those schools which produce shoddy goods, it is believed will lose custom. And it would appear that in the government's view shoddy goods mean 'poor' results in national tests ... Given that schools are also required to provide a fixed National Curriculum it is tempting to refine the business model slightly and see the education market as a system of franchises, what one writer has called 'Kentucky Fried Schooling'. (Hargreaves, quoted in Ball, 1990b, p. 11)

Ball (1990a) argues that the likely outcome of the Education Reform Act will be further inequality between favoured schools in the leafy suburbs and under-resourced schools in the inner cities; this will clearly have an impact on 'racial' and 'sex' inequality.

Jones (1989) argues that the anti-equity rhetoric of the Tory party at the end of the 1980s led to political gains for them. The replacement of the discourse of equal opportunities and egalitarianism with one of quality and standards popularized Tory policies and marginalized their opponents. In this discourse egalitarianism threatens the social and moral order of society. Neo-liberals deny that sexism and racism result in inequality. Their individualism supports the idea that the market is open to all to enter as the reward of individual effort and virtue. Connell (1990) writes that the state is 'an active player in gender politics'. It is 'a significant vehicle' of both 'sexual and gender oppression and regulation'. He argues, however, that the state is not a static entity and constantly undergoes change which allows new political possibilities to emerge (Connell, 1990, p. 532).

The discourse of standards and quality marginalizes issues of class, race and sex equity to the extent that, in the late 1990s, they are seldom on the agenda for discussion either in initial teacher training or in post-qualifying and professional development courses. The impact of these new discourses on the learning of students from the different social groups is ignored, and this can only lead to further inequality.

Explicit discussion about the social context

- discussion of inequality in education and society must be part of the learning process
- discussion about how the social context affects learning must be part of the learning process

- the interrelationship between personal and social is valid discourse in the class-room

To address the power imbalance brought about through the social construction of knowledge and the surface approach to learning requires awareness and discussion both of the social construction of knowledge *and* of the social construction of learning. Murphy makes this point in relation to knowledge:

> The social construction of knowledge is a product of negotiation. In order to understand key ideas in subjects students need to understand, and have access to, this process of negotiation. This suggests a need to examine critically the status of subject knowledge claims and whose cumulative wisdom is reflected in teachers' practice and in the curriculum guidelines they work within. This examination needs to include gender, ethnicity, race and socio-economic class to determine which individuals and groups the knowledge is accessible to, and/or valuable for. (Murphy, 1996, p. 9)

We have discussed how knowledge is socially constructed, and if young people are to grow up with a less ethnocentric, gendered and heterosexist view, an alternative view of the world needs to be suggested which encompasses the experiences of different social groups. People can be encouraged to examine the social construction of knowledge. Similarly they can learn to recognize ways in which inequality is structured into the organization of institutions and into the processes by which such institutions operate; to recognize the role of the state and the ways in which they are affected by these processes.

Throughout this book we argue that learning must be made explicit. Chapter 5 outlines one approach to meta-learning – learning about learning. In Chapter 3 we discuss making learning explicit in relation to learning in the group. Part of this discussion about how we learn must also include an explicit discussion about how the social context affects learning. Classroom teachers are beginning to build meta-learning into their day-to-day work with young people. Some feminists have developed parallel ideas in their development of women's studies courses which adopt what feminists have called a 'feminist pedagogy'.

> Feminist pedagogy . . . aims to create awareness of 'difference' and of the process by which social divisions such as race, sex and socio-economic class, structure individual experiences and opportunities . . . A feminist pedagogy provides students with access to alternative discourses to help them understand how identities are shaped and meanings and truths constructed . . . Feminist pedagogy advocates making students theorists by encouraging them to interrogate and analyse their own experiences in order to gain a critical understanding of them. In a similar way, students can become theorists about subject knowledge as it is presented. (Murphy, 1996, pp. 14–15)

Weiler (1991) argues that Freire is the most influential theorist of liberatory education (see Chapter 6) and that his pedagogy, like feminist pedagogy, shares the view that oppression exists in people's material conditions of existence and as part of consciousness. Freire (1970) states that learners' perceptions of the world are culturally induced and their personal meanings or constructs can only be understood in their unique social and political context. Freire uses the term 'conscientization' to describe the process by which one's false consciousness is transcended by education. Both liberatory and feminist pedagogy see consciousness as containing a critical capacity that allows us to transcend the dominant discourse. Both see human beings as subjects and actors in history. Both have a commitment to justice and liberation.

Other writers (Mezirow, 1978, 1981; Reed, 1981; Cunningham, 1983) discuss what they call 'the empowering learning process', which involves the transformation of social consciousness and focuses on the experiences of learners and the historical development of inequality. Mezirow (1978) sees an important area of learning as one which frees people from habitual ways of thinking and acting and involves them in 'perspective transformation'. This is the process of becoming critically aware of how and why our assumptions about the world in which we operate constrain the way we see ourselves and our relationships. The Transformatory Approach stresses the importance of this 'reframing' process, and this is seen as the most important aspect of changing the meaning of experience.

Habermas (1974) describes an important reflective process occurring in a context of purpose which he calls 'critical intent'. He sees this as the investigation and reconstruction of social and moral involvement to achieve enlightenment and ultimately emancipation. In his view, a group of people with critical intent bringing their informed judgement to bear on the apparent issues or problem is an act of reflection. This process generates critical ideas or theories about the validity of the questions which are considered, the inferences drawn, and the reconstruction of new ones. Reflective activity with critical intent is, for Habermas, the heart of the process which frees the human mind.

The Transformatory Approach to Learning supports the notion of 'freeing the human mind through reflective activity', although we recognize that this is not problem-free. Feminists (Murphy, 1996; Weiler, 1991) have challenged the critical or liberatory pedagogies that emerged in the 1960s and 1970s. They challenge these pedagogies because of their assumptions of a collective experience of oppression and because feminist teachers have become increasingly aware of the way in which sex, race, sexual preference, age and physical ability divide students from one another and teachers from students.

In Chapter 3 we argue for cooperative and collaborative learning which promotes affective, social and cognitive gains. Collaborative group learning is also an essential way of organizing learning for social equity and justice. Murphy (1995) argues that for equity in the classroom to become a reality, classroom practice needs to enable problem-solving and cooperative learning. This involves engaging students and teachers in 'critical reflection on group processes' (Hansen et al., 1995). Putting this into practice requires changes in the way in which educational organizations are organized, and shifts in the way in which students and teachers perceive themselves and each other. These required changes are assumed in the Transformatory Approach to Learning.

Attempting to implement these pedagogies without acknowledging the conflict not only of divided consciousness but also the conflicts among groups trying to work together to name and struggle against oppression . . . can lead to anger, frustration, and a retreat to safer or more traditional approaches. (Weiler, 1991, p. 130)

This approach questions whether the oppressed cannot act also as oppressors and challenges the idea of a commonality of oppression. It raises questions about common experience as a source of knowledge, the pedagogical authority of the teacher, and the nature of political and pedagogical struggle.

Freire (1970) repeatedly states that his pedagogical method cannot simply be transferred to other settings, but that each historical site requires the development of a pedagogy appropriate to that setting. As indicated earlier, central to Freire's pedagogy is the practice of conscientization; coming to a consciousness of oppression and a commitment to end that oppression. The role of the teacher is to instigate a dialogue between students, based on their common ability to know the world and to act in it.

In the two previous chapters we argued that learning needs to encompass the emotional, social, spiritual and cognitive dimensions. Learners also need to discuss the interrelationship of these aspects of learning. This is necessary if learning experiences are to allow discussion about sexism, racism and other inequalities. However, education for social justice must include more than exploration of the effects and experiences of inequitable social practices in the classroom; this alone is not sufficient to ensure that the education offered to children will be anti-racist, anti-sexist or anti-heterosexist in effect. Changes in organizational policy and practice must be made (see Chapter 8).

Challenges to liberatory pedagogy raise the question of whether education can, or indeed should, be the means of social change. Feminist pedagogy has raised three areas of concern in considering ways in which Freirean and other liberatory pedagogies can be enriched and expanded. These include examination of:

- the role and authority of the teacher
- the claim that personal experience and feeling is a source of knowledge and truth
- the question of similarity of experience, which has been challenged mainly by women of colour and by post-modernists

This chapter now turns to the question of difference.

Recognizing the different experiences of people

- diversity needs to be recognized within social groups

The Transformatory Approach to Learning recognizes that people in the same social group may have experiences in common, and also that within social groups there will be a broad range of experiences. Feminists have also been concerned with this issue and have questioned the category 'women' as well as the assumption of the inevitable unity of 'women'. Instead feminist theorists have increasingly emphasized the importance of recognizing difference as a central feature of feminist pedagogy.

In the actual practice of feminist pedagogy, the central issue of difference, positionality, and the need to recognize the implications of subjectivity or identity for teachers and students have become central. Moreover, the question of authority in institutional settings makes problematic the possibility of achieving the collective and non hierarchical vision of early consciousness-raising groups . . . (Weiler, 1991, p. 138)

Institutional authority highlights the contradiction of trying to achieve democratic and collaborative ideals in a hierarchical organization. It also raises the question of the meaning of authority for teachers from some social group whose right to speak or to hold power is itself under attack in a patriarchal, racist, homophobic and inequitable class society.

Feminists point out that there is not a universal and common women's experience, but rather deep divisions in different women's reality, and in the kinds of knowledge they have. The recognition of differences raises challenges to liberatory pedagogy by revealing tensions among students as well as between teacher and students. The problem for liberatory pedagogy is that if we recognize the complexity of people's identities, and appreciate that each of us has partial knowledge, and that there are conflicting differences between us, how can we develop a liberatory pedagogy which facilitates active struggle against different forms of oppression? Reagon (1983) calls for 'coalition-building', a recognition and validation of both difference and conflict and an attempt to build coalitions around common goals of social justice and empowerment.

This chapter highlights some of the issues which must be considered in relation to the social context of learning. It stresses that each of us is positioned in terms of sex, race, socio-economic status, sexuality, physical ability and age. Our identity is formed in relation to this, and both our own and others' expectations of us are affected by these factors. The learning process includes explicit discourse about the constraints on learning resulting from social inequality; about our experiences of ourselves as learners and how these are affected by the social context; about reframing our experiences to allow for the possibility of new perceptions and action for liberation. In Chapter 5 we propose an action learning process to facilitate this discourse.

FIVE

Cycles of Change: The Action Learning Process

Learning is complex. The learner is complex, the context is becoming increasingly more complex, the process is complex. All aspects interrelate and affect the rest; it is a dynamic relationship. In practice the learner, context and learning process are intertwined. Individuals' learning always takes place within a context, involving process.

The next stage of exploring the Transformatory Approach to Learning considers the learning process. This is one of the three elements in the Transformatory Approach, the three being: the learner, the learning context and the learning process. The learner and the context have been discussed in the previous chapters. We now concentrate on the process.

Whitaker writes about the importance of the process in bringing about change:

> process is concerned with an enhanced view of human potential. It is concerned to create conditions in which the people involved can grow and develop and become more than they currently are . . . survival in a fast changing world may well depend upon the ability of pupils to develop skills in adaptation, flexibility, co-operation and imagination. (Whitaker, 1995a, p. 8)

Ferguson (1982) suggests that the key in satisfying the needs of a fast-changing and uncertain future is in looking to the nature of learning rather than to the curriculum and methods of instruction; in focusing less on structure and curriculum and more on practice and process. This shifts from learning in order to know towards learning in order to be.

In this chapter we make an important distinction between the learning process and the action learning process. Process learning has been described as:

> that reflective activity which enables the learner to draw upon previous experience to understand and evaluate the present, so as to shape future action and formulate new knowledge. (Abbott, 1994)

Watkins *et al.* point out that process definitions do not include *all aspects* of the process of learning. The action learning process:

- enables actions for change. This is a key concept in the Transformatory Approach to Learning. The action learning process is the vehicle through which individuals change and bring about changes in their environment.
- engages people in an action learning cycle. This is a process of reflection on experiences, learning from reflections, applying learning to new contexts in further action, bringing about change.
- involves meta-learning; learning about learning.
- includes the cognitive, affective and social dimensions of learning. This is part of the action learning discourse.
- explores the interconnection of the learner, context and process.
  (Watkins *et al.*, 1996)

We propose that action learning is effective:

(1) for individual learners, working alone;
(2) for individual learners, on a one-to-one basis with a tutor, or supervisor;
(3) for groups, to facilitate group learning;
(4) for learning organizations, within an action research process.

In this chapter we discuss such questions as: What is the action learning process? How are cycles of learning understood? How does engagement in the action learning process help people learn about learning? What is the learning discourse? What are the links with the action research process?

ASSUMPTIONS ABOUT THE ACTION LEARNING PROCESS UNDERPINNING THE TRANSFORMATORY APPROACH

We start the analysis of the action learning process by exploring our assumptions in more detail.

- the action learning process transforms individuals and groups
- action learning changes the meaning of experience
- the process involves understanding, constructing knowledge, making connections, taking control and taking action
- learning never stops; all experiences contribute to learning throughout life
- reflection on experience is an essential part of action learning
- reflection on self as learner and context of learning is essential in the action learning process
- making the learning explicit is an essential part of action learning
- action is an essential stage in learning
- applying the learning is an essential stage of action learning
- feedback is an important aspect of reviewing, learning and taking action
- learning about learning is essential for effective learning
- the effect of the emotions on learning is valid discourse

- the effect of the learning context, and the interconnection of the context, learner and process, is valid discourse

We use the same format as in the previous chapters, discussing the assumptions in turn. We have grouped assumptions together where there is logical connection. We start by exploring the purpose of the action learning process, within the Transformatory Approach.

The purpose of action learning

- the action learning process transforms individuals and groups
- action learning changes the meaning of experience
- the process involves understanding, constructing knowledge, making connections, taking control and taking action
- learning never stops; all experiences contribute to learning throughout life

We describe the learning process in the Transformatory Approach as 'action learning'. We argue that action learning is transformatory. It can lead to change in individuals and in groups. The process of action research, which is similar in some respects to action learning, can transform organizations (see Chapter 10).

Biggs and Moore (1993) differentiate between quantitative and qualitative conceptions of learning. They point out that quantitative and qualitative levels are not antagonistic but feed each other.

A quantitative level of conception includes:

- increasing knowledge
- memorizing
- reproducing and applying. (Applying, in this conception, refers to facts being adjusted to contexts.)

In a qualitative level of conception, learning is:

- understanding the meaning of content
- seeing something in a different way
- changing as a person; changing the meaning of experience, by coming to be in charge.

Quantitative conceptions, or absorption models of learning, relate to the concept of surface learning, and qualitative conceptions link with the concept of deep approaches (see Chapter 2). Biggs and Moore point out that underlying the shift from quantitative to qualitative is a constructivist view of leaning:

- people actively construct knowledge for themselves
- knowledge is based on categories derived from social interaction not observation; it is the way you come to look at things as much as what you are looking at
- people determine their own knowledge.
  (Biggs and Moore, 1993, p. 22)

Wittrock suggests:

> methods of teaching should be designed to stimulate students actively to construct meaning from their own experience rather than stimulating them to reproduce the knowledge of others. (Wittrock, 1977, p. 180, cited in Biggs and Moore, 1993)

Important educational implications arise from this view:

- What is learned may not be what the teacher intends to be learned. The major determinants of learning are internal to the learner.
- What is learned depends on what is already known. The most important determinant of learning is existing knowledge. New knowledge affects the outcome, but not as powerfully or directly as we may assume.
- Learning is an ongoing process; it is continuous and active.
- Learners have final responsibility for their learning. In adopting a constructivist view, one must allow learners to develop self-direction and not force 'correct' constructions onto them.
- Constructed meanings share common characteristics. Through language and shared social experiences, people's constructions allow communication and acknowledgement of mutual validity.
- Teachers who see their role as passing on established truths will be threatened if students question their utterances.
  (Biggs and Moore, 1993, pp. 22–3, drawing on Candy, 1991, and Driver and Oldham, 1986)

This constructivist view underpins the Transformatory Approach. We believe that knowledge is constructed; meaning is derived from experience. It is only when action comes as a result of reflection that learning has occurred. We use a very practical situation to illustrate this:

> I theoretically understood the workings of my car. I attended car maintenance courses for women. I could explain what to do, but I remained consciously incompetent. I knew that I could do it, but something stopped me. It was my belief about myself as a woman in this society that stopped me. I knew it was partly because I am a woman, and because of my 'learned helplessness', that I continued to believe I could not fix it. I believed that it was best to leave it to the AA man, even though it meant waiting around for two hours.
>
> It was only when I changed my view of myself as a learner, and thought about how I felt towards the task, reflected on what stopped me from doing it, that I was able to lift the bonnet of my car, confidently, and apply my knowledge to changing the battery. My feelings and beliefs about myself had changed. Then I could say that I actually learned. I took control, and acted on, and applied my learning. Now I feel good about fixing my car. I don't always fix it. But I can now decide whether I want to, or not. That is the difference.

This example illustrates that:

- learning is constructed
- what is learned depends on the way you look at things
- learning is self-determined.
  (Biggs and Moore, 1993, p. 22)

Action learning is a process in which reflection, learning and application need to be balanced in a dynamic relationship. Change comes when learning involves understanding the reasons why people behave in the ways they do. For example, women may have a particular view of themselves in relation to particular areas. In the example, there is a change in that person. There has been a change in the meaning of experience. She has come to be in control. She has choice.

In all change there are gains, losses and disturbances; within the Transformatory Approach this is recognized. Absorption models of learning ignore the struggles and confusions about learning and bringing about change. In the Transformatory Approach the process involves unravelling complex views about people as learners and the complexities of the learning context. This is done through the action learning process. Although our example above is very practical, the same principles apply to all learning. The process with which we engage in relation to academic learning still requires that we reflect on ourselves as learners, in order that our learning is most effective. What is important is that the process involves affective, social as well as cognitive considerations. The process focuses on ourselves as learners, and our understanding of the context in which we are learning.

In our experience, people who have been successful academically may not see the need for action learning: 'We don't need to learn how to learn. We are successful learners as we have done well academically.' This view may also be prevalent in higher education establishments where students are awarded higher grades for critiquing, arguing and intellectual reasoning. These are highly important skills, and as Biggs and Moore (1993) suggest levels of conception are not antagonistic. The world may be perceived differently through knowledge and understanding but knowledge and understanding may not in themselves bring about change. Bringing about change requires attention to process.

Freire (1970) highlights three vital elements in the learning process: praxis, problematization, conscientization. Praxis, in this process, is the continuous sequence of experience and reflection, involving critical thinking and dialogue. This is based on the premise that we will be able to act deliberately if we do not understand how previous specific actions succeeded or did not.

In problematization, Freire suggests that we need to focus on difficult or frustrating parts of learning, areas which need to change. He believes that if these are ignored or rationalized, cognitive dissonance or learned helplessness will result. People come to believe they are unable, or no good at certain things, and it is this belief, rather than any other reason, that prevents them from learning.

Freire describes conscientization as the process through which learners, by a deepening awareness of the social and cultural contexts in which learning is taking place, are able to develop a capacity to understand and transform that reality.

This continuous sequence of experience highlights the notion of learning cycles.

The cycle of learning

- reflection on experience is an essential part of action learning
- reflection on self as learner and context of learning is essential in the action learning process
- making the learning explicit is an essential part of action learning
- action is an essential stage in learning
- applying the learning is an essential stage of action learning
- feedback is an important aspect of reviewing, learning and taking action

Central to the Transformatory Approach to Learning is the learning cycle. We draw on Kolb's (1971) process referred to as experiential learning, and Dennison and Kirk's (1990) 'Do, Review, Learn, Apply' cycle.

Kolb's approach suggests a cycle of discrete mental processes following concrete experience (see Figure 5.1). This process includes reflecting on various experiences, to make sense of them, which enables the experiences to be assimilated into our framework of concepts and constructs. New learning allows us to formulate fresh concepts, and thus we can act upon our changed constructs.

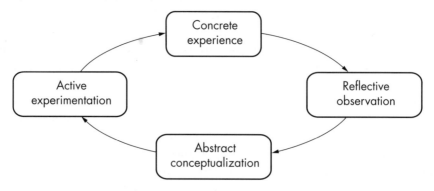

Figure 5.1 The experiential learning cycle

Whitaker (1995a) distinguishes between incidental and deliberate experiential learning. He highlights the importance of structured learning experiences punctuated with deliberate periods of reflection and critical thinking. He suggests that for learning to be effective it is as important to focus on how the learning is being conducted and managed, as it is on what is to be learned. Indeed we would argue that the 'content', what is to be learned, in the Transformatory Approach to Learning, includes the process. The process becomes part of the content. A further discussion on this is developed under discourse about learning (p. 77).

Dennison and Kirk's (1990) cycle of learning, developed from Kolb (1971), outlines a process of reflecting, analysing, evaluating, making connections and planning action for change (Figure 5.2).

This cycle highlights activity in learning (Do), the need for reflection and evaluation (Review), the extraction of meaning from this review (Learn) and the planned use of learning in future action (Apply).

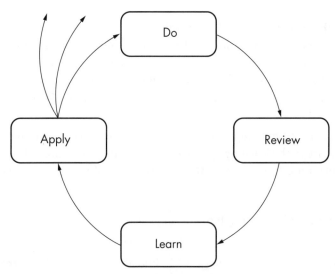

Figure 5.2 The 'Do, Review, Learn, Apply' cycle of learning

Cycles of learning may not take the total picture into account. Within the cycle there may be an emphasis on cognitive processes; emotional and social aspects of learning may be less prominent; the learning process may be viewed as a conscious and rational process. A linear approach may be taken. However, making connections between past, present and future does not always follow in a linear fashion. The cycle may play down the difficulties of 'unlearning' old patterns, and 'letting go' established and safe structures. Additionally, learning cycles may not take account of the unconscious and motivational aspects of action. There may be assumptions that learners have total control of the situation, ignoring power dynamics, constraints and the learners' social position (see Chapter 3).

Boud *et al.* (1985) include affective as well as cognitive aspects in their analysis of the process of reflection and identify three stages:

- returning to the experience
- attending to the feelings
- re-evaluating the experience

In group situations where there is a learning facilitator, an important role can be played, in attending to feelings:

In the 'DO' stage the facilitator encourages the learners to engage in a variety of stimulating, relevant and informative learning tasks. They will negotiate with learners to give them opportunities to plan and organize some areas of study. In the 'REVIEW' stage facilitators provide constructive feedback. They structure group situations when learners reflect together on their work. Facilitators encourage effective learning by helping learners explore how their emotional state helps or hinders the learning process, in groups as well as on their own. In the 'LEARN' stage they help the learners make the learning explicit by asking questions to tease out their new insights, connections, understandings and meanings. To develop reflective learning the facilitator structures situations in order that the learners evaluate their learning. In the 'APPLY' stage the facilitator helps the learner to approach new situations differently in the light of these understandings. (Watkins *et al.*, 1996)

When working one-to-one, in a tutorial or supervision setting, a framework following a similar structure to the learning cycle can make limited time more effective (see Table 5.1). Action planning forms part of the 'Apply' stage of the learning cycle. There are

Table 5.1 Framework for using the learning cycle in one-to-one situations

Stage of tutorial/supervision meeting	Principles for the helping role
Exploration of situation Reflecting	– active listening – asking open questions – being non-judgemental
New understanding Learning	– empathizing – reflecting back – sharing insights
Action Applying the learning	– establishing clear, negotiated goals – action planning

key processes and associated skills, identified by Watkins and Butcher (1995), which also relate to the learning cycle: (a) taking stock, self-assessment; (b) clarifying goals, selecting priorities, making choices; and (c) deciding on a course of action, devising strategies and goal-setting. At best, the process becomes continuous: one plan can lead to another. Reviewing the progress which has been made on a plan leads to learning and to modifying the next steps – a further plan (Watkins and Butcher, 1995). This process highlights learning cycles within the cycle itself.

At any stage of the cycle feedback is important. This is crucial in helping individuals reflect, learn and bring about actions for change. This will include giving positive feedback, as well as feedback used as information on which to base changes, if appropriate. Feedback includes giving information to another person about how their behaviour is affecting others. The information presented may be confirming to the other person: it may lead them to some new perceptions of themselves; they may use it to modify their actions; or they may choose to disregard it. Giving feedback within a structured, supportive context does not guarantee change, but it is more likely that individuals will hear feedback, and not react in a threatened or defensive way.

Characteristics of effective feedback

- It describes the giver's feelings and reactions, rather than judges the receiver's behaviour
- It follows the behaviour being responded to closely in time
- It describes specific observed behaviour, what was seen and heard, and does not involve guesswork
- It focuses on sharing ideas and information, rather than giving advice
- It focuses on potential use and value to the receiver rather than upon the 'release' value to the giver
- It is limited to the amount of information that the receiver can use, rather than upon the amount the giver would like to suggest
- It is shared at an appropriate time, in an appropriate place, and given in such a manner that it can be received

  (*Spectrum* (1996), 7 Endymion Road, London N4, training handout)

The cycle of learning is used frequently. In further learning occasions the facilitator may provide support to the learner, in exploring how the learner dealt with new situations. In this way the facilitator may help overcome the difficult and frustrating areas, discussed earlier, the 'problematization' element of the learning process (Freire, 1972), and help in the letting-go and relearning stages.

Cycles of learning may be useful for the individual learner and for a group of learners working collaboratively. Where the cycle is used in group settings, the social and cultural contexts in which learning is taking place can be analysed. Group and social dynamics may be explored. Learners may be able to develop their awareness of themselves in the group context and develop a capacity to understand and transform that reality.

The facilitator's role within this includes making the purposes of the learning process explicit, rather than the learning itself; providing a safe and challenging environment, where learners can take risks; ensuring the group agreement is adhered to (for example, listening, giving everyone a voice); and providing feedback. It is crucial to make the purpose of the learning process clear to the learner, especially to people who may be unfamiliar with this way of working. A degree of freedom is associated with the approach. This may be uncomfortable if the learner holds a different perception of the teacher's and learner's role. Individuals may be used to direction, clear instructions, and explicitly stated end results or learning outcomes. Handling freedom, open-ended situations and different interpretations needs to be learned. This requires learning about learning.

Cycles of learning are useful at the level of organization through a process of action research (see Chapter 10). Both action learning and action research are central to the Transformatory Approach. Both focus on reviewing learning and taking action as a result. Both are cyclical processes involving reflection on practice and personal learning. Both have the self as central in the process. In action learning, the learner is responsible for the learning process and for bringing about change. In action research the practitioner is responsible for defining the issues, and areas to be developed and changed. Both result in change; change as a person; change in the meaning of experience, being in control. Both are more effective if carried out collaboratively, when group and organizational change result.

Meta-learning

- learning about learning is essential for effective learning

One of the assumptions highlighted in the Transformatory Approach is learning about learning. We suggest that meta-learning can lead to effective learning; the learners can bring about actions for change as a result of:

(1) understanding themselves as learners;
(2) understanding the context in which they are learning, and the effect it has on them; and
(3) understanding the learning processes.

We argue that learning about learning results in a greater awareness of the affective, social and cognitive aspects of learning. A context which emphasizes learning about learning leads to an increase in deep approaches and long-term improvements in academic performance (Biggs, 1988). Others identify meta-learning as a necessary process in becoming an effective learner (Novak and Gowin, 1984; Nisbet and Shucksmith, 1986; Biggs and Moore, 1993).

> Effective learners have therefore gained understanding of the processes necessary to become effective learners. This has been described as 'meta-learning' . . . (Watkins *et al.*, 1996)

Many authors use the term 'meta-learning' to describe learning *how* to learn, suggesting that people become meta-learners as they become more conscious of learning *how* to learn. We are suggesting another stage in meta-learning, where people become more conscious of the personal and social factors affecting their learning; learning *about* learning.

The following quote illustrates learning *how* to learn, as opposed to learning *about* learning:

> The task of helping our students to learn (as opposed to covering the content of the course) is a daunting one, since no tutor can possibly help every individual student to improve their learning *efficiency*. What we can do, however, is to encourage students to be aware of their own learning development and to *increase their own understanding of how best to learn* . . . One way to facilitate this 'meta-learning' (i.e. learning about learning) is to encourage students to *reflect* on their own learning. Understanding how to learn is particularly important for new learners, since the quicker they can recognize what works effectively for them, then the more effective their learning will be . . . I am not suggesting that it is easy, and in some ways the more students have been successful without conscious reflection, the less willing they might be to try it! (Open University, pp. 3–4, our emphases)

Meta-learning in this definition includes learning about approaches to learning (see Chapter 2), for example the individual's style of learning; strategies used; systems to support learning (for example, where the learner is going to study; identifying individuals who will support the learning process, identifying appropriate times of day for study).

> Studies of approaches to learning demonstrate that study skills which focus on surface matters such as reading, note taking and time management are largely ineffective, whereas a focus on approach to strategy and review is more effective. Learners need occasions to review their strategies of learning. (Open University, developed from Selmes, 1987; Ramsden, 1988; Gibbs, 1992)

These areas are important. However, our definition of meta-learning also includes individuals reflecting on, and learning about:

(1) their own beliefs about themselves as learners;
(2) how their emotion affects their learning;
(3) the group context in which they are learning;
(4) how they are affected by their external environment, for example, their families' views about learning; and
(5) the wider social, political and cultural climate.

We are suggesting that the action learning process includes learning how to learn, learning about approaches to learning, and learning about learning through learning discourse – discussion leading to understanding about the involvement of the whole person in learning.

Discourse about learning

- the effect of the emotions on learning is valid discourse
- the effect of the learning context, and the interconnection of the context, learner and process, is valid discourse

Within the Transformatory Approach, learners need an understanding of themselves as learners. To achieve this, it is important for learners to reflect on all aspects of themselves. This contrasts with the prevalent views of learning, where the intellectual dimension of the person dominates and the emotional and social aspects are mostly ignored.

In approaches to effective learning, Watkins *et al.* (1996) incorporate aspects of the learning discourse which focus on the emotional and group context, as well as cognitive dimensions.

In the Transformatory Approach to Learning, the effect of the emotions on learning is seen as valid discourse. Social and cultural dimensions are also considered. This can be achieved through reflection, diary-writing and explorations with peers.

> Part of the public school ethic has been to develop character by concealing emotions and feelings and suppress them while at the same time discouraging intuitive

thinking and imagination by extolling the virtues of rationality, logic and deductive thinking. It is, of course, no coincidence that the polarization of these attributes has been a central feature of gender socialization. (Whitaker, 1995a, p. 20)

It is interesting to note how gender perceptions are expressed in regard to different forms of learning. This view is reflected in our experience of working with groups of females and males of all ages. Perceptions of gendered and other socially constructed roles may be unlearned through the process of discourse, as part of the learning cycle (see Chapter 4).

Earlier in this chapter we highlighted the purpose of action learning as helping people change perceptions, change as a person, change the meaning of experience, by taking control and coming to be in charge. This recognizes that learning requires the whole person *being* in the process. As Rogers puts it:

> It is a quality of personal involvement – the whole person in both his [sic] feeling and cognitive aspects being in the learning event. It is self-initiated even when the impetus or stimuli comes from the outside, the sense of discovery, of reaching out, of grasping and comprehending, comes from within. It is pervasive. It makes a difference in the behaviour, attitudes, perhaps even the personality of the learner. It is evaluated by the learner. He knows whether it is meeting his need, whether it leads toward what he wants to know, whether it illuminates the dark area of ignorance he is experiencing. The locus of evaluation, we might say, resides definitely in the learner. Its essence is meaning. When such learning takes place, the element of meaning to the learner is built into the whole experience. (Rogers, 1969, p. 5)

This discussion highlights the importance of the process having significant meaning for the learner. It recognizes that the learning process is closely interlinked with the person, their thoughts, their intuition, and a whole spectrum of feelings. As we argue, learning discourse needs to consider all dimensions of the person, the affective, spiritual, social and cognitive. Jung (1971) suggests that human completeness also consists of the intuitive. All these aspects need to be part of learning discourse, if the learner is to change the meaning of experience and take control.

The complexity and the multi-dimensional nature of individuals means that the process of learning and learning outcomes may be unpredictable and not easily measured. Nevertheless, there are stages in the learning process which may be structured and designed to help the learning become more explicit. Structured and deliberate learning experiences, with periods of reflection and critical thinking, are important if learning is to be explicit and more effective.

The process of learning takes place within a context.

Learning is influenced by:

– the form of organization;
– the style of management;
– the climate of relationships, between individuals and between groups.
(Watkins *et al.*, 1996)

As well as the immediate environment, learning is influenced by wider social and political contexts. The effect of the context on learning is crucial in the learning discourse (see Chapters 3 and 4). This, we believe, is aligned to the concept of conscientization (Freire, 1972) described earlier. Through a deepening awareness of the organization, social, political and cultural contexts in which learning is taking place, learners are able to develop a capacity to understand and transform that reality. As we stress at the beginning of the chapter, learning is complex; the interconnection of the learner, process and context is crucial for understanding.

To ensure congruence, and maximize learning opportunities, there needs to be support for the Transformatory Approach at all levels, at individual, at classroom, and at the organizational level.

> ethos is the linchpin of any action a teacher or school takes on behalf of the pupil. Central to the ethos are issues such as support, approachable staff and pupil empowerment. (Carey, 1993)

The outcomes of learning depend on the processes in which the learner is engaged (Biggs and Moore, 1993). Throughout this chapter we stress that within the Transformatory Approach the outcomes of learning include change at individual, group and organizational level.

The processes of learning outlined in the Transformatory Approach help individual learners, groups and organizations:

- take responsibility for their learning
- construct, rather than absorb, knowledge
- find meaning in knowledge and relate that to their experiences
- make learning personally significant
- reflect on their own learning and learning strategies
- deepen understanding about different aspects of their learning
- explore the effects of social contexts on their learning
- explore the effects of wider social, political and cultural issues
- identify insights and new understandings
- use feedback
- make learning explicit
- identify actions for change
- plan to use new learning in other situations
- set further learning goals

Through the action learning process, learners identify personal values and direction, find new ways of collaborating with others, test new ideas, skills, behaviour and ways of being. The action learning process helps learners 'let go', or 'unlearn', ways of being which close learning down. It will help learners take risks, and bring about actions for change. We believe that this approach helps learners find excitement, and a lifelong commitment to learning.

Summary of Part 1

In Part 1 we present our Transformatory Approach to Learning, and explore the assumptions underpinning this approach.

- We argue that the Transformatory Approach leads to change at individual, group, organization, and societal levels
- We consider traditional theories of learning and make connections between the Transformatory Approach and these theories
- We adopt an organismic approach, which recognizes that learning involves affective, social and spiritual dimensions, as well as cognitive dimensions
- We view learners as having a wealth of experiences which they bring to learning, and stress that learning continues throughout life
- We explore the interrelatedness of the learner, the process, the group and social context
- We draw on a cycle of learning to illuminate the learning process
- We emphasize the importance of the group in facilitating effective learning for change
- We recognize the social constraints on learning and explore ways of addressing these constraints
- We argue that the learning process is the vehicle through which individuals change, and bring about changes in their environment
- We argue that learning is complex, and draw attention to the cohesion and comprehensiveness of the Transformatory Approach to Learning

Part 2
Educational Metamorphosis

SIX
Developing Educational Frameworks

In Part 2 we look at education within organizations, for example, in schools, colleges, universities or other working contexts, where education is planned, formal and has explicit goals.

Chapter 6 provides a theoretical context within which the Transformatory Approach can be understood and applied within an educational setting. It develops a typology of different models of education, and explores the goals and concepts which underpin them: the Functionalist; the Client-centred; the Liberatory and the Social Justice models. It examines the ways in which the Transformatory Approach to Learning, discussed in Part 1, embodies the practical application of the Liberatory model of education.

We start by exploring the usefulness of models, and their value in enabling educationalists to locate their practice within a theoretical framework.

MODELS OF EDUCATION

The theoretical framework we present outlines four models of education; the Functionalist, Client-centred, Liberatory and Social Justice (see Figure 6.1).

Models are simplified representations of the overall picture. They act as tools for analysis, evaluation and exploration, and help clarify educational approaches adopted. Theoretical models rarely match up to practice; it may be that educationalists draw on several models, but by identifying different approaches, the underlying aims and philosophy will be clarified for practitioners.

The Functionalist model relates most closely to practice in educational establishments. The Client-centred model influenced practice for 20 years between the mid-1960s and mid-1980s, especially in primary schools and the lower years of secondary school. The Liberatory model (sometimes called emancipatory education) has been associated with adults' learning, although there have been some pockets of practice influenced by this approach in all phases of education. The Social Justice model is an oppositional model, and in practice could not be adopted in mainstream educational establishments, although some individual teachers in particular curriculum areas have adopted some of its principles. We have included this model because it

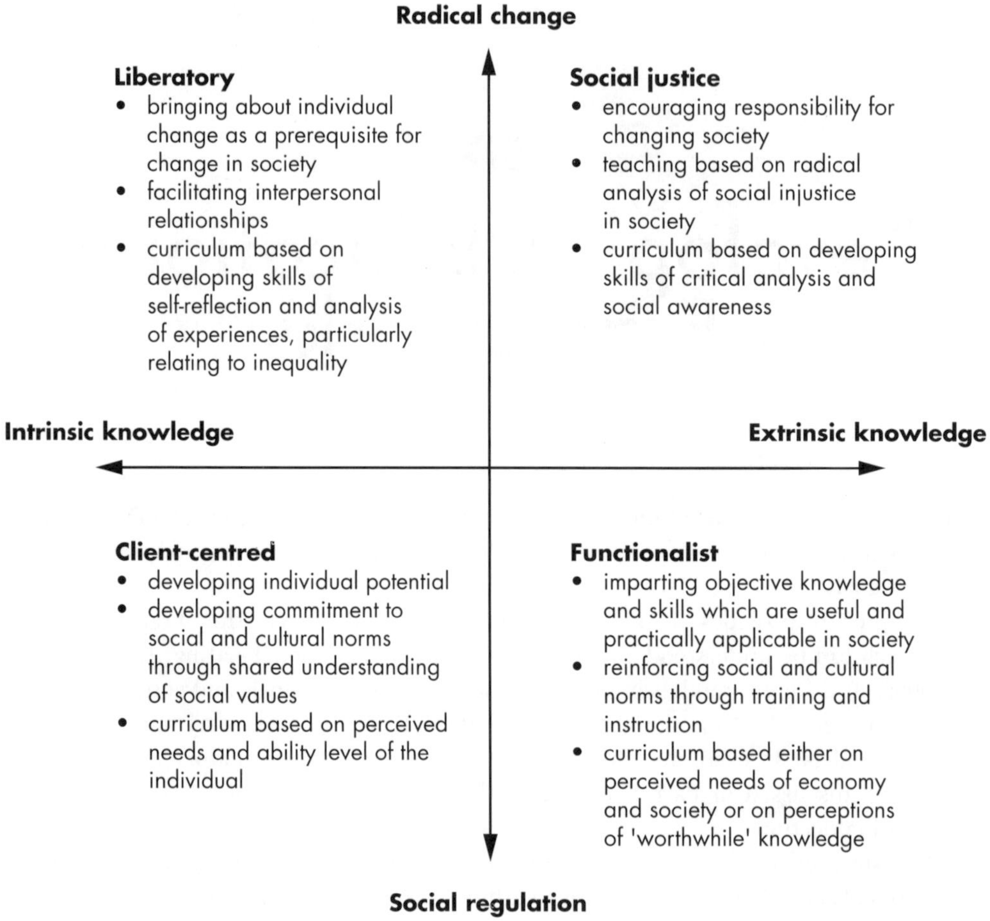

Radical change

Liberatory
- bringing about individual change as a prerequisite for change in society
- facilitating interpersonal relationships
- curriculum based on developing skills of self-reflection and analysis of experiences, particularly relating to inequality

Social justice
- encouraging responsibility for changing society
- teaching based on radical analysis of social injustice in society
- curriculum based on developing skills of critical analysis and social awareness

Intrinsic knowledge ←→ **Extrinsic knowledge**

Client-centred
- developing individual potential
- developing commitment to social and cultural norms through shared understanding of social values
- curriculum based on perceived needs and ability level of the individual

Functionalist
- imparting objective knowledge and skills which are useful and practically applicable in society
- reinforcing social and cultural norms through training and instruction
- curriculum based either on perceived needs of economy and society or on perceptions of 'worthwhile' knowledge

Social regulation

Figure 6.1 Typology of models of education

is useful when making comparisons, and clarifying positions within the other models. Following our analysis of the four models, we make links with the Transformatory Approach to Learning.

These models are mapped as two-way continua. One continuum is concerned with knowledge. At one extreme, knowledge is viewed as extrinsic; that is as objective facts which are taught by an 'expert'. This knowledge is perceived as conventional wisdom – of either the policymakers in education or those in opposition to them. At the other extreme, knowledge is viewed as intrinsic; it develops from interaction with the environment, and making personal sense and meaning from our experiences. People construct knowledge for themselves (Biggs and Moore, 1993; see Chapter 5).

The other continuum is concerned with the nature of society. For example, with notions of stability and change; the question of whether society exists as a reality in its own right, or merely as a collection of individuals; with maintaining the status quo, in terms of the organization of society, or challenging structures and organization of society. The radical-change–social-regulation continuum is concerned with the purpose of education – either to socialize young people into the norms and values of society, or to bring about radical change in the society.

There are four quadrants and four models. The Liberatory and Social Justice share a commitment to radical change, though they are at different ends of the knowledge continuum. The Functionalist and Client-centred models share a commitment to social regulation and shared social values, whilst being at either end of the knowledge continuum.

The Liberatory and Client-centred models are similar as their focus is on intrinsic (subjective) knowledge, whilst being opposed in relation to their position on the change–regulation continuum. The Social Justice and Functionalist models share a belief in knowledge being extrinsic (objective) and are also in opposition on the change–regulation continuum.

The chapter presents a more detailed exploration of the four models, and a discussion of the limitations of each. The characteristics of the four models are then outlined in Table 6.1 (pp. 93–5), including their fundamental goals, the method used to achieve them and the key principles on which the curriculum is based in each model.

The Functionalist model of education

This is the most familiar model of education in schools, colleges, universities and other working contexts. The primary goal is to teach specific skills and knowledge, and for students to reach a set standard of behaviour, attitude and work, defined by the educational establishment, workplace or state.

The Functionalist model of education was paramount up until the end of the 1950s. In the 1960s and 1970s, there was a shift toward a more progressive, child-centred model. The growing trend in the 1980s and 1990s has been back towards the Functionalist model. Criticos writes:

> There is no doubt that there are two major competing epistemologies. The dominant epistemology underpins most of mainstream education. This dominant epistemology, an analytical and objective way of knowing, does not tolerate experiential learning, action research, holistic medicine and other alternative ways of knowing and working. (Criticos, 1993, p. 158)

The Functionalist model is mechanistic, focusing on the cognitive dimension of education. Teaching and knowledge acquisition is paramount. The predominant view of the curriculum is a body of knowledge (Hirst, 1974). Those who focus on content view the primary task of education as delivering concepts and facts (Cheney, 1987; Finn and Ravitch, 1987; Hirch, 1987). The model is based on the belief that the teacher is an expert in a particular field of knowledge. Teachers give information by using didactic pedagogic strategies – lectures, talks by other 'experts'; and the student is seen as a passive recipient of knowledge. The curriculum content is non-negotiable. Students are viewed as differing in terms of their intelligence level.

Divisions in society are not challenged in this model, as students are educated according to perceptions of their abilities. The division of schooling into grammar and secondary modern reflected this belief, as the taught curriculum for different schools is based on what is seen as relevant for those particular students. This reflects the cultural prejudice in England which has propagated the view that only a few need 'educating'; the masses need 'training'. More recent emphasis on setting and streaming, and developments of assessment and its publication in league tables, arise from this model, and welfare-into-work proposals seem to be an extension of the 'training' ethos.

Vocationalism fits this approach, to prepare young people for the world of work. It assumes the students are educated for a particular function in society and prepared to be good workers.

A similar view of education is that of a body of 'worthwhile' knowledge to which everyone should have access (Hirst, 1974). This view developed in parallel with the Client-centred model, but differs from it as its starting-point is not relevance of knowledge for the individual, but relevance of particular knowledge for everyone in society. The notion of 'worthwhile' knowledge rests on value judgements about knowledge which are both culturally and historically specific. Decisions about what constitutes 'worthwhile' knowledge are made by the same people who decide what constitutes 'worthwhile' education. Stanton writes about knowledge in higher education:

> the dominant epistemology of knowledge, which informs higher education, is based on a sense that replicability is the final test of truth, that knowledge is analytical, abstract and logical. The task of education is the distribution of knowledge, or the 'banking' method of education. Random experience is inadequate as a means of knowledge. We are taught to distrust personal experience as a guide, to identify universal truths from logical, preorganized, abstractions. (Stanton, 1986, cited in Criticos, 1993, p. 159)

Whether the curriculum is based on worthwhile knowledge or on societal and economic needs, in this model knowledge is transmitted by the 'expert' rather than constructed by the students. The curriculum is also based on the notion that different knowledge bases develop different skills: for example, different forms of problem-solving and rational thinking.

Limitations of the Functionalist model of education

The Functionalist model is congruent with one of the four pillars which Delors (1996) describes as forming the foundations of education – learning to know. The problem with this model is that education may become elitist; people who are not in possession of the 'worthwhile' knowledge are excluded from all walks of life in which this form of education is deemed necessary. Their constructed knowledge will not have the same status. Those who are in possession of 'worthwhile' knowledge may also see themselves as superior; however, they may lack aspects of learning which others have who are not regarded as educated. The Report to UNESCO (1996) puts greater emphasis on 'learning to live together' in the twenty-first century:

by developing an understanding of others and their history, traditions and spiritual values and on this basis, creating a new spirit which, guided by recognition of our growing interdependence and a common analysis of the risks and challenges of the future, would induce people to implement common projects or to manage the inevitable conflicts in an intelligent and peaceful way. (UNESCO, 1996, p. 22)

The Functionalist model does not stress 'learning to live together', nor does it stress the other two pillars of education: 'learning to be' and 'learning to do' (UNESCO, 1996). 'Learning to do' does not only involve learning skills (which may be incorporated into a Functionalist model), but also includes

the acquisition of a competence that enables people to deal with a variety of situations, often enforceable, and to work in teams, a feature to which educational methods do not at present pay enough attention. (Delors, 1996, p. 23)

Those who support the process model argue that the teaching of facts to people is ineffective unless they are taught how to construct their own schema for internalizing the information and organizing it so that it becomes their own (Costa, 1991; Day, 1981; Worsham, 1988). The latter writers see the primary task of education as the development of thinking abilities for processing, acquiring and relating information to own experience. In the twentieth century the increase in knowledge has outstripped our abilities to learn it all in a lifetime. The need for greater information-processing skills has therefore received greater attention, and the teacher's role has shifted to some extent from information-giver to facilitator.

The Functionalist model is mechanistic; it fails to take a holistic approach to the educational needs of students. In a technological age these needs change rapidly. In the new millennium, knowledge will soon become out of date. Young people will need to learn how to learn, they will need to be flexible, they will need to be able to make connections between their learning in one sphere and learning in another, and most of all, they will need to be able to apply their learning to different situations.

The Functionalist model does not address approaches to learning, cycles of learning, learning strategies and meta-learning. In the Functionalist model, the approach to learning is surface rather than deep (see Chapter 2). The model does not stress connections at a variety of different levels; either between different bodies of knowledge, between knowledge and personal experience, or between personal meaning and understanding which may be applied to the knowledge. Emotional and social aspects of learning are not addressed, and the model does not acknowledge what the learner brings to the learning situation. Finally, the model does not recognize or address social justice or social transformation.

The Functionalist model stresses the importance of rational thinking and stresses the specific; that is objective, abstract, logical, sequential thinking. As a result, the view is uncluttered, although incomplete. This view is similar to looking through a telescope; the telescopic lens magnifies and clarifies one aspect of the situation while failing to see everything outside its range of focus.

Vocationalism raises implications for contemporary society, in which around 30 per cent of 16- to 25-year-olds are unemployed. The disaffection of some groups of pupils may reflect their belief that they have no obvious role, and therefore no value, in the economy.

> It is increasingly apparent that even in the most prosperous societies on earth, there are growing numbers who are becoming alienated, and in some cases disaffected, in spite of the immense economic progress made in the late twentieth century. (Barber, 1996, p.15)

Another criticism of this model is that it places people in particular roles and does not allow for the possibility of mobility. Divisions between young people in school both reflect divisions in society, but also contribute to the perpetuation of social divisiveness. The ways people are divided according to 'ability' affects their perceptions of themselves as learners. They may be affected in different ways; for example, they may be alienated from the system of education and reject it, or they may internalize messages about being academically inferior. Either way the situation is iniquitous, as it disadvantages young people because they either do not have access to, or may not benefit from, formal learning situations. Those seen as 'successful' in this model may also be disadvantaged, as being successful academically does not automatically ensure success as a learner in its broader sense. Nor do contemporary successful academic learners necessarily possess the learning skills needed in the new millennium. Society also suffers as social division leads to unrest and dissatisfaction.

The Client-centred model of education

This model developed in the 1960s and 1970s. It is based on the egalitarian ideals of encouraging each child to achieve their maximum potential. It attempted to challenge some aspects of social injustice by providing the same educational opportunities for all, including nursery provision, and access for all to higher education (for example, the Open University). It developed alongside ideas of comprehensive schooling, the demolishment of selective schools and selection at eleven, and the introduction of 'mixed-ability' teaching.

The Client-centred model promotes the learning needs of individual children. The teacher provides the experiences that the individual child needs. The key features include discovery learning, participatory learning, open-ended questioning, and discussion (see Chapter 1 for a discussion of Piaget's influence). It attempts to relate knowledge to the young person's everyday life and experiences, and for knowledge to be more meaningful and relevant. It operates on the assumption that young people are rational decision-makers, can be self-directed and learn autonomously. Learners are encouraged to make choices about their learning experiences, within limits placed on them by teachers and the school context.

In this model, it is still accepted that young people have different intelligence levels and different talents, interests and skills. There is an attempt to counteract divisions in society by providing equal educational opportunities for all in the state system, and developing the unique abilities of all children. Education in this model is based on the principle of 'drawing out', rather than 'putting in'.

The emphasis shifts from coercive approaches based on rules, regulation and punishment for infringements, to attempts to motivate pupils, and develop their commitment to the values and norms of the organization. This necessitates the development of a relationship between teacher and student. The teacher has to be interested in finding out each learner's abilities, interests and skills.

In this model, the needs of the economy become secondary to the needs of individuals. The primary goal is to maximize the potential of each person, and the underlying inference is that society will benefit accordingly.

This model represents a shift towards the organismic view. In this model the cognitive dimension of learning is still dominant. However, there is recognition of the role played by social and emotional factors. Because the focus is on understanding and meaningful experiences, the approach to learning is at a deeper level.

Limitations of the Client-centred model of education

This model, like the Functionalist model, does not incorporate meta-learning; it does not address approaches to learning, cycles of learning, or learning strategies. The Report to UNESCO (1996) on learning in the twenty-first century stresses the importance of learning about learning throughout life:

> The concept of learning throughout life thus emerges as one of the keys to the twenty-first century. It goes beyond the traditional distinction between initial and continuing education. It meets the challenges posed by a rapidly changing world. This is not a new insight, since previous reports on education have emphasized the need for people to return to education in order to deal with new situations arising in their personal and working lives. That need is still felt and is even becoming stronger. The only way of satisfying it is for each individual to learn how to learn. (UNESCO, 1996, p. 22)

The Client-centred model assumes people can attain their maximum potential given the necessary experiences in the classroom. The problem is that it suggests that once a person has developed particular skills, for example, autonomy, they will be able to exercise their personal power in bringing about change in personal circumstances and lives. The model does not address the constraints in society and inequalities which may affect the achievement of potential. The goal of the model is to enable young people to fit in society rather than to challenge social injustice.

One criticism of the Client-centred model is that by over-emphasizing personal meaning and understanding, one detracts from the acquisition of knowledge, which is viewed as more relevant for the needs of society. This suggests 'falling standards' in formal education. This model does not focus on learning contexts, or take oppression and the experience of oppression into account.

The Liberatory model of education

The Liberatory model has never become mainstream educational practice although individual teachers have attempted to incorporate some of the underlying principles into their practice. Perhaps the best known proponent of this kind of approach is Freire

(1970). The goal of this model is to achieve enlightenment and emancipation from oppression through a process of individual change. Grundy describes it as follows:

> the emancipatory interest is concerned with empowerment, that is, the ability of individuals and groups to take control of their own lives in autonomous and responsible ways ... At the level of practice the emancipatory curriculum will involve the participants in the educational encounter, both teacher and pupil, in action which attempts to change the structures within which learning occurs and which constrain freedom in often unrecognized ways. (Grundy, 1987, p. 19)

This model is based on the notion that groups of people can be more powerful than individuals in bringing about changes. It shifts from a stress on individual responsibility, to suggest that people should collaborate, identifying issues in their community and society which affect their wellbeing and act to bring about changes.

It purports that emancipation involves a reflective process of learning which involves critical investigation and reconstruction of social and moral values, and sharing of subjective experiences. The model argues that personal meanings and constructs can only be understood in their unique social and political context.

The role of the teacher in this process is to instigate a dialogue between themselves and their students, based on their common ability to know the world, and to act as subjects in the world. The role of the young person is to actively engage in the process. This suggests that relationships between teacher and pupil are less hierarchical and less boundaried than in the previous two models.

The social and political context of learning is central to this process. In order to bring about social change, critical investigation, reconstruction of social and moral values, sharing of subjective experiences, emotional processes and relationship skills are addressed.

This model of education is concerned with shifting the balance of power and working towards a fair and just society for all its members. Like the Client-centred approach, it also represents a move towards the organismic view. The focus is on understanding and meaningful experiences, and the approach to learning is at a deeper level. Unlike the Client-centred and Functionalist approaches, this model is based on subjective reflection and action for change and incorporates the stages of the action learning cycle (see Chapter 5). The cycle is used in relation to actions, and learning for political change.

Limitations of the Liberatory model of education

One problem with the Liberatory model is that the authority and power of the teacher, particularly those forms of power based on the teacher's position, in terms of their race, class and gender, is not addressed. However, this model of learning does not necessarily require a teacher or facilitator. For example, women's consciousness-raising groups were based on the principle of shared power, sharing experiences, forming generalizations and abstracting with a view to personal-political change.

It is difficult to conceive of this model being adopted in any form within the current educational climate, since teachers and educational establishments have less autonomy, and are faced with increasing direction on how and what to teach. Students are expected to be less challenging and more conforming in a climate of decreasing resources.

One criticism of this model is that it places too much emphasis on individual and group responsibility for change.

The Social Justice model of education

The goal of the Social Justice model is to bring about far-reaching social change. Like the Liberatory model, it starts with a critical evaluation of society, but it is the strategy for achieving change that is different.

It does not view change as dependent upon individual change, individual responsibility or self-reflection, but on political action; education involves critical evaluation of injustice in society as a step toward political action, for example by an exploration of issues such as inequality, how power operates, and resource allocation. The curriculum is knowledge-based but may include the teaching of action skills, e.g. through organizing petitions or demonstrations.

As in the Functionalist model, teaching is based on imparting a particular body of knowledge which has been constructed by theoreticians. Teachers are more likely to impart this knowledge through didactic pedagogic strategies and, as in the Functionalist model, the learner is seen as a recipient of knowledge. However, it differs from the Functionalist model in that the purpose of knowledge is to empower people to act for social change.

This model is mechanistic in that it has a single focus. The teacher presents ideas and does not facilitate learning processes. It assumes the learner will internalize and bring meaning to the ideas. The learner is expected to be committed to the ideals underpinning the theories. The model is seen as providing knowledge which is inspirational about possibilities for change.

Limitations of the Social Justice model of education

As with the Liberatory model, it is argued that it is not possible to develop the principles of the Social Justice model within educational organizations as their function is to act as major socializing institutions. They are not in the business of promoting radical change. Some aspects of the knowledge base of this model were previously incorporated into the curriculum, for example through political education and sociology. Since the 1980s the political and sociological content of the school curriculum has been drastically reduced.

One criticism of this model may be that fairness and justice in society have to be modelled at every level, including the interpersonal level. For example, the Liberatory perspective may argue that before we can understand fairness and justice in society, we need to explore fairness and justice in our own relationships, relationships in the classroom and in the work situation. Therefore, a model that does not address subjective reflection and interpersonal power dynamics is inadequate and ineffective. It could be argued that political change will only come through personal change resulting from this process.

CENTRAL CHARACTERISTICS OF THE FOUR MODELS OF EDUCATION

Table 6.1 summarizes the central characteristics of the four models, including goals, learning, views of the learner, role of the teacher, knowledge base and evaluation. The table illuminates major differences and similarities in approaches to education.

THE TRANSFORMATORY APPROACH TO LEARNING IN RELATION TO THE FOUR MODELS OF EDUCATION

The Transformatory Approach to Learning is not a model of education. As we already argue, a model of education is a simplified representation based on theoretical analysis which, in practice, may not exist in its pure form. Nevertheless, we believe that by considering the four models, educationalists can more easily identify the underlying values and goals which underpin their practice. In order to improve or change practice, it is useful to understand the principles on which it is based.

The Transformatory Approach to Learning is based on many of the theoretical assumptions associated with the Liberatory model of education; it develops a practical application of this model for individuals, groups and organizations, and offers pointers for change. The Appendix shows how the assumptions of the Transformatory Approach to Learning discussed in Part 1 match the theoretical assumptions underpinning the four models of education.

The Functionalist model does not incorporate any of the assumptions about learning as we define it (see Appendix). The Client-centred and Social Justice models share some theoretical assumptions with the Transformatory Approach to Learning.

Each model of education assumes that learning takes place. Our definition of learning incorporates the notion that learning results in a change in the meaning of experience, and consequently a different approach to our experiences, and perception of ourselves. For example, we may believe someone is selfish because they do not exchange presents on a significant day. An alternative way of perceiving this experience may be, for example, to look at our own expectations about giving and receiving gifts, our own patterns, what meaning giving and receiving has for us, and whether or not others attach similar meanings to it. This reflection leads to a different meaning of this particular experience and to perceive ourselves and other people differently.

Learning in the Transformatory Approach results in action from insights and new understandings. In the above illustration, for example, we would feel and behave differently; instead of feeling angry, resentful or hurt, we could feel content with the situation, and continue to behave in a loving, warm and generous way.

If we apply the idea that learning always results in some change in the individual, it is useful to explore what change may be brought about as a result of education based in each of the four models. In the Functionalist model the hoped-for change in the individual will be in terms of increased knowledge, competence, skills, confidence and clarity about role in society (input–output model). In the Client-centred model the hoped-for change in the individual would be in terms of increased knowledge, competence, skills, autonomy, self-empowerment and clarity about role in society. In

Table 6.1 Central characteristics of the four models of education

	Functionalist	Client-centred	Liberatory	Social justice
Goal	Acquiring knowledge and skills to fulfil role in society	Encouraging personal growth to achieve maximum potential, within accepted social norms and values	Facilitating individual change as a prerequisite for bringing about social change	Developing critical social analysis as a means of achieving social justice
Learning in relation to change	Learning results in change in the learners' view of their abilities and competences	Learning results in change in the ease with which the learner can solve problems and make connections	Learning results in a conscious change in the way the learner responds and acts in the world	Learning results in change in the way the learner views the world
View of learning	Mechanistic: based on psychological theories of behaviour, and positive/ negative reinforcement, e.g. Skinner	Organismic: based on psychological theories of child development, e.g. Piaget	Organismic: based on critical insight theorists, e.g. Freire, Habermas	Mechanistic: underpinned by behaviouristic model of learning and sociological critical analysis, e.g. Marx
View of society	Conservative view in which stability and the importance of social order is stressed	Society offers opportunities for individuals to succeed	Society maintains oppression through exploitation of particular groups within it	Economic inequality results in social and political disadvantage for certain groups

	Functionalist	Client-centred	Liberatory	Social justice
View of the learner	Passive recipient of knowledge; limited capacity for learning according to prescribed social roles	Active negotiator and problem solver; variable capacity for learning which may be underestimated	Reflective, active, change agent; considerable capacity for learning	Critical actor; equal capacity for learning but learning limited by position in the economy
Influences on learning	Extrinsic factors, for example, the need for good examination results and a job	Intrinsic factors, for example, natural curiosity or personal gratification	Both intrinsic and extrinsic factors, for example, the desire to change; peer and social factors	Extrinsic factors in society, including social injustice
View of relationship between learners	Competitive: individual achievement is measured in relation to others	Interactive: context enables individual achievement which is measured in terms of self-development	Collaborative: working toward shared vision and outcomes which are seen as more effective than individual achievements	Cooperative: individuals work side-by-side on their own tasks to achieve a joint vision or goal
Role of the teacher	Expert, transmitting knowledge and developing skills	Facilitator of relevant experiences	Facilitator of self-reflection, sharing of experiences and application of learning	Transmitting knowledge and developing social-analytical skills
Role of the learner	Accepting role allocated within society and taking responsibility for achieving within the confines of this role	Accepting social norms and values and taking responsibility for developing potential	Taking responsibility for personal, group and social change	Challenging the norms and values of society; being responsible for bringing about social change

	Functionalist	Client-centred	Liberatory	Social justice
Curriculum base	Accepted 'wisdom' of the society determined by experts, e.g. in academia, industry or government	Determined by the teacher depending on the needs of the young people	Subjective experiences of teacher and the group; determined by them: flexible and changing	Critical evaluation of the knowledge base and accepted 'wisdom' of society as determined by experts
Process of learning	Absorbing ideas and developing skills	Interactive, using the group as a resource	Interactive, using the group as a resource, reflecting on subjective experience	Absorbing ideas and developing skills
Teaching methods	Lecture, films, comprehension exercises, demonstrations	Collaborative group work, projects, discovery learning	Discussion, agenda-setting, problem-solving, action learning, action research	Lectures, discussion, critical analysis, oral history, direct action
Organization of learning	Arranged in rows, teacher at front	Arranged in groups, teacher mingling	Flexible arrangement, teacher's position fluid	Arranged in rows, teacher at front
Evaluation of learning	Summative: testing knowledge and skills. Regular assessment published in league tables	Summative and formative: to inform decision-making about next stages of learning, including self-evaluation	Formative: to facilitate reflection and action-planning; negotiated by the group, through action learning	Summative: assessing understanding and critical analysis

both the Functionalist and Client-centred approaches learning would not result in a change in perception either of the learning experience or of ourselves.

The Social Justice model assumes that the ideas being taught will lead to changes in the individual in that their perception of the world will change; they will never be able to look at a particular situation in the same way again. For example, if we learn about the history of women's oppression over the centuries, we will perceive the actions of women in the feminist movement differently. However, it does not necessarily follow that we will perceive ourselves differently, or look at the ways that we may oppress other women. An individual may be inspired by an idea to change society but may not change personally in any way as a result of this.

The Transformatory Approach stresses the importance of both individual and social change and sees them as interrelated. Social change cannot come about without individual change; individual change leads to social change. We argue that if individual change is truly established then it results in a change in relationships between individuals which ultimately affect social relationships, organizations and society, a view closely aligned with the Liberatory model.

SEVEN

Facilitating Change in Classrooms

Part 1 of the book is concerned with exploring the Transformatory Approach to Learning. The Transformatory Approach is useful when thinking about learning in any setting, including formal education. Part 2 is concerned more directly with educational organizations. This chapter is about putting the Transformatory Approach into practice in the classroom in any phase of education. It is concerned with developing congruence between the Transformatory Approach to Learning, the goals of the Liberatory model of education explored in Chapter 6, and working with people in the classroom.

The chapter asks such questions as: What is the teacher's role in relation to the learner? What is the role of the learner? How are the principles of the Transformatory Approach translated into practice? Collaborative group work is explored as essential to the process of implementing the transformational approach in the classroom. Equality, respect and fairness are outlined as key values which underpin the approach taken. Case studies are included in this chapter to illustrate aspects of the Transformatory Approach in the classroom.

THE LINKS BETWEEN THE LIBERATORY MODEL OF EDUCATION AND THE TRANSFORMATORY APPROACH TO LEARNING

In Chapter 6 we outline the goals for the Liberatory model of education and compare them with the goals of other models of education. The goals for the Liberatory model are:

- bringing about individual change as a prerequisite for change in society
- facilitating interpersonal relationships
- curriculum based on developing skills of self-reflection and analysis of experiences, particularly relating to inequality

In the same chapter we explored the characteristics of the Liberatory model of education in detail. These are summarized in Table 7.1.

Table 7.1 Characteristics of the Liberatory model

Characteristic	Liberatory model
Goal	Facilitating individual change as a prerequisite for bringing about social change
Learning in relation to change	Learning results in a conscious change in the way the learner responds and acts in the world
View of learning	Organismic: based on critical insight theorists, e.g. Freire, Habermas
View of society	Society maintains oppression through exploitation of particular groups within it
View of the learner	Reflective, active, change agent; considerable capacity for learning
Influences on learning	Both intrinsic and extrinsic factors; for example, the desire to change, peer and social factors
View of relationship between learners	Collaborative: working towards shared vision and outcomes, which are seen as more effective than individual achievements
Role of the teacher	Facilitator of self-reflection, sharing of experiences and application of learning
Role of the learner	Taking responsibility for personal, group and social change
Curriculum base	Subjective experiences of teacher and the group; determined by them, flexible and changing
Process of learning	Interactive; using the group as a resource, reflecting on subjective experience
Teaching methods	Discussion, agenda-setting, problem-solving, action learning and action research
Organization of learning environment	Flexible seating arrangement; teacher's position fluid
Evaluation of learning	Formative: to facilitate reflection and action planning; negotiated by the group

In Chapter 6 we show how the Transformatory Approach to Learning has most in common with the Liberatory model of education. We argue that while models describe educational frameworks, our approach to learning is built on a set of assumptions about learners, the learning context and process, which gives guidance for practice. Resnick (1987) has contrasted learning in institutions with everyday learning and argues that learning in the classroom needs to be more like learning outside the educational organization. Resnick (1987) writes about learning in schools, but her assertions are equally true of all phases of education.

Learning in institutions

- is decontextualized
- tends to be individualistic
- is assessed by others
- requires symbolic thinking

Everyday learning

- involves general skills and knowledge
- has a 'real' context
- is cooperative/shared
- is self-assessed
- engages directly with objects, situations and people
- involves situation-specific skills and knowledge

Resnick cites evidence that educational organizations are not contributing in a direct and obvious way to experiences outside, but also that knowledge acquired outside the learning organization is not always used to support learning inside.

Schooling is coming to look increasingly isolated from the rest of what we do. (Resnick, 1987, p. 15)

The idea of making learning in organizations more like learning outside is congruent with the Liberatory model of education. 'Everyday' learning has many of the features which promote effective learning. It focuses on the experiences of learners and has the potential for bringing about individual change in order to bring about social change.

This chapter continues by emphasizing the importance of the Transformatory Approach to Learning centred in a holistic view of education which is concerned with the whole person.

EDUCATING FOR WHOLENESS

We argue that if education is informed by the Liberatory model and the Transformatory Approach to Learning, we will educate the whole person, and include an emphasis on the affective and social as well as cognitive dimensions of learning. The dominant Functionalist model focuses attention on the cognitive domain. This is mechanistic, highlighting knowledge and skills development.

As we argue in Part 1, the division of cognitive and affective is an arbitrary classification; no true separation of the two can meaningfully be made. Forty years ago, Bloom (1956) noted 'the erosion of affective objectives' from educational practice, and the way in which the cognitive bias in school testing, the slower rate of development in affective objectives, and the belief that the affective would develop without teaching had contributed to this erosion. Education for wholeness includes addressing the affective domain as well as the cognitive, spiritual and social domains and is equally important in all phases of education. Whitaker writes:

> The holistic approach to education strives to restore an appropriate balance to the learning process by giving equal status to experience, imagination, creativity and intuition as it does to knowing, thinking, remembering and reasoning. Holistic education sees the purpose of learning as directed towards being capable in the world, rather than only knowing about the world. This involves a reconsideration of both the curriculum we offer to pupils and the nature of the learning experiences that deliver it. (Whitaker, 1995a, p. 20)

Education for wholeness includes personal and social development and may be considered in the following framework:

1. Personal development

(a) Emotional
- recognizing and accepting the whole variety of emotions
- encouraging a feeling of self-worth
- understanding the causes of feelings
- recognizing the difference between feelings and actions
- handling stress and anxiety

(b) Cognitive
- improving skills of analysis, differentiation, categorizing, judging
- understanding the processes of learning
- recognizing and exploring artistry and creativity
- making connections, seeing patterns
- making generalizations and abstractions

(c) Spiritual
- feeling a sense of purpose and meaning
- understanding the opportunity for learning in every experience
- being able to detach from problems and seeing them from a higher perspective

2. Social development

(a) Education for social responsibility

This includes the recognition of responsibility for:
- personal power and its non-exploitative use
- addressing local and global issues

- awareness and understanding of inequalities relating to sex, gender, sexual orientation, class, race, age and physical ability, and acting on this
- social change and social justice
- the political decision-making processes

(b) Education for relationships with others

This includes developing interpersonal communication skills, for example:
- improving ability to work collaboratively
- giving and receiving feedback
- dealing with conflict and negotiating disagreements
- communicating wants
- expressing anger without its being destructive
- taking another's perspective
- improving empathy and sensitivity to others' feelings
- analysing and understanding relationships
  (Askew and Carnell, 1995)

The framework presents separate dimensions; in practice they are interlinked. If young people are educated in a mechanistic way they are likely to be alienated from themselves and from society. Educational organizations need to develop a curriculum which provides coherence for the learner, and provide time and guidance for the learner to reflect on and make connections. Other writers also make this point:

> Until we realise that the key to understanding human affairs and activities lies more in making connections between the various factors than in struggling to define a pecking order of relative importance, we are unlikely to satisfy our desperate need to raise the quality of learning (Whitaker, 1995a, p. 21)

The ability to make connections in different contexts is dependent upon a curriculum which is not planned and taught in separate and unconnected units (Hargreaves, 1994). Ferguson (1982) argues that schools have been the greatest single social influence during the formative years and that as such they have been the 'instrument of our greatest denial, unconsciousness, conformity and broken connections'. She suggests that learning disabilities are caused by the separatist and often alienating experiences of many students in the classroom.

The roles of the learner and of the teacher are radically different in the classroom which focuses on education for wholeness.

THE ROLE OF THE LEARNER

The role of the learner in the Liberatory model of education and in the Transformatory Approach to Learning is to be reflective, active, and an agent for change. The learner has considerable capacity for learning. (This is true for teachers as well as students.) In Chapter 6 we compare different views of the learner inherent in the four educational models (see Table 7.2).

Table 7.2 Educational models and their views of the learner

Characteristic	Functionalist	Client-centred	Liberatory	Social Justice
View of the learner	Passive recipient of knowledge; limited capacity for learning according to prescribed social roles	Active negotiator and problem-solver; variable capacity for learning which may be underestimated	Reflective, active, agent for change; considerable capacity for learning	Critical actor; equal capacity for learning, but learning limited by position in the economy

In Chapter 2, we argue that one of the assumptions about learners in the Transformatory Approach is that learning is an essential aspect of self-actualization. Self-actualization is the goal of personal change; individual change is the goal of self-actualization. In the Transformatory Approach, we argue that action learning can facilitate individual change, self actualization and social justice.

THE ROLE OF THE TEACHER AND THE TEACHER'S RELATIONSHIP WITH LEARNERS

The role of the teacher is radically different in the Transformatory Approach to Learning. The Functionalist model of education views the teacher as 'expert'. In this role the teacher transmits knowledge; their power base is superior knowledge. In the Liberatory model the teacher is a facilitator of self-reflection, sharing experiences and learning in order to enable others to become reflective learners. In the Transformatory Approach to Learning the teacher is also a learner. Delors writes:

> Better still, school should impart both the desire for, and pleasure in, learning, the ability to learn how to learn and intellectual curiosity. One might even imagine a society in which each individual would be in turn both teacher and learner. (Delors, 1996, p. 21)

The view that teachers are learners is not normally stressed. However, to think of ourselves as learners brings about a profound shift in our view of both ourselves and other learners. If we think of ourselves as learners, we are continuously involved in the cycle of learning (see Chapter 5). We engage in a process of reflecting on our teaching, make generalizations, form theories from our experience, and apply this learning to our approach in the classroom. We also learn about ourselves by reflecting on our relationships in the classroom. For example, How clear are our boundaries? Does certain behaviour trigger our anger? How attached are we to a particular image of ourselves? Do we take certain behaviours personally and become emotionally involved, or can we detach and see others' behaviour as no reflection on our worth as teachers? How strong is our self-esteem?

In the classroom there are countless opportunities to reflect and learn about ourselves, and the more we learn, the better our relationships with other learners will be.

The dominant model of teacher education focuses on how to teach rather than how to facilitate learning. It is unusual, in our experience, for initial training to focus on teaching people how to learn or about learning. Even less so for teachers' professional development to focus on their own experiences of learning. This is congruent with the Functionalist model. Boud *et al.* argue that it is a mistake to assume that teaching leads to learning:

> While we commonly assume that teaching leads to learning, it is the experiences which teaching helps create that prompt learning, not primarily the acts of the teacher. We have all had the experience of being exposed to countless hours of teaching which had no discernible effect on us, but from time to time we are engaged by something which the teacher says or does which touches our experience, has meaning for us and moves us on to further work. The teacher creates an event which the learner experiences and may learn from. In fact, the event is an important learning experience for the teacher as well. (Boud *et al.*, 1993, p. 9)

Other writers (Gage, 1972; Whitaker, 1995a) explore the distinction between teaching and learning:

> A distinction can be made between theories of learning and theories of teaching. While theories of learning deal with the ways in which an organism learns, theories of teaching deal with the ways in which a person influences an organism to learn. (Gage, 1972, p. 56)

When applied to educational organizations, the Transformatory Approach shifts the emphasis away from teaching to enabling and facilitating learning. Rogers has argued that learning organizations and teachers need to shift from a focus on teaching, which:

> leads them into a host of questions which are either irrelevant or absurd so far as real education is concerned ... such as content and course coverage to facilitating learning. (Rogers, 1969, p. 125)

Goodlad's (1983) study showed that less than 1 per cent of teacher talk required that students think beyond the recall level, and evidence such as this has emphasized the need for approaches that engage the young person actively in learning. Thinking more effectively includes learning to question appropriately, solve problems, look for alternatives, make decisions and create new ideas. These approaches to learning are congruent with the holistic approach which we discussed in Chapter 1. Wood (1993) describes his vision of the classroom in the year 2015, in which the teacher will spend less time giving information and more time 'on attending to aspects of an individual pupil's learning processes'.

The case study below (from Askew and Carnell, 1995) describes one teacher's attempt to move away from teaching in a didactic way towards facilitating learning in her mathematics classes. It illustrates some ways in which young people can be encouraged to take more responsibility for their learning which frees her to pay attention to their learning processes.

CASE STUDY – DEVELOPING PERSONAL AND SOCIAL SKILLS THROUGH MATHEMATICS

Caroline Dawes

Many people think of Mathematics as being 'culture-free', that it is a neutral subject not affected by context or opinion or the passing of time, and that it has little to contribute to the personal-social domain. The perceived intrinsic importance of Mathematics, due to its compulsory nature at school, implies that the development of mathematical skills is quite enough for a Maths teacher to deal with. I feel that Mathematics has a more proactive role to play in the development of personal-social skills.

Linking factors – an example of a lesson with Year 11

The 'Linking Factors' worksheets formed the basis of a statistics project with a middle-ability Year 11 group. My main aim was to enable the students to apply the theory which they had recently covered to some 'real' statistics. However, a secondary aim was the enhancement of various personal-social aspects.

The students were asked to work in small groups and think of a hypothesis relating to two bits of information given in the table (for example, the lower the GNP, the lower the life expectancy). Their task was then to present their findings in the form of an illustrated talk to convince the rest of the class of their results. They had to decide on methods to prove their hypotheses and also the most effective way of displaying their data. The rest of the class would have the chance to quiz the group on their findings (the roles being those of cynical customers to salespeople).

This way of working gave the students ample opportunity to develop and enhance different personal-social skills. In particular, some students presented information through basic graphs. This was evidently satisfying for them and did raise their self-esteem, in a subject in which they lack confidence. Working in groups meant that strategies were adopted for dividing up the work load and allocating roles for actual presentations.

Opportunity was thus given for the development of leadership skills. The process of preparing and delivering a presentation was a chance to develop self-confidence as well as effective communication skills, and the degree of control which the students were given with this work helped provide them with a sense of ownership and autonomy. My role was one of facilitator and fellow-learner, as the students asked me for resources and advice, and as they presented their own findings and arguments. Occasionally I would play devil's advocate in order that both arguments were heard, especially those of a potentially stereotypical nature (e.g. large population causes poverty in a country, rather then the other way round).

Obviously one lesson cannot develop all the personal-social skills mentioned, for all the students in a class, that is far too simplistic. But if this lesson was a typical Maths lesson, and if it was considered in conjunction with similar lessons being delivered through other subjects, then I think that it would be an effective way of enhancing the development of personal and social skills.

However, this was not a typical Maths lesson, and the resistance to taking part was interesting. There were comments such as 'This is Maths not Sociology' and 'Can't we just do something from the text book?'. It was apparent that the students sectioned their skills into subject areas and that they were not readily transferable. There was a general feeling, at first, that since non-mathematical skills were involved, the exercise was somehow less worthwhile. Nevertheless, once the students were involved, the skills learnt in other lessons, especially those regarding group dynamics, were in fact transferred to the Maths context.

The emphasis in this work was problem-posing rather than problem-solving, which Lerman suggests has a fundamentally revolutionary character. He draws parallels between an Authoritarian model and the oppression of various social groups, and between the problem-posing approach and freedom.

Developing personal-social skills through SMP

SMP (Schools Mathematics Project)

The SMP booklet scheme is used in the first two years with mixed ability form groups of 31 students. When I first started using SMP I was not very happy with having administration and stock control as major priorities, as I found that I was not actually helping students with their Maths. Motivated by the idea of freeing myself from as much administration as possible in order that I might have more contact with students, and inspired by the prospect of actively developing personal and social skills, I made a conscious decision to organize my classroom slightly differently.

My SMP classroom – a typical lesson with Year 8

As soon as I enter the classroom the monitors are asking for the keys to open the filing cabinet, cupboard and computer stock cupboard. While I am taking the register, the booklets are brought to the table, the equipment and answer books are put on top of the filing cabinet and the computer is wheeled in.

This method works very smoothly. The students remind each other if someone has forgotten to do their job and there are standard jokes about P45s. Students volunteer to be monitors and they change every time the module changes, so everybody has a chance.

The responsibility is readily accepted, and the students feel that they play an important role in the lesson. The computer monitors take great pride in setting up and loading the software and organizing from their rota the next pair to work on the machine. The equipment monitors check the equipment and chastise anyone who has not signed out their equipment. The students are not passive receptacles waiting for resources to be handed to them but are an essential part of the organization of the SMP system and frequently suggest ways in which it could be more efficient.

The role of facilitator

With this Year 8 class who have been working with me for a year and a half, my role has changed so much from the central person (traditional teacher) to a facilitator, that I often feel that I am just another aspect of the system which the students control, like the filing cabinet, or the equipment box. However, my role is, of course, much more important than any of the other resources available to the students.

I used to think that a facilitator had less direct influence on a person's learning. However, I have learnt through working with SMP that being a facilitator gives you *more* control over the motivation of the students. The fact that the students have such autonomy and readily accept the responsibilities of their time and resources management means that the teacher is freed from the minutiae of the system and can concentrate on the wider-reaching aspects of her role. My role is now one of mentor and guide, who tries to inspire and support individuals and provides direction to the whole class.

It is interesting that within a teaching model such as this, which is basically the Self-Empowerment model, the teacher being didactic at any time is very effective. The students take any direct instructions or information very seriously, and it is seen as essential advice which must not be ignored. At times I find myself talking quite severely to the whole class. For example, 'You must organize your time so you do as much Maths as possible' and 'Each of you is responsible for making sure you get as wide an experience of different areas of Maths as possible before you start Year 9 [when they are put into sets] and you must bear this in mind when deciding what booklet to do,' etc. The fact that I am imposing something on the students is not viewed negatively, but shows them that I care about their progress, that it matters to me that they are working at their full potential and that I want them to do well. I believe very strongly that this idea of the teacher caring about what the students do is essential for effective learning and is an aspect which often seems to be excluded from the theoretical model of facilitator.

What the students say . . .

It is easy, as a teacher, to employ methods in the classroom which we feel facilitate the students' development; and, indeed, it is easy to become quite self-righteous about it. However, when actually analysing it I was struck by doubt as to whether the further development of students' personal-social skills was in fact enabled by the honourable methods I was employing. Did the students feel they were developing skills other than those mathematical? Did they agree with my philosophy and methodology? Did they realize what I was trying to achieve? Did they care?

I asked my Year 7 and 8 classes to write down how they felt they had got on in Maths since they started the SMP scheme, what they felt they had achieved, what they felt they could improve on, etc., but also asked them to think about all the skills they had learnt or developed, not just mathematical skills, and asked for their opinion on the way we did SMP and the organization of the lessons.

Here are the results (some examples):

. . . about classroom organization:

I think it is a very good sequence of having monitors for taking all the equipment out and people can have turns at doing everything and the teacher is helped by it, and the children also get some experience of how to sort out the equipment. *(Manmeet, Year 8)*

I like the responsibility of having to get my own review sheets etc. I seem to be more in control of my work. *(Natalie, Year 7)*

. . . about responsibility

We get our own equipment review sheets, etc. I thinks it makes us more responsible too. When I was the computer monitress I learnt to be more responsible at home, because I had the responsibility of getting out the computer and putting it away. I felt I could take on more responsibility at home too and in other lessons. *(Rukshana, Year 8)*

. . . about deciding what they learn

You can say what booklets you would like to do and you know what you are doing. You know what booklet would be right for you. When I was at my old school the teacher told you what maths you were doing. Whereas now you feel much, much older. *(Sarah, Year 8)*

. . . about self-assessment

The students have very strong feelings about marking their own booklets, and I was surprised at how negative some opinions were. This seems to be an area of weakness of the system relating to the amount of feedback students are given about their work.

It is brilliant that Ms Dawes lets us mark our own booklets because it makes us feel more responsible and grown up. *(Manisha, Year 8)*

I don't like marking the booklets because I think we could be doing other booklets, anyway it is dead boring. I think it might be a good idea if we mark each other's booklets because it might make it more interesting to see how other people do things. *(Natalie, Year 8)*

. . . about the role of the teacher

These student responses showed differing opinions and understanding of the role of the teacher as facilitator. It is interesting to note the difference between the comments of Year 7 students and those of Year 8.

On Thursdays and Fridays I have Maths two periods and Ms Dawes my Maths teacher doesn't teach me she only helps me sometimes. *(Hawa, Year 7)*

When we all started on booklets we had been told the process of doing the booklet and marking it, doing the review sheet and handing it in. First of all when I marked the booklet I thought it was a bit weird. I can remember when we were told that we could use the school's equipment which I found acceptable, but when we were told to choose our own booklets and get our own review sheets from the filing cabinet, it put over the wrong impression on me, that the teacher would be doing nothing while we would be working on booklets and review sheets. *(Michelle, Year 7)*

Sometimes if the booklet you are doing is quite hard and you need some help in the lesson, you can put your hand up and either Ms Dawes or another helper will come over and help you. This is good because you can understand the problem more clearly and get the answer right. *(Emily, Year 8)*

. . . as recommendations

If somebody came to me and said 'How would you change the Maths system' I'd say 'I would never, never, never change it in any way.' *(Claire, Year 7)*

I think the booklets and review system might work in religious studies because you could have a different box for each religion and each booklet concentrates on different parts of the religion, like food, customs, praying, etc. The booklet and review system could also work in French but it might also be more difficult. *(Natalie, Year 8)*

Recommendations for change

From these responses I think it is clear, on the whole, that the students do appreciate why I run SMP as I do. The fact that they know what the objectives are means that their personal-social skills are being developed and, it seems, being transferred. I think it is clear from the difference in the responses of Year 7 and Year 8 that I need to be more explicit as to the reasons for my delivery of SMP at the beginning of students' time in school.

The motivation behind my way of working was not initially based on noble ideas of student development but solely on freeing me from tedious administration in order that I could have more direct contact with individual students and thus raise their achievement. I was actually asked by my second in department when he was in my lesson one day how I managed to avoid long queues at the teacher's desk when staff in other SMP classes were constantly being asked for booklets or resources. I briefly explained my system from the administration angle and he agreed in principle but was still worried about potential loss of booklets and equipment.

It seems clear to me that in order for students to learn to be responsible for resources they have to be given that responsibility first. However, in a classroom ethos which does not treat the student as an active participant who shares the responsibility for her learning and the administration of the system, mixed messages will be received about trust and responsibility and the system will be taken advantage of and will break down.

Reference

Lerman, S. (1986) 'Learning mathematics as a revolutionary activity', in Lerman, S. and Nickson, M. (eds) (1992), *The Social Context of Mathematics Education: Theory and Practice*. Southbank Press.

Caroline's description of her role as a facilitator of a Mathematics class highlights many of the principles underlying the Transformatory Approach to Learning. For example, she enables learners to move from dependence on her, towards independence and interdependence; learners have control over what they are learning; collaborative learning is organized where appropriate; learners are encouraged to reflect on the learning experience and learn more about learning. Caroline also makes her approach to learning explicit and discusses this in the classroom.

Effective learning only happens if there are effective teacher–pupil and peer relationships. The skills to develop interpersonal relationships are learned by teachers and taught (Cowie and Rudduck, 1990).

The case study in the next section illustrates other principles underlying the Transformatory Approach, including action learning, the development of inter-personal relationships, and issues relating to group and social context.

ACTION LEARNING IN THE CLASSROOM

In the Transformatory Approach, effective learning is viewed as resulting in change of the individual and, ultimately, of society. By action learning we mean learning that brings about action for change (see Chapter 5). Change in individual learners includes change in the perception and meaning of experience which results in behaviour change. Change is extremely difficult and takes a long time; we have to let go of practices which we have come to rely on. This can be experienced as frightening and threatening. Risk-taking is undertaken in a climate of support. One way of providing this support and structure for change is to use a cycle of learning which makes several stages of the process explicit. The cycle of learning which we draw on is Dennison and Kirk's (1990). We briefly look again at each of these stages.

DO

The 'Do' stage of the cycle includes all the tasks and processes that the learner engages in, which are traditionally seen as the nub of education. This may include learning at two of the different levels of learning suggested by Nisbet and Shucksmith (1984).

1. basic and subject specific *skills*, e.g. the teaching of literacy and numeracy skills
2. broader learning *strategies*, e.g. the teaching of study skills such as note-taking, accessing information and organizing learning

Educational organizations focus on this stage of the cycle, particularly on subject-specific skills and knowledge. The next stage, the review, is not traditionally emphasized in educational organizations and is incorporated in the remainder of the learning cycle, which we now go on to discuss.

REVIEW

In the review stage, learners evaluate the process of learning they have gone through. This includes emotional, social and cognitive aspects; for example, how emotional aspects help or hinder the learning process, how successfully individuals worked within a group. This reflection on the process of learning ensures that learning will be at a deeper level than would ensue from an emphasis on product and outcome.

Promoting learning about learning demands that learners can discuss the tasks and processes they are involved in, and their own state in regard to learning. For example, they may discuss their style of learning (see Chapter 2).

LEARN

In the learn stage a range of themes may be identified and learners' strategies compared. Learners begin to notice patterns in their approach to specific experiences. This stage also includes making connections and generalizations and forming new concepts. Teachers help students make the learning explicit, including through asking high-order question to tease out new insights and understandings.

APPLY

In the apply stage the learner identifies learning situations in which they wish to try out new strategies and approaches. The teacher helps the learner plan future action differently in the light of new understandings, by promoting transfer of learning, planning of strategies and goal-setting. Applying new learning is not a simple and straightforward matter – many things affect how we can apply new learning. The cycle of learning is continuous. When we apply new learning in a new context, we again review the outcomes and reflect on learning.

The case study below illustrates the use of this cycle in the classroom. This case study describes work with a group of young men. The central aim is to develop a collaborative work culture as part of a project which focused on an exploration of equality and equal opportunity issues.

CASE STUDY – COLLABORATIVE AND GROUP WORK
Bernadette Mitford

A few years ago I worked with a group of 20 young men as part of a curriculum innovation on equity issues. One issue which emerged during this work was that the young men seemed to be very competitive with one another, and it appeared that their skills of negotiation over, for example, conflict resolution could be improved. I decided to do some work in the classroom which specifically focused on developing collabora-tive group learning. I decided to focus this work around the preparation and eating of food. During the work I was looking for opportunities to discuss equity issues if opportunities arose. I was also keen to look for opportunities to discuss the young men's experiences and feelings, since I thought this would develop empathy and help break down the competitive ethos. I was interested to read Epstein's account of her work on anti-racism and her emphasis on taking opportunities to explore issues of inequality as they arise:

> On the other hand, learning which involves a high level of emotional involvement and exploration of feelings enables children (and adults) to make cognitive gains. However, while provision for both cognitive and affective learning are a necessary condition for developing anti-racist education, their presence alone is not sufficient to ensure that the education offered children will be anti-racist, anti-sexist or anti-heterosexist in effect. In order for this to happen, one must also plan for – and take advantage of opportunities offered for – explicit exploration with children of issues of inequality. (Epstein, 1993, pp. 145–6)

It seemed to me that work with food provided an ideal opportunity for relating our discussion in the classroom about equity issues to personal experience. The young men worked in groups of four over a half-term. The instruction given to them was to create a meal in their group; to plan what to make; to do the shopping and to invite at least one other person from outside the class to eat. The proviso was that each course in the meal must have been made by at least one person in the group. I hoped that cooking and eating together would provide a safe atmosphere in which to explore other issues. Epstein talks about the need for this in relation to discussing equity issues:

> An essential part of an anti-racist pedagogy, then, is to create, as well as take, opportunities to explore equality issues with children, in a context in which they feel they are safe and can express feelings, while making cognitive gains. (Epstein, 1993, p. 146)

I made it clear to the class that one of my goals was to look at how we work collaboratively. I put my position to them: my belief that working collaboratively leads to more effective learning for all; my commitment to the idea that collaboration is important in the world of work, and vital for the development of society; my conviction that we have to learn particular skills if we are to collaborate effectively. I was aware that devising activities which require collaboration and cooperation is not an easy matter. The most obvious tasks over which young people must collaborate are those which result in a single end product, or activities which cannot be carried out without the participation of all; I thought that cooking was a good activity. It may be that young people sit together and talk while working, but that the activity is only very 'loosely' directed toward them acting jointly. Collaboration may be along a continuum from independence to interdependence.

In thinking about how to develop collaborative group learning I felt that the following questions were important to ask:

- How will we decide who will work together?
- Will it work best if groups are based on friendship or on the basis of individual strengths and resources, so that these can be shared?
- Do all the tasks need to be collaborative?
- Will there be some tasks which the group decides to allocate to individuals within the group?
- Will the groups be mixed in terms of experience, class or ethnicity?

In the end I left it up to the young men to decide with whom they would work, and it was interesting that, on the whole, they chose to work with people from the same ethnic group as themselves. This may have been so that they could choose to make a dish which was familiar to all in the group. For example, young men from India chose to make curry; from the Caribbean some chose Akee and salt fish; from Turkey some boys chose to make kebabs. This provided a wonderful opportunity to talk about experiences of shopping, cooking and preparing food in different cultures.

I wanted to develop a sense of responsibility for the work, and built a lot of reflection in. At the end of each class I asked the young men to review their work both individually and as a group. I focused this review on the process of collaborative group learning rather than on the product.

Review of work

Individual

- In what way did you affect the decisions made by the group?
- Were you happy about all the decisions that were made?
- Were you able to express your views?
- Do you feel that you were able to contribute as much as you would have liked?
- What significant contribution did you make?

The group

- Who do you feel had most influence in the group?
- What were the most striking things about the way in which the group worked?
- What would be the most useful issues to discuss with the group in order to take the group forward?
- How were individuals encouraged to use their particular expertise?

The task

- Was the task achieved?
- How was conflict managed?
- What was the single most important issue discussed by the group?
- What class, gender or race issues emerged?

At the end of the series of classes I also asked the young men to review and evaluate the work of the group and the way the group had functioned by using the checklist at the end of the case study (see p. 114).

My personal reflections on the work

I felt that this work had been very rewarding for a number of different reasons. On the level of developing skills:

- the young men appeared to enjoy the cooking, were very skilled and knowledgeable about cooking and were able to bring their own experience of preparing food into the classroom;
- cooking provided an excellent medium for work on English as a second language.

In terms of collaborative group learning:

- the review at the end of each lesson and at the end of half-term was approached very seriously. Cooking was organized every fortnight. In the intervening week the young men discussed their reviews and set targets for the following week. They also planned what they would cook.
- I believe that the groups developed negotiation and conflict-solving skills as the weeks progressed.

In terms of discussion about equity issues:

- There were some opportunities to talk about roles, stereotypes and expectations. These were all informal exchanges of view which often took place around the table as we ate. Often I 'dropped' in a question as I went from one table to the other and left it for the young men to discuss or not.

My learning

I think the most important learning for me was that if I give young people responsibility in the classroom they achieve far more than if I attempt to maintain control over their learning. I was amazed at how much they knew about food preparation. I was pleased by the way they reviewed their joint work and that they saw the benefits of this review. Whether or not the work had any impact on attitudes and beliefs about roles, expectations and stereotypes, I do not know. In future, if I repeat this work I would build in a review at the end and, possibly, at the beginning to find out more about their thoughts about roles, expectations and stereotypes. I also noticed that attitudes differed between cultural groups. For example, young men from African-Caribbean descent appeared to be much more knowledgeable about food preparation than young men from some other cultural groups. I would like to build in some discussion about this in future. For example, it would be useful to make my observation explicit to the group and ask about whether my observation seems valid to them and discuss possible explanations. Perhaps we could develop a hypothesis and test it out with research in the rest of the college.

Half-termly review of how the group is working

- Individually, place a cross somewhere on the continuum from 'very like my group' to 'not at all like my group'.
- Discuss your responses in pairs. Compare the issues that have emerged for you with the rest of the group.
- Choose one or two areas which have not worked. What actions can you take as a group to make this area work better?

Effective group work

1. The climate is friendly, individuals are relaxed and all members are on task.

very like my group _____ not at all like my group

2. Everyone is working. Everyone has a role.

very like my group _____ not at all like my group

3. Everyone understands what they have to do and is clear about their role and responsibilities.

very like my group _____ not at all like my group

4. Everyone listens to each other. All ideas are given a hearing.

very like my group _____ not at all like my group

5. Conflict and disagreement arise. The group manages this and finds solutions. Everyone agrees to keep to the decisions made.

very like my group _____ not at all like my group

6. People are open and honest. They make constructive suggestions for change. Complaints are accepted and solutions found in the group.

very like my group _____ not at all like my group

7. People can share their feelings in the group.

very like my group _____ not at all like my group

8. The role of leader in the group changes from week to week or alternates in any one week.

very like my group _____ not at all like my group

9. When action needs to be taken all participants are clear what the group has decided to do. Individuals understand and take responsibility for the action they have agreed to take.

very like my group _____ not at all like my group

10. There are regular group reviews. Attention is paid to how the group is working. The group looks after itself.

very like my group _____ not at all like my group

(Adapted from McGregor, D. (1960) *The Human Side of Enterprise*. McGraw Hill)

Like Caroline's case study, Bernadette's embodies some of the principles of the Transformatory Approach in practice. For example, reflection on self as a learner and the group context is seen as essential, the learning is made explicit, individuals are seen as needing to learn how to learn in a group, collaboration is seen as an important contribution to individual learning.

When planning for effective learning, the tasks and processes need to promote:

- active learning
- collaborative learning
- learner responsibility
- learning about learning
  (Watkins *et al.*, 1996)

When planning classroom practice incorporating the Transformatory Approach to Learning, we need to have a clear rationale and aims which are devised with learners; negotiate the programme; base the curriculum on the perceived needs; ensure that learning relates to change in the individual, group and organization; and recognize learners' different cultural backgrounds. We need to plan for a variety of individual, small-group and whole-group work; incorporate and build on learners' experiences; plan for progression of learning and regular self-assessment and evaluation.

During the learning experience we need to introduce concepts of meta-learning; make commitment to learning and joint endeavour explicit; explore concepts of trust, challenge and risk; pinpoint successful and unsuccessful previous learning; make the aims explicit; emphasize student responsibility for learning; incorporate a range of action learning experiences and work in a variety of groups for different purposes. We need to build in time for reflection on learning and facilitate students in setting goals to apply learning to other contexts.

Evaluation of learning needs to facilitate learners in evaluating their own learning in ways which are congruent with the Transformatory Approach to Learning. The explicit aims will form the basis for the evaluation. The teacher will also need to evaluate how clear the goals were; whether the programme was flexible, responsive and relevant; how the students were encouraged to take responsibility for their own learning; whether the work was sufficiently challenging and rigorous; and whether sufficient time was given to reflection on learning. Evaluation includes considering how students are enabled to set goals which enable them to apply learning to other contexts, and how individual lessons are linked and connections made to work carried out before, and in other learning contexts. Finally, we need to evaluate how successfully students are involved in evaluating their own learning.

EIGHT
Transforming Organizations

Our central argument is that change in organizations follows from change in the people who work in them. Change in society follows from change in people, groups and organizations. It is only by individuals taking action to alter their own environment that there is any chance for deep change (Fullan, 1993). Individuals need support and encouragement for this change process at all levels: recognizing what they are learning, how their learning affects the organization, how the organization affects their learning, and how change within the organization can influence wider changes. This process applies to all people, at all levels, in the organization. For example, an organization cannot be learning unless the same learning principles are applied to how the organization is managed. The requirements of managing in a changing environment are closely interlinked with processes of learning (Lessem, 1991).

LEARNING IN ORGANIZATIONS

The concept of 'wholeness' in relation to the experiences of learners, and approaches to learning, was explored in Chapter 7. Here we explore the idea of 'wholeness' in relation to the learning organization and the learning community. We believe that for the Transformatory Approach to flourish, a culture of learning is needed throughout the organization and community:

> All members of the organization are in a process of review, reflection and improvement: the teachers see themselves as members of a professional community. (Louis and Kruse, 1995)

The organization itself impinges on individuals' learning through the nature of its culture – values, composition, ethos, relationships, traditions – and its effectiveness as a learning organization. This indicates the importance of looking wider than the classroom experience. As discussed in the last chapter, learning will also be affected by the development and nature of relationships with other learners, teachers and other adults, which can affect learning positively or negatively. Schools, through their forms of organization, can influence the feelings and efficacy of both teachers (Hoy and Woolfolk, 1993; Lee et al., 1991) and pupils (Rudduck et al., 1996).

What is a learning organization?

We argue in Chapter 2 that individuals want to learn; that they need to take risks to develop and maximize their potential. We also argue that if organizations are to survive, grow and adapt, they too must change. Change requires learning, and learning leads to change. Hence the concept of the learning organization.

Schools become learning organizations when:

- Connections are made with learning in different contexts, promoted by methods such as investigation, action research, and engaging adults other than teachers in classrooms;
- Boundaries within school and with its external community are undefended;
- Roles are blurred: teachers see themselves as learners, pupils see themselves as teachers;
- Leadership is shared and open, resource allocation is transparent and power and decisions are shared;
- There is a high focus on effective learning;
- The school and its key leaders model effective learning by encouraging evaluation, feedback, exploration and initiative;
- The climate is one of high expectations, joint learning and shared responsibility for learning;
- Diversity is explicitly valued and the affective domain is explicitly considered. (Watkins *et al.*, 1996)

Botkin *et al.* (1979) distinguish between maintenance and innovative learning. Maintenance learning is associated with conventional, analytical-based management, including rules for dealing with the known and problem-solving. It is designed to maintain an existing system, and is indispensable to the stability of society. Innovative learning brings change, renewal, restructuring and problem-reformation to individuals and organizations. In turbulent times, learning of this kind is essential for long-term survival (Botkin *et al.*, 1979). Innovative learning requires anticipation, considering trends, making plans and participation. This is more than sharing decisions, but cultivating an attitude of cooperation, dialogue and empathy. Learning in organizations has often been associated with Botkin's concept of maintenance learning. New theories of organizational learning stress the need for innovative learning; the concept closely aligned with our Transformatory Approach.

Defining the learning organization

The term 'learning organization' developed to describe changes and learning processes experienced by commercial and manufacturing firms who sought a competitive edge on the market; it is increasingly used in education circles. The learning organization

facilitates the learning of all its members and continually transforms itself (Pedler *et al.*, 1988)

facilitates participative (horizontal) and innovative (vertical) development within and between people and institutions, commercially, technologically and socially. (Lessem, 1990)

is one in which the general management style is to delegate responsibility in an attempt to foster employee involvement, personal initiative and generate effective internal communications. (Smythe *et al.*, 1991)

Jones and Hendry (1992) identify indicators of learning organizations: transformation, change, participation, innovation, altering the way people work, adapting, and fostering involvement. Similarly, Hayes *et al.* (1995) highlight characteristics of the learning organization: anticipating future problems, paying attention to the external environment, continuously seeking improvement, problem-solving based on conceptual analysis and understanding, rewards given for growth, initiative and creativity.

Hayes *et al.* (1995) and Garratt (1987) highlight dimensions of successful organizational learning: learning in the organization must be greater than, or at least equal to, the rate of change in its environment. In addition, the organization not only demonstrates the will to manage change, but also takes the necessary steps to acquire or develop the capability to do so; the organization learns to improve its performance on a continuous basis; everybody is expected to add value through their work, and is supported in so doing; a general learning culture is valued, recognized and rewarded.

Senge (1990a) asserts that learning organizations are possible because, deep down, we are all learners; not only is it in our nature, but we love to learn, teams can learn and organizations can learn. However, Senge criticizes managers who reward people who excel in advocating their views, rather than enquiring into complex issues. He also notes that people protect themselves from the pain of appearing uncertain or ignorant, a process which blocks out any new understandings which might threaten them. In our experience of working with teachers and other learners, providing a 'safe', supportive, yet challenging learning context can facilitate an environment where people feel free to express uncertainty and explore new ideas. This unblocking can be powerful and lead to new understandings. However, organizations need to provide a culture to encourage learning at all levels. We argue that action research provides a vehicle for this (see Chapter 9).

Argyris (1990) calls avoidance of learning 'skilled incompetence' in that teams of people may be incredibly proficient at keeping themselves from learning. To learn privately or in a group or organization can be threatening. For example, in our experience, strategies for meetings are carefully structured to avoid learning; no time may be given for quiet reflection. This raises important issues for 'learning on the job', that is, embedding learning experiences in day-to-day working experiences.

Senge (1990b) offers five disciplines of the learning organization, acting as antidotes to 'learning disabilities': systems thinking, personal mastery, mental models, building shared vision, and team learning. He states that these need to be developed in tandem.

A learning organization is a place where people are continually discovering how they create their reality. And how they can change it. (Senge, 1990b, p. 12)

Jones and Hendry (1992) acknowledge these disciplines, but identify other important processes: changing power structures, leading change, and expressing concern for social and ethical issues.

Learning organizations are dynamic; they are flexible and open to new ideas and to change. They anticipate future problems, and seek continuous review (Hayes *et al.*, 1995). These characteristics provide the optimum environment within which the Transformatory Approach can flourish. However, there are other important dimensions that the Transformatory Approach emphasizes: explicit learning, the person within the organization, collaboration, and the learning context.

An explicit focus on learning

Making learning explicit, through the learning cycle and meta-learning processes, is crucial for effective individual learning (see Chapter 5). We argue that any learning within organizations, whether at an individual, group or whole-institution level, also requires learning to be explicit. For example, at group level, there can be a continuous review of what the group is learning, how the group can change their practice in future, and how change in the organization is affecting the group.

Similarly, where change has occurred across an organization, review can focus on which systems seem to be working better and why; which new systems are not working; how change is resisted and why; what personal dilemmas and threats prevent learning. This review can be introduced within a continuous cycle of learning, as Handy suggests:

- The wheel of learning cannot be left to chance, so the organization has a formal way of asking questions;
- It is clear about its roles, future and goals, and is determined to reach them;
- It is constantly reframing the world and its part in it;
- It cultivates negative capability, in that disappointment and mistakes are accommodated as part of the learning whole;
- It is a caring organization, in that it wants everyone to learn, and makes that explicit to everyone.
  (Handy, 1991)

This closely resembles the learning cycle underpinning the Transformatory Approach (see Chapter 5).

Throughout our book we stress the need for individual learners to explore the affective and social dimensions of learning, as well as the cognitive. Some writers who are concerned about organizational learning are also interested in this multitude of dimensions to learning. Kingsland (1986) suggests a combination of cognitive, affective and behavioural activity for innovation and learning, using the overlapping sets of Feel, Think, and Do. Handy (1991) and Kingsland (1986) indicate broad perspectives which support a holistic cycle. Learning is made explicit and emphasizes a personal dimension, extending beyond the cognitive, behavioural and mechanistic views of learning and change.

An explicit focus on the person within organizational learning

Concepts of learning organizations may remain mechanistic if they do not take full account of affective, social and behavioural contexts. Organismic approaches pay attention to the expertise of individuals, what they bring to the situation, in terms of their experience, talents, and psychological state (Dubin, cited in Watkins *et al.*, 1996). Individual hopes, fears, disappointments, dreams are considered. An 'organismic' approach to a learning organization stresses an interconnection of parts, permeable boundaries, and a view of individuals as multi-dimensional. This approach is clearly visible in the view of the developing learning organization, described by Watkins *et al.* (1996) on page 117.

Hayes *et al.* (1988) provide research evidence from a 'people first' approach, which is in line with the Transformatory Approach to Learning. They view employees within an organization as having similar characteristics to the learner identified in Chapter 2. Assumptions for creating a successful learning organization include:

- People inherently want to do their best;
- Human resources are too valuable to leave untapped;
- Creative talents and skills are widely distributed at all levels of an organization and society;
- People will voice concerns if they feel the organization will respond appropriately;
- Work is more interesting when people are challenged;
- People take a pride in training others;
- Removing artificial differences in the ways people are treated will result in better performance;
- Real responsibility motivates high performance;
- People make, and implement, better decisions when they work together.
  (Hayes *et al.*, 1988)

Clearly there are major benefits for organizations, groups and individuals. The implications of stressing the personal dimension for teachers' learning is discussed in Chapter 10.

An explicit focus on collaboration

If an organization does not learn, it will decay. However, learning is not required simply to keep the organization alive; this is particularly pertinent to educational establishments. In recent years, within a competitive, political context, it has been necessary for educational establishments to be seen to develop a 'competitive edge' in line with market-led educational reforms. The survival of educational establishments may rest on their ability to present themselves as 'top competitors'. For some educationalists the idea of adapting competitive strategies from industry is anathema. As we stress throughout the book, collaboration leads to more effective learning, both within and between organizations.

Collaboration between learning organizations subverts any central government pressure for educational organizations to compete against each other as a means of raising educational standards (Hall and Wallace, 1993). A new climate of political reform is urgently needed to ensure that educationalists are able to work with politicians in collaborative learning ventures.

Fullan (1993) suggests there may be other 'moral' as opposed to 'competitive' purposes for considering the lessons from industry in relation to becoming a learning organization.

> a deeper reason is that education has a moral purpose . . . to help produce citizens who can live and work productively in increasingly complex societies (Fullan, 1993)

This 'moral' purpose seems to fit with the Functionalist model of education discussed in Chapter 6; its major goal is to prepare people to work in society. However, the Liberatory model, which is more closely aligned with the Transformatory Approach to Learning, includes goals which support individuals reaching their potential. Through collaboration, and individual, group and organizational learning, change results for a more just and equitable society. Educational establishments need to become learning organizations not simply to survive, but to contribute to, and have influence upon, the kind of society envisaged in the Liberatory model. In a highly complex and rapidly changing world, educational organizations can offer a model in which change itself is a focus for learning.

An explicit focus on the learning context

In the Transformatory Approach we highlight the dynamic interaction between the learner, the context and the process. The context in which the organization is learning will influence it, and vice versa. Little and McLaughlin observe:

- context matters, and locally shared interpretations of practice triumph over abstract principles;
- institutional perspectives and priorities are mediated by structural conditions of teacher isolation and independence, and by the complex web of communities within schools;
- there is a creative tension between individuality and community;
- the greater the appreciation for context specificity, the less categorical statements appear to be a sound basis for policy.
  (Little and McLaughlin, 1993)

Little and McLaughlin recognize that by emphasizing the complexity of within-school contexts, they risk the impression that complexity is chaotic. This view of chaotic complexity in schools feeds the emphasis towards a management style of social control and regulation. However, Little and McLaughlin emphasize that complexity is patterned rather than chaotic, and that it is inevitable. This view of patterned complexity feeds the emphasis towards a management style that is unfamiliar and unpractised. This demands risk-taking, an open approach, flexibility, acquiring new skills. This fits with our assertion that learning comes from welcoming change, rather than trying to control or avoid it, and from thinking of new ways of approaching the unfamiliar; developing 'mindsets which can help us manage the unknowable' (Stacey, 1992). As we stressed at the beginning of the chapter, the requirements of management, in a changing context, are similar to the processes of learning.

We also stress that an organization cannot be learning unless the same learning principles are applied at all levels. As well as facilitating change in students, the organizational context must also facilitate change for everyone within its community. A focus on support for teacher learning, resulting in organizational improvement, is emphasized by Stoll and Fink.

- Treating teachers as professionals;
- Promoting high quality staff development;
- Encouraging teacher leadership and participation;
- Promoting collaboration for improvement;
- Developing ways to induct new members of staff;
- Functioning successfully within their context;
- Working to change things that matter.
  (Stoll and Fink, 1996)

Promoting a learning organization has implications for the style of leadership and relationships between the adults in a school. In a context which is hierarchical, male-dominated, with a strong competitive ethos, learning will be adversely affected because it inhibits reflection, collaboration, support, trust, guidance and feedback.

Rosenholtz (1989) identifies characteristics of particular school contexts which she describes as 'moving' or 'stuck'. 'Moving' schools have shared school goals, norms of collaboration, norms of continuous improvement, certainty and optimism. 'Stuck' schools have little attachment to goals, norms of self-reliance, a numbing sameness, and fatalism. 'Learning-enriched' schools encourage higher achievement by the pupils (Rosenholtz, 1989). A learning-enriched school is one where all members of the community are involved in a process of review, reflection and improvement, where the teachers see themselves as learners. These schools have become learning organizations.

Our exploration of the principles of organizational learning highlights the importance of explicit learning, the personal dimension, collaboration, and the learning context. Effective learning strategies develop in organizations when certain steps and phases are implemented, congruent with the principles outlined above.

EXPLORING ORGANIZATIONAL CHANGE

Morgan (1986) reminds us that the word 'organization' derives from the Greek *organon*, a tool or instrument, loaded with mechanical or instrumental significance. Morgan coins the word 'imaginization' to break free of this mechanical meaning by symbolizing the close link between images and actions. He believes we can create revolutions in the way we organize, by being aware that we are always engaged in imaginization.

> There is a close relationship between the way we think and the way we are . . . in using metaphor to understand organization we . . . are simply encouraged to learn how to think about situations from different standpoints. We are invited to do what we do naturally but we do so more consciously and broadly . . . Our images or metaphors *are* theories or conceptual frameworks. Practice is never theory-free, for it is always guided by an image of what one is trying to do. The real issue is whether or not we are aware of the theory guiding our action. (Morgan, 1986, pp. 335–6)

Morgan's approach to organizational analysis arises from a belief that organizations are generally complex, ambiguous and paradoxical. He suggests that one of the basic problems of modern management is that 'the mechanical way of thinking is so ingrained in our everyday conceptions of organizations that it is often very difficult to organize in any other way' (p. 14).

Morgan (1986) strongly suggests that every metaphor may be found in every situation; organizations can be many things at one and the same time. A 'machine-like' organization designed to achieve specific goals can simultaneously be: a species of organization that is able to survive in certain environments and not in others; an information-processing system that is skilled in certain kinds of learning but not in others; a cultural milieu characterized by distinctive values, beliefs and social practices; a political system where people jostle to further their own ends; an arena where various subconscious or ideological struggles take place; an artefact or manifestation of a deeper process of social change; an instrument used by one group of people to exploit and dominate others; and so on. We have summarized Morgan's organizational metaphors in Table 8.1.

In identifying why planned change does not always work it is striking to see how useful Morgan's metaphors can be. Everard and Morris suggest that agents for change can fail because:

- they can be over-rational in introducing change;
- they can operate at such a different level that they are unable to see how others perceive the change;
- they over-rely on power and position and neglect the values, feelings, ideas and experiences of others who are affected by the change;
- they can fall into the trap of explaining problems which necessitate change to individuals rather than to methods and systems, thus causing defensiveness; and,
- they might be trying to deal with an insoluble problem.
  (Everard and Morris, 1990)

Mechanistic and bureaucratic strategies will fail if organismic and cultural aspects of change are under-emphasized, or political positions are overlooked as a source of conflict, and when people's feelings and emotional responses to change are ignored.

Table 8.1 A summary of Morgan's metaphors of organization

Metaphor	Way of thinking
Machine	This is mechanistic and bureaucratic. The organization is made up of interlocking parts that play a clearly defined role in the functioning whole.
Organismic	There is concern about understanding and managing organizational needs, relations between species, and the evolutionary patterns found in the organizational ecology. This draws attention to how the organization grows, develops, and declines and how it is able to adapt to changing environments.
Brain	This draws attention to the importance of information-processing, learning, and intelligence, and provides a frame of reference for understanding and assessing.
Culture	Organization is seen to reside in the ideas, values, norms, rituals, and beliefs that sustain organizations as socially constructed realities.
Political	This is about different sets of interests, conflicts, and power plays that shape organizational activities.
Psychic prison	People become trapped by their own thoughts, ideas or beliefs, or by preoccupations originating in the unconscious mind. Favoured modes of organizing manifest an unconscious preoccupation with control, or a desire to minimize or avoid anxiety-provoking situations. Ways of organizing may be designed to protect people from themselves.
Flux and transformation	This rests in understanding the logics of change shaping social life: organizations are self-producing systems that create themselves in their own image; produced as a result of circular flows of positive and negative feedback; the product of a dialectical logic whereby every phenomenon tends to generate its opposite.
Instruments of domination	Organizations often use their employees, their communities, and the world economy to achieve their own ends, and the essence of organization rests in a process of domination where certain people impose their will on others. This metaphor is particularly useful for understanding how actions that are rational from one viewpoint can prove exploitative from another.

Some changes are planned, some not. Some are imposed, some initiated by the organization itself. There are forces for change operating from both within and outside the organization; change is endemic. There are implications at micro and macro levels (Carr and Kemmis, 1983). Whatever the change, strategies need to support learning, while attending to political, social, affective and cultural complexities.

The social complexity of educational change is highlighted by Fullan. This involves several phases:

- Initiation – when the decision is made to adopt a change;
- Implementation – when the change is put into place;
- Continuation, or institutionalization; and,
- Outcome – the positive or negative effects of the change.
  (Fullan, 1991)

Fullan suggests change is a process, not an event. 'Educational change depends on what teachers do and think – it's as simple and complex as that' (Fullan, 1991). It is beneficial if the change being introduced is itself developed, and if both the change and those involved change together, in a process of 'mutual adaptation' (Fullan, 1992).

> The recognition that (educational) development needs to be preceded by attitudinal change is salutary and consistent with the oft-stated maxim that teachers must feel 'ownership' of change if it is to be implemented effectively. Externally imposed innovation often fails because it is out of time with the values of the teachers who have to implement it. (Bush, 1995, p. 139)

At each stage of the change process: initiation, implementation, continuation, and outcome (Fullan, 1991), there are opportunities for the organization to learn about itself. The ways in which the institution learns and innovates can create new ways of approaching the change process to 'help move beyond bounded rationality' (Morgan, 1986, p. 107). It becomes a cycle of development. Change helps individuals, groups and the institution to learn; the organization learns from innovation informing the change process. Again there are important implications for action research as a change strategy (see Chapter 9).

Transforming organizations

We argue that the organization is transformed through learning. Learning and change in organizations follows from learning and change in individuals and groups. It is a dynamic relationship; the organization influences people's learning, and people influence the organization's ability to learn.

Phases of learning have been identified which can be applied to organizations as well as to individuals (Jones and Hendry, 1992; Pedler *et al.*, 1988): foundation, formation and continuation, transformation and transfiguration. These move through stages of basic skills development, learning how to learn, supporting the desire to engage in further learning, becoming independent, innovatory, self-motivated and confident.

The transformation stage is about thinking and doing things differently. It begins to look at power relationships, culture, and decision-making strategies. Thinking differently includes absorbing local, national, and global cultural differences. The transfiguration stage refers to the fully developed person or organization; this relates to individuals' 'self-actualization' (see Chapter 2). At this level, leaders and managers act as facilitators for learning. Collaborative team work is emphasized:

> This form of organization develops without hierarchy of personal status. Teams and groups at this level bring about innovatory work and communication systems. (Jones and Hendry, 1992, p. 29)

At the transfiguration stage, the organization, or individual, steps outside its existing frameworks and patterns of thinking, is able to 'let go' that which is keeping it 'stuck', and puts into practice a new set of operational styles (Jones and Hendry, 1992).

The five stages do not necessarily represent 'phased' progression (Jones and Hendry, 1992). Some organizations get stuck at the early stages, some remain at the transformation state, unable to make the 'mind-shift' to get to the transfiguration phase. Jones and Hendry claim it is possible for an organization to be established from the beginning at the transfiguration phase, visiting and revisiting other phases of learning to acquire the skills, knowledge, and learning enabling it to progress with its transfiguration development systems. Our experience indicates that whole organizations do not pass from one phase to another in unison; one part of the organization may be far more advanced in its activities and thinking than another.

Groups within organizations can develop independently. We argue that to transform any organization there needs to develop a shared vision. Groups within the organization may be able to act as agents of change, but their ability to bring about major shifts will be constrained by the ethos of the organization within which they are based. A shared vision needs to reflect work and learning in the classroom; approaches to professional development and learning; approaches to work with others in the community. This congruence provides a powerful ethos, and change is more likely to become embedded within the 'deep structure of the organization' (Bernstein, 1967).

Jones and Hendry cite Hawkins (1991), Nevard (1991) and Henson (1991), who discuss the 'spirituality' of organizations where the practice of reflection and exploring philosophical ideas is important. Day-to-day work practice includes structured reflection. This fits with our Transformatory Approach, which stresses the importance of structured and explicit individual reflection for learning, and developing new understanding to bring about change.

Reflective rationality assumes that complex practical problems demand specific solutions which can be developed only inside the context in which the problem arises, and in which the practitioner is crucial. These assumptions are the basis of action research and extend the concept of professionality: a capacity for autonomous professional self-study through the testing of ideas by classroom research procedures (Stenhouse, 1975).

We argue that whole-organizational learning can be organized and managed through action research (see Chapter 9). Commitment to change in the action research process comes about from reflection on experience rather than imposition from managers or from external pressure. However, there is always pressure from outside to change, and government legislation is imposed. We still argue that action research can be adopted even when change is imposed. People in educational organizations involved in collaborative action research processes discover the best way to implement imposed change in their particular organization.

The learning organization will be affected by the plans, the strategies and the definitions of success of people other than the learner. These result from a complex process of synthesis by teachers, managers, inspectors, government policy-makers, and many others. Recently teachers have been disempowered from professional decision-making. Learners themselves are rarely given a voice in this process (Rudduck et al., 1996). Collaborative action research, however, encourages all those involved within an organization to adopt the role of learner. Through the process of action research the organization can more readily become a learning organization, involving all members of the organization (see Chapter 9).

We relate this to the concept of the 'stuck' and 'moving' school (Rosenholtz, 1989). The 'stuck' school feels powerless to effect change. In the 'moving' school there is a spirit of optimism and feeling of control which allows the organization to work collaboratively to improve any situation. There is a paradox here of course: action research will only happen in a moving school, but the way to get the school moving is through a process of action research. A small group may be able to act as catalysts, gradually involving others in collaborative action research.

The role of action researchers as agents for change

Educational organizations may go through the appearance of change, while the reality continues as before: 'innovation without change' (Hoyle, 1986a). The role of the agent for change is to ensure that change is 'real'; facilitating individual, group and institutional change in practice. Successful change depends on recognizing the cultural, political, social, affective, and cognitive dimensions of organization.

From our reflections on the complexities of change, learning and action research, and drawing on the ideas of Lippett et al., 1958; Watkins, 1995; Fullan, 1991, 1993; Bolam, 1986; Hall and Oldroyd, 1991, we have developed strategies for change for the action researcher.

Strategies for the agent of change

The context for learning and change
Understanding the complexities of organizations

- have organizational learning as the goal; understand the difference between organizational culture change, and the implementation of single innovations
- start where the system is; recognize the importance of multiple perspectives for analysing the organization; use organizational metaphors
- understand and recognize different political strategies; avoid subversive factionalism, coercion and positional power
- pay attention to individual people's feelings and different group cultures
- be aware of the changing external environment; predict the implications for the organization
- build flexible, dynamic matrices, and exploit different forms of interorganizational relationships
- value the individual, the group and the organization in the learning process
- fight for resources; encourage the organization to make a public commitment though resourcing; keep resourcing issues public; use resources to back value decisions and strategic action

---

The learning and change process
Understanding the complexities of the learning and change process

- recognize and guide different phases of the change process; initiation, implementation, continuation and outcome
- recognize and guide different phases of the learning process; formation, continuation, transformation and transfiguration
- ensure changes and change strategies are congruent with the values of the organization
- do not expect change to happen quickly; it may be years between initiation and institutionalization; implementation happens developmentally
- analyse the forces in the organization which have positive and inhibitory influences on change; recognize insoluble problems and do not waste energy on them
- be aware of feelings and different levels of disturbance provoked by change; do not work with people who are disinterested; do not assume everyone will change
- encourage mutual adaptation, groups and individuals developing the change and being developed by it; recognize the needs of different groups; encourage their sense of ownership
- support strategies for change with practical training and embedded work experiences

The role of the agent for change / action researcher
Understanding the complexities of the role

- analyse your own standpoint and values; do not assume you are implementing your own view; exchange your reality with others
- have a vision and evolutionary plan but do not be blinkered; seek public commitment of managers
- have clear priorities to stay healthy; analyse your personal resources; say no; do not set out to please everyone; stay positive and keep a sense of humour
- choose appropriate ways of working with others which are congruent with your own values; recognize the need for support; work collaboratively with others in the organization; share ideas
- build resources; set up support networks; find and work with reliable people who are committed and enthusiastic; establish and maintain helpful relationships; build for success; often celebrate with others, and praise others for their contributions
- manage how you would like to be managed, based on principles that are congruent with the work; make decisions based on values; anticipate and welcome conflict; use it to challenge your perspective and strengthen arguments
- work on different aspects at different levels; kindle interest in different areas
- be courageous, yet patient; use a combination of encouragement, support, and pressure; be open and flexible; expect disappointments but do not hold on to them

---

The individual learner
Understanding the complexities of learning

- value personal learning as the route to system change; simultaneously push for change while allowing self-learning to unfold
- be prepared for a journey of uncertainty; do not over-organize; know when to let go
- see problems as sources of creative resolution
- develop a theoretical perspective; use theoretical perspectives to inform practice
- analyse problem areas; carry out regular reviews, get feedback from others
- take risks; see mistakes as positive opportunities for learning; make decisions for action using intuition, knowledge and political awareness
- take time to reflect on what is being learned; make learning explicit; seize learning opportunities
- make the learning cycle explicit; reflect on practice, work out own meaning, apply new insights, bring about actions for change, reflect on the changes

The strategies demonstrate the practical transferability of the Transformatory Approach to Learning within an organizational context. They provide strategies for individual learning and organizational learning. They draw together the main issues discussed within the chapter: features of the learning organization, explicit learning, the personal dimension, collaboration, the learning context, the implications of organizational metaphors for change; change perspectives, change strategies, and the role of action research.

Throughout the chapter we have been concerned with learning and change within the organization. We have stressed the importance of teachers seeing themselves as learners and the organization seeing itself as learning. In the Transformatory Approach, the community within which the organization is based is viewed as a learning community, and as being a resource for learning. Fullan makes a similar point:

> It is simply not possible to realize the moral purpose of teaching – making a difference in the lives of students – without similar developments in teachers. Moreover, many of the new goals of education for students – having a sense of purpose, habits of and skills of inquiry, ability to work with others, and to deal with change – are precisely the skills of change agentry ... Teachers must succeed if students are to succeed, and students must succeed if society is to succeed. (Fullan, 1993, p. 46)

In 1969, Rogers appreciated that the unstatic nature of the world meant that people needed to learn how to change, and how to learn. Once again, educational organizations are facing the most profound changes which, in terms of educational reform and school improvement, have been extensively debated (Fullan, 1993; Hargreaves, 1994; Hopkins *et al.*, 1994; Larson, 1992; Stoll and Fink, 1996; Whitaker, 1995b).

Barber highlights the need for still more radical change:

> We need to go beyond school reform ... to reconstruct our entire approach to education. We need to redesign the whole process of learning ... it is not sufficient to reform schools – the role of school itself in the learning process needs to be questioned too. (Barber, 1996, pp. 248–9)

Educationalists and politicians need to work collaboratively for these changes to come about. We are optimistic that changes in government policies and state reforms will provide supportive, non-blaming, yet challenging contexts for learners and learning organizations. This will be necessary to provide the cultural emphasis on learning that is long overdue.

Summary of Part 2

In this Part we explore the Transformatory Approach in practice within formal education settings

- We discuss a variety of models of education and highlight the links between the Liberatory model and the Transformatory Approach to Learning
- We outline the main principles of the Transformatory Approach to change in classrooms and organizations
- We demonstrate how a cycle of learning is used in practice in educational settings
- We look at how collaborative group work is put into practice in the classroom
- We illustrate how the Transformatory Approach to Learning is applied at the organizational level
- We propose that organizations can embrace change, through the Transformatory Approach to Learning

Part 3
Reframing Professional Development

NINE

Learning on the Job: Action Research

The process of learning is the vehicle for change within the Transformatory Approach to Learning. Action research has at its core a continuous cycle of reflection, learning and actions for change. This is also pivotal for action learning (see Chapter 5).

Action learning and action research are central to our Transformatory Approach to Learning. Both focus on review of learning and taking action as a result. Both are cyclical processes involving reflection on practice and personal learning. Both have the self as central in the process. With action learning, the learner is responsible for the learning process, and for bringing about change. With action research the practitioner is responsible for defining the issues, and areas to be developed and changed. While the processes and principles of action learning and action research are similar, there are important distinctions.

Action learning is primarily a personal activity, and has an internal focus (see Chapter 5). It is concerned with individual learning, learning about learning, factors affecting learning and actions for change. The action learning cycle can be very focused and short-term. In Chapter 7, we relate the action learning cycle to practice. This process can be applied to a specific piece of learning and could, for example, be a part of every session, or part of a review of day-by-day learning. In action learning, the learner focuses on their own learning, in any situation or relationship.

In action research, the learner focuses on their professional practice. For example, classroom practice, or processes of communication, or decision-making. Action research always focuses on interactions within a particular context: for example, interactions between people or the effect of interventions on the context.

Action learning is part of the process of action research, because the practitioner investigates the relationship between their practice and their internal learning process. Action research is broader, and more public, as it affects other people.

This chapter is about action research as a form of teachers' professional development, and as a vehicle for individual, group and organizational change. It makes important links between action research and our Transformatory Approach to Learning (see Chapter 1). We make four assertions:

- action research is more effective than many other forms of professional develop-ment; its *raison d'être* is to bring about change in practice;
- collaborative action research is more effective than individual action research; bringing about change with others is more significant and lasting;
- action research can contribute significantly to the development of the learning organization, involving all members of the organization in a process of reflection, learning and change (see Chapter 8);
- action research provides an effective means of self-actualization, and bringing about radical change.

This chapter explores the purposes, advantages and limitations of action research. It compares it to other forms of research, and discusses its importance in professional development, and in bringing about individual, group, organizational and societal change.

EXPLORING ACTION RESEARCH

Action research is defined by Kemmis as a form of research carried out by practitioners into their own practices. It aims to improve the rationality and justice of

- social or educational practices,
- understanding these practices, and
- situations in which the practices are carried out.
  (Kemmis, 1993, p. 177)

Action research starts with questions arising from concerns in everyday work. Investigation takes place in the practitioner's own workplace, and no effort is made to 'control' the research context or design an 'experiment'. The findings of action research are fed directly into practice, and aim to bring about change.

Action research has a spiralling nature of action, reflection, learning and application; it is essentially developmental, longitudinal and multi-dimensional, requiring reflection at many different levels. The focus of research is ever-changing; it tells an unfolding story.

Action research does not have its own particular research techniques. Action researchers are likely to use the techniques employed by interpretative researchers (ethnographers, case study researchers, historians, etc.) rather than those such as statistical analysis and experiments, used by empirical-analytical researchers. This is because the 'objects' of action research are not only behaviours, but actions, and the viewpoints and historical context which give them meaning.

Contrary to the case in the physical sciences, the 'objects' of action research are not viewed as 'phenomena', neither are they like the objects of interpretative research, focusing on the intentions, point of view and perspectives of the practitioner. The 'objects' of educational action research are educational practices; that is informed, committed practice: praxis. Praxis is action informed by practical theory, which may in its turn inform and transform the theory which informed it. Practice in this context is not viewed as any behaviour, but as action which seeks to find a solution to a problem. Kemmis argues that the practitioner is the only one who can study praxis:

> only the practitioner can have access to the perspectives and commitments that inform a particular action as praxis, thus praxis can only be researched by the actor him/herself. The dialectic of action and understanding is a uniquely personal process of rational reconstruction and construction. (Kemmis, 1993, p. 183)

While it is only practitioners who can research their own practice, the interpretations of other participants inform the practitioner and contribute to the process of reconstruction.

Techniques do not distinguish action research, its process does. As already described, this process stresses a spiral of self-reflection, and a commitment to the improvement of the practitioner's understanding and practice.

Somekh (1995) states that action research methodology bridges the divide between research and practice. It is concerned with understanding practice and bringing about changes to practice. It rejects the two-stage process of other research, where in stage one researchers first carry out research and disseminate it to practitioners, and in stage two apply knowledge gained from the research to practice. In action research practitioner-researchers have 'a felt need . . . to initiate change' (Elliott, 1991, p. 53) or 'a moral responsibility to act' (O'Hanlon, 1994).

Action researchers do not use particular meta-techniques for establishing reliability or validity:

> Rigour derives from the logical, empirical, and political coherence of interpretations in the reconstructive moments of the self-reflective spiral (observing and reflecting), and the logical, empirical, and political coherence of justifications of proposed action in its constructive or prospective moments (planning and acting). (Kemmis, 1993, p. 185)

The validity of action research is tested by evaluating the impact of actions in a continuous process of data-collection, reflection and analysis, interpretation, action and evaluation (Altrichter and Posch, 1989). At a later stage, it is further validated through communication to other practitioners, who will make comparisons with their own experience, and judge the work to be worthwhile or not.

Three criteria are usually applied in the evaluation of action research:

- Action researchers engage in the formation and development of critical theories about their practices and their situation. The criterion here is 'true statements'; the truth of a statement is evaluated through discourse. What is stated should be comprehensible, accurate, truthfully or sincerely stated, and 'right' or appropriate in its context.
- Action researchers engage in applying and testing their practical theories to their own situation. The criterion here is authentic insights which are grounded in the participants' own circumstances and experience.

- Action researchers engage in the resolution of questions and the selection of strategies. The criterion here is prudent decisions.
(Kemmis, 1993, p. 185)

We present tables comparing the unique characteristics and principles of action research with other approaches to educational research. While action research draws on the techniques of qualitative and quantitative research, there are some fundamentally different principles underpinning the methodologies. Table 9.1 highlights the distinctions between action research and other forms of educational research. Table 9.2 highlights differences between action research, qualitative and quantitative research.

Somekh argues that action research is a radical research methodology which challenges the assumptions and status of traditional research:

> Not surprisingly it inspires loyalty among those who benefit from its democratic inclusiveness and practical relevance, and is subject to attack by those who value the modernist certainties of traditional research grounded in experimental design.
> (Somekh, 1995, p. 11)

Our own experience of action research, and experience of working with teachers developing action research in their schools, confirms this. We have found it a liberating experience, providing practical possibilities for change, while providing opportunities for challenging practice, reflection and learning. Action research promotes

- an understanding of the complexity of learning;
- an understanding of interpersonal relationships;
- an understanding of the organization and learning contexts;
- an understanding of change processes.

We believe action research is more effective than many other forms of professional development. It is 'transformational' in that it challenges the professional culture of teachers (Elliott, 1991).

ACTION RESEARCH AND TEACHERS' PROFESSIONAL DEVELOPMENT

Teachers use investigative skills as part of their everyday work. In day-to-day classroom practice, teachers carry out many aspects of the action research process by analysing, recording, and using information to improve their teaching, and other work in school. Carrying out action research allows teachers to conduct day-to-day reflection and action, in a more conscious and formal way. Action research is not seen as additional work, but as an essential process in transforming practice. This is fundamental to our Transformatory Approach. By engaging in action research, as an integral aspect of daily work, teachers learn, and can make changes to their practice. Action research provides powerful support for the development of professional practice (Somekh, 1995):

Table 9.1 Characteristics and principles of action research compared to other forms of educational research

Characteristics and principles	Action research	Educational research other than action research
Subject of research	Practitioner investigates own practice	Researcher investigates other people and/or other people's situations
Intention	Practitioner is committed to change their practice	Researcher uses research to answer research questions, formulated at start of research
Role of researcher	Primarily a practitioner, using research to transform practice	Primarily a researcher with specific expertise in research methods, and area of research
Process	Self-reflective spiral of planning, acting, reflecting, learning, and applying learning to the next stage	Linear process determined by the rationale for the research; starting with research questions which determine techniques for investigation
Focus	Determined by the practitioner, identifying the area of their practice they wish to change	Usually decided by a research team, or research funders
Decision-making	Embodies democratic principles; decisions are made by practitioners themselves; knowledge gained is owned by the practitioner	Decisions about research are made by the researcher; knowledge gained is owned by researcher
The relationship between theory and practice	Practice informs theory, theory informs practice, in a cyclical process	Theory informs practice in a linear process

Table 9.2 Differences between action research, qualitative and quantitative research

	Action research	Qualitative research	Quantitative research
Purpose	To bring about informed change	To illuminate meaning and understanding	To increase knowledge and find universal laws and generalizations
Framing	Concerned with the whole picture and everything that impacts on it	Concerned with understanding phenomena within specific settings and contexts	Focused on specific behaviour, not on context
Rationale for planning	Research planned to investigate practice	Research planned to investigate phenomena	Research often planned to test hypotheses
Techniques	Draws on both qualitative and quantitative techniques, studying particular situation or group(s) of people	Draws on ethnographic and case study methods, focusing on a particular group(s) or situation; techniques allow for unexpected outcomes	Uses measuring techniques, for example, surveys or experiments, usually involving large samples of people
Rigour	Based on logical coherence of interpretations in the reflection and learning spiral, and the action deriving from this	Achieved through discussion of bias and constraints; use of techniques such as triangulation, pilot studies	Uses measuring instruments or statistical analyses, and meta-techniques used for establishing reliability and validity; establishing possibility for replication of findings
Objective–subjective dichotomy	Enables practitioners to clarify, question and reconstruct values on which practice is built	Recognition of the subjective nature of research	Sets out to be objective and value-free

Evaluation	Evaluated in terms of reflective questions such as; 'Has it clarified issues in practice?' 'Has practice been informed by new learning?' 'Has it led to more effective practice?'	Evaluated in terms of questions such as; 'Has it illuminated personal meaning?' 'Has it contributed to understanding of the situation?' 'Does it make sense in its context?'	Evaluated in terms of questions such as 'Is it true?' 'Are the results reliable?' 'Can the results be duplicated?'

> Professional development is professional learning with an action orientation, and it seems clear that action research incorporates a lot of the features which cognitive psychologists see as essential for effective learning. (Somekh, 1995, p. 7).

Somekh (1995) argues that action research provides a 'high quality intellectual life' for teachers; professional practice is enriched by the intellectual challenge of research. Frequently it leads to the development of a new kind of professional dialogue with colleagues, especially when undertaken collaboratively. Prawat (1991) stresses the importance of 'dialogue or discourse during learning'. Discussion amongst teachers about their research helps learning about learning, an essential element in becoming an effective learner (see Chapter 5).

Action research is learning which is integrated with working experience, 'learning on the job'; a good example of situated learning (Brown *et al.*, 1989). Learning in the context of practice means that practitioners do not have to imagine the practical applications of what is being learnt. Nor do they have to manipulate ideas in an abstract form, which may be subsequently difficult to translate into practice.

Action research is learned through practice, rather than following a set of prescribed methods or techniques. Elliott suggests three different kinds of reflection:

- personal reflection: the self as a *de facto* component of the situation under study;
- problematic reflection: the self as actor, evoking responses and reactions within it;
- critical reflection: the self as an unconscious exponent of 'taken-for-granted' beliefs and assumptions.

Reflection is an active process of self-scrutiny and self-challenge.
(Elliott, 1993b)

Action research needs to document some aspects of the researcher's reflection, in order to establish the validity of the research (Somekh, 1995). The involvement of the self as a full participant in the situation under study adds to the complexity of this process:

> The self is a research instrument and the practitioner researcher must demonstrate reflexive awareness of the many factors which may have influenced his/her

interpretations, judgements and decisions . . . However, all research is essentially an enquiry into phenomena, practices or concepts, and its focus is outward-looking. Too much emphasis on the importance of the self in action research can distract the practitioner-researcher from the substantive focus of the study. There is a tendency for some action research to become ingrown and 'contentless', so that self-exploration and personal growth seem to become the whole focus and purpose of the research. This may be effective as a form of therapy, but it is difficult to justify calling it research. (Somekh, 1995, p. 13)

Educational action research, as with other forms of research, needs rigour if it is to be professionally challenging. Action research needs to be critical and analytical. While it focuses on practice, it needs to be located within a wider social and political perspective, to avoid the pitfalls highlighted by Somekh.

ISSUES IN CARRYING OUT ACTION RESEARCH

Action research raises a number of ethical questions (James and Ebbutt, 1980). The researcher is a practitioner, and the research involves an investigation into his/her own practice and that of colleagues:

- it is not possible to draw a line between data which has been collected as part of the research, and data which is available to the researcher as part of the job;
- ethical issues concerned with how much control colleagues have over written reports of their work;
- when an outsider is working with the practitioner-researcher as a co-researcher or facilitator of the research, the roles and responsibilities of both partners need to be clearly defined.
  (James and Ebbutt, 1980)

Kemmis suggests that the problem of whether action researchers can research their own praxis in an undistorted way, and whether new understandings are biased, 'subjective' or distorted, is illusory:

- It supposes that it is possible to analyse praxis from a perspective which is value-free, neutral or 'objective'. Since human praxis must always embody values and interests, then a value-free 'objective' social science cannot by definition be possible.
- Seeing action research as biased or distorted ignores the purpose of action research as enabling the practitioner to be self-reflective and, therefore, discover previously unrecognized distortions of interpretation and action. Any distortions will be expressed through language, also subject to influence by values and interests. Consequently, any interpretation of meanings from action will always be a relative rather than absolute emancipation from injustice or irrationality. Undistorted communication is the ideal-typical and the action-researcher will pursue this ideal through critical self-reflection.
  (Kemmis, 1993, p. 183)

Hammersley argues that one of the problems of educational action research is that it reflects what teachers are concerned about, and not necessarily what they ought to be concerned with.

> Teachers do not have any uniquely privileged position in deciding what are important educational issues. Thus we should not dismiss those topics pursued by educational researchers on the grounds that no teachers are concerned with them, even if this is true. (Hammersley, 1993, p. 217)

Kelly concurs:

> The issues which teacher researchers study tend to be questions of classroom management rather than socially or sociologically important problems. I do not accept that action research should be restricted to the questions which are important to practitioners, or that the practitioners' viewpoint is necessarily 'right'. (Kelly, 1985, p. 144)

Hammersley (1993, p. 220) challenges participatory democracy as an element of action research. He argues that in everyday life we do not treat everyone's opinions on all topics with equal value; we judge them in terms of their likely validity and take into account their source. The authority of research, he argues, derives from the fact that it is governed by norms of systematic investigation and rigorous analysis: this gives it intellectual authority.

Somekh points to the methodological problems when reporting action research:

> Action research knowledge is generated by the individual through detailed examination of, and reflection upon, particular experiences and events; and it is different from 'propositional' knowledge which claims generalizability across situations. However, once this knowledge is written up in a report it becomes, de facto, more like propositional knowledge for prospective readers. (Somekh, 1995, p. 18)

Nevertheless, writing is a useful tool which encourages the action researcher to take the process of reflection and analysis to a deeper level. This is frequently described by the teachers with whom we work. Often reluctant to start, teachers are surprised by the additional insights they gain when writing up their accounts.

Somekh writes:

> Ultimately the problems of reporting action research reside in the provisional nature of knowledge. Definitive statements are not easy to make in a world where knowledge is personally and socially constructed. This is where post-modern writers illuminate the problem interestingly by de-stabilizing our felt need to find answers. (Somekh, 1995, p. 18)

Action research involves reflection and learning from experiences, and then applying that learning to new situations; the development of skills including the ability to analyse and make connections; development of the ability to generalize; and the formation of new concepts. The principles of ownership, responsibility and power-sharing are embedded in teachers' learning through the process of action research in their own school. Engaging in action research develops professional expertise, observation skills and analysis. It makes teachers even more aware and sensitive to the work context, and can add a more exciting dimension to the task of teaching; action research is intrinsically interesting and worthwhile.

ACTION RESEARCH AND CHANGE

Action research can bring about change at different levels: individual, group, organizational, and societal. The benefits of action research often highlight individual personal/professional development, rather than its contribution to the development of the learning organization (see Chapter 8). Action research can be a powerful process of reflection, theorizing, learning and change. It has potential for reconstructing approaches to education and learning, and influencing social change.

Action research is viewed by Lewin (1946) as a democratic approach to research, because the practitioners are involved in every phase of the process. It leads to independence, equality and cooperation, resulting in social change (Lewin, 1946, p. 46). Kemmis argues that action research should not be viewed as a technique to introduce democracy, but rather as the embodiment of democratic principles:

> it allows participants to influence, if not determine, the conditions of their own lives and work, and collaboratively to develop critiques of social conditions which sustain dependence, inequality, or exploitation in any research enterprise, in particular, or in social life in general. (Kemmis, 1993, p. 179)

One of the strengths of action research is its importance in educational reform within a democratic society. Through action research the processes of educational reform remain in the control of those most closely involved, for example, teachers, students, and others. This contrasts with the 'disenfranchisement' of teachers (Elliott, 1993a) and the 'paternalism' of traditional educational research (Nixon, 1981). Rudduck (1987) makes a related point:

> there is an urgent need to analyse the structures that govern the production and distribution of research knowledge and the right to engage in research acts. Teacher research is, at one level, a means of countering the hegemony of academic research which teachers are often distanced by. (Rudduck, 1987, p. 5)

Participatory democracy stresses the control people should have over their own lives and contexts. Action research transforms educational organizations and praxis, to achieve social justice, by being practical and critical.

We present three studies of teachers' work, illustrating action research starting-points in particular contexts. They highlight collaborative action research at classroom, team and organizational levels.

We work with professional groups, in two different capacities. Teachers, and other professionals, attend MA and Advanced Diploma courses. They may be involved in action research within their organizations already, or may take the opportunity to conduct a short piece of action research for their course work. Writing up this experience can form part of their course assignments. We also work in schools, and in other organizations, with groups of teachers and other professionals. Two of the accounts describe the work of MA course participants; the other account is work we helped facilitate, with a group, in the teachers' own setting. A discussion of issues emerging from these accounts follows.

PETER, A HEAD OF A PRIMARY SCHOOL WORKING TOWARDS RAISING SELF-ESTEEM

How did you begin?

The school's morale was low. Unusually, the teachers seemed at a low ebb; some were less than enthusiastic. The children didn't seem to be achieving as much as they could, so as the head, I felt I needed to do something. I discussed it with our senior management team, and we decided that the next whole-school INSET day should be devoted to gathering information and raising awareness about our own self-esteem. So we organized the day, and it was very useful as we looked at ourselves, what caused us stress, and how we could communicate more effectively as a team.

Part of the day involved discussion in small groups, which we recorded. This focused on school factors which support high self-esteem, and factors which lower a sense of self-worth. We followed it up with a series of staff meetings about action research, to discuss how we could extend the work, and through a bit of direction from me, everyone agreed to do some work with their classes. We thought that what made us feel good as a school team of teachers could be transferred to the classroom. We did the same exercises with the children that we had done, with some modification; for example, we asked the children what made them feel good in school and what sort of things made them feel bad. We collected this information from all the classes and gave the results back to the children. The children next worked in groups to plan changes to increase the 'good' factors. I went into classrooms more to work with the teachers and we had whole-school assemblies where we shared what was happening in each of the classrooms. There was a conscious awareness about the research element, as we had based our changes on the information we had collected from the children.

What was the learning?

Well, my biggest mistake was not to have all the staff there for that first INSET day. It was only for the teachers, and if you are trying to bring about whole-school change, then that has to be everybody. We need to get everybody involved, and it is hard to do that if there are still boundaries between the different categories of staff. Some support staff felt excluded and others didn't want to get involved.

I learned a lot about my relationship with the staff, and something new about my role in introducing change. Because the whole thing was about collaboration and the importance of communication, it affected my management and the role of the senior management team. I think we were more aware of how we were making decisions, and the impact it had on others. We tried to draw everyone into the processes of decision-making. I was also aware of how the teachers were working differently. Because we had a new emphasis on the learning processes, we were having different sorts of conversations with, and about children. I am sure this is good. Of course I can't say yet what the children are learning, but there is a different sort of atmosphere, which is bound to rub off on them.

What action are you taking as a result of this learning?

Our next stage of action research involves asking the children to give us feedback about how they feel about their work in school now we have done this work together. I've tried to engage all the staff, but that is difficult. And I'm trying to think about the ways in which we might involve all the governors. I've heard of a scheme where each governor 'adopts' a class and gets to know the children in that class, and visits them when they are working. I'd like to involve the governors in finding out if the children are experiencing change as a result of our action research. We also want to work with parents in a different way. I think we can involve them in action research in the future. There is so much we can do, but we can only take on so much at a time. It is like decorating your home. You start painting in one room and then realize the room next door needs attention.

I get lots of ideas, but I am aware that it is important not to introduce too many changes too quickly. That makes me think about my role, and the difference between leadership, collaboration, and coercion. I'd like to support the teachers in writing up their accounts.

SHONA, A TEACHER WITH RESPONSIBILITY FOR STAFF DEVELOPMENT FOR THE SCHOOL
How did you begin?

Well I got the new post and I went on a course to try to obtain support; it seemed a daunting task, and I wanted to meet with other teachers who were in similar situations. I was interested in the idea of action research when it was introduced, and I thought it could help me, in my situation. I thought I could do some research into the perceptions of other people in my organization, to find out what their previous experiences of staff development were, what their needs were, and what they thought the best strategies would be to develop this area, in our organization. I spent a lot of time talking with people, a cross-section of staff, if you like, and I analysed their responses and wrote it up in a report with a plan of action, and some thoughts about policy.

What was the learning?

I needed to be clear about my purpose and goals; being clear about what aspects of my practice and my organization's practice needed to change; being clear why some things are important issues, and others not; to find out if is this just my perception, or if others feel the same. To find out what I need to know; to find out what do others say; what is in the literature; what do other colleagues feel, both in my organization and outside.

One thing that bothered me was that I could never tell if what I was doing was part of my research, or part of my job, but that didn't seem an issue after a while. Once I decided what to focus on, that helped clarify lots of other things as well. I suppose that is because the same issues are at the root of so many problems for staff.

I am learning a lot about people's attitudes to learning, especially about responsibility for learning. There needs to be more of a shift from 'someone out there breathing down my neck' to 'let me see what I can take on for myself'. There are some members of staff who can't learn enough, they are always attending training workshops and courses, and having a go at changing their way of working. Others don't want to know; they avoid discussions; they are cynical; they say things in the organization will never change, but I think individuals themselves have to change.

I am also learning a lot about people's attitudes towards the organization. I was surprised by the strong responses; hearing people say that they didn't feel part of the organization and how my role was seen as part of the management's strategy.

My main learning is that change is slow. I am often disappointed by people's reactions. I get frustrated by cynicism. I see small changes, but I want to work at a faster rate. I have to work where people are, and to move on from there. So I have learned about myself too, and how I might need to change my strategy in future.

What action are you taking as a result of this learning?

I think the main thing has been to recognize people's different needs. I am also very aware of the different levels of response in different departments. Things have to be tailor-made. It is no good foisting stuff on people; they will reject it immediately. Change strategies have to match the group.

I also became aware of my isolation. Although I work with people across the entire organization, I need people to talk things through. So I've set up a small working group who help me with ideas. I am also working more with people of a similar role in other organizations. Networking is very important. We share lots of ideas and strategies; we contact each other regularly to find out what we are doing as a response to external initiatives. People put lots of really interesting literature my way. E-mail is great for keeping in touch and for debating the ideas in the reading and discussing how it relates to our practice. That has been another really important thing for me, being able to take on board the theoretical issues, to inform my practice. It helps me distance myself, and not take things personally. I'd like to set up a programme of action research for staff to see how it could bring about changes in the organization. It is too early for that though. The climate isn't right. I went to a conference and heard about an entire school being involved in action research. That sounds exciting, but I don't think we are ready for that. Introducing the idea, in my organization, would put a lot of people's backs up, but I would like to work where that was common practice. I could start with just a few colleagues; we could be part of an action research support team.

SARAH, A CLASSROOM TEACHER CONCERNED ABOUT ACHIEVEMENT OF BOYS

How did you begin?

We were becoming more and more concerned about a large group of boys in the school whose examination results were not as good as we had expected. Our attendance checks also showed that boys in Year 11 were absent from school more often than the girls in Year 11. We thought that it would be useful to involve Year 11 classes in this action research and planned a series of lessons in PSE. We paired up and I observed another teacher's PSE class, and she observed mine. These lessons were set up so that each class focused on investigating a different aspect. My class chose to look at the difference between boys and girls in their feelings, attitudes and perceptions of taking GCSEs. This meant that the research was at different levels. The young people were doing some research into achievement, I was looking at the effects of the classroom intervention, and the year team was looking at this intervention in terms of the results for the whole year.

What was the learning?

I think the young people learned more about collaborative group work; they learned about research, particularly about constructing questionnaires; they talked about their feelings and perceptions about GCSEs, and the process itself helped them focus on their own achievement and learning. I was interested in finding out whether classroom intervention of this kind made any difference to the achievement of boys. At the end of the series of lessons I asked the young people to reflect on their work and learning in class. I collated their individual comments and fed them back for further discussion. Two things emerged. The first was that they said it was useful, it related to their experiences, and focusing on it helped them think about their own learning, but that they would like to have thought about it earlier.

The second was that some of the young people thought a focus on gender differences was too narrow and suggested that it would be interesting to see if there are differences in perceptions of other social groups.

My colleague gave me feedback about how I work with boys and girls; my expectations about their work, how my language differed, and about messages my body language conveyed. I was surprised by her feedback. I thought I was treating the boys and girls in a similar way, but my colleague picked out subtle differences; for example, my tone of voice was different and I gave the boys less responsibility.

What action are you taking as a result of this learning?

We decided that the work had many positive effects, but that it was too late to make very much impact on the achievement of young people in Year 11. We also thought that we would like to focus on the achievement of all pupils in the school and on maximizing the potential of everyone in the organization. We have decided to refocus our classroom work in Year 7 in September. We are going to start by asking some of the girls and boys who took part in this project to talk to the new Year 7 in assembly. We intend planning some research for the new Year 7 pupils to carry out about attitudes to learning. We would like to extend looking at difference to explore difference between young people in other social groups. We hope this will lead to other changes and further learning, both for us and for the young people. We are going to continue with the pair observation work. We found that really useful.

EMERGING ISSUES

These studies illustrate the value of action research in personal/professional develop-ment and in bringing about change to practice. Teachers, and other professionals, become empowered by taking control of their practice, and influencing the context. Carr and Kemmis (1983) propose that the exercise of critical analysis, and rational debate, can free the individual from some of the constraints of institutional power structures. This highlights the importance of working collaboratively, and engaging in critical debate with colleagues. Action research

> may be investigated by an individual, but its momentum is towards collaboration, because the emphasis on social interactions and inter-personal relationships has the effect of drawing other participants into the research process. The focus of the research is likely to be an issue which is of concern to the group. (Somekh, 1995)

Establishing collaborative groups is essential

- to support each other in 'becoming critical', without which action research would be ineffective in bringing about change, because it could do little more than collude with the existing power structures to reinforce the status quo;
- to develop 'collaborative critical endeavour', providing an effective means of empowering the self and bringing about radical change in society. Without this collaboration, individuals' judgement would be contaminated by uncritical assumptions which are culturally determined.
(Carr and Kemmis, 1983).

Collaboration overcomes the problems of teachers working in isolated situations:

> The problem of isolation is a deep seated one. Architecture often supports it. The timetable reinforces it. Overload sustains it. History legitimates it. (Fullan and Hargreaves, 1992)

Considering the ways in which action research is introduced raises important issues for senior management. At best, action research comes from professionals' desire to change their practice. At an organization-wide level, issues of coercion and power need to be addressed. Collaboration is the key, rather than 'contrived collegiality':

> Collaborative cultures comprise relatively spontaneous, informal and pervasive collaborative working relationships among teachers which are both social and task centred in nature. Contrived collegiality is more controlled, regulated and predictable in its outcomes and is frequently used to implement system initiatives on the head teacher's preferred programmes. (Hargreaves, 1994)

Action research processes are valuable in:

- exploring multiple perspectives of interactions, interpersonal relationships, and actions in particular contexts;
- deepening understanding of the complex situations in which practitioners work;
- generating 'situational understanding' (Dreyfus, 1981) as the basis for action;
- informing actions;
- bringing about improvement in the practice being researched.

Action research adds complexity to learning. Professional practice is enriched, as it leads to the development of new insights and understandings, and new ways of thinking and talking about learning.

TEN

Time for Change: Conceptualizing Teachers' Learning

In times of change, learners will inherit the earth, while the learned find themselves beautifully equipped to deal with a world that no longer exists. (Ascribed to Eric Hoffen; exact reference unknown)

Hoffen's observation portrays the need for lifelong learning; a fundamental premise of our Transformatory Approach to Learning. Our view of continuing professional development for teachers is based on the Transformatory Approach. We reject a deficit stance, suggesting teachers need improvement, but see change as an essential part of being a professional; a positive aspect, where learning is embraced as an important part of living in a rapidly changing world.

This chapter explores our understanding of planned professional development for teachers. It is based on our own action research over five years. In Chapter 9 we highlight our work on MA courses with teachers. One goal of this work is to facilitate teachers becoming action researchers. (For a full discussion see Chapter 9.) In this chapter we are concerned with improving teachers' learning through course design. We draw on observations from teachers who have participated in our courses, to illuminate the main principles of the Transformatory Approach, when applied to teachers' professional development. We begin by looking at different perspectives of professional development, and then outline the principles of our approach.

PERSPECTIVES ON TEACHERS' PROFESSIONAL DEVELOPMENT

The way we view professional development 'is a direct outgrowth of the way in which we view teacher roles' (Wise *et al.*, 1984, cited in Blackman, 1989, p. 2).

- if we view the teacher as an applier of a craft, then we will focus professional development primarily on the methods and techniques of teaching;
- if we view teachers as functioning in isolation from one another, we will focus professional development upon the activities of the classroom;
- if we view a teacher as a functionary, then managers of the school system will be the sources for the agendas of professional development.

(Blackman, 1989, p. 2)

If teachers are viewed in these ways, the focus is on 'what the teacher can *do*, rather than what the teacher *is*, and can become' (Blackman, 1989, p. 2). However

- if we view the teacher as a professional, we will address issues related to decision-making, practice and professional knowledge about human development, learning, and school purposes;
- if we view teachers as members of school staffs, and as members of the profession at large, we will address not only matters of classroom practice, but matters to do with the school and its sphere of the education programme, and matters related to the school system which might include questions involving long-range planning and issues of concern to the profession–at–large;
- if we view teachers as professionals, we also consider them capable of creating their own agendas for professional development.
  (Blackman, 1989, p. 2)

Blackman suggests that if we alter our views of the teacher's role, from that of technician to that of professional, we alter the focus of the agenda for professional development; the locus of concern is broadened, and the source of the agenda changed. The view of the teacher as professional permits us to get beyond the technologies of teaching, to gain a fuller understanding of what we seek to do in schools and why.

This positive view of the teacher as a professional fits with the Transformatory Approach to Learning. We view the teacher as a learner, engaged in a process of action learning, and action research, reflecting on experiences, developing understanding, gaining insights into practice, making important professional judgements and bringing about actions for change. We see teachers operating in a complex classroom, engaging with other learners, young people and adults, within complex organizations. The teacher is not a technician who merely 'delivers' a curriculum, but is a professional learner and educator, who is creative, can interpret policies and programmes of study according to the needs of learners, and most importantly, create learning conditions within the realities of their particular school context. Our view of the teacher is related to the Liberatory model of education rather than the Functionalist model (see Chapter 6), yet it is the Functionalist model that has dominated much of planned professional development experience. Many weaknesses have been identified, especially in relation to course-led models of professional development. Planned experiences such as these:

- take place off site, and are geared to individuals, rather than groups of staff;
- fail to link with the needs of departments or schools;
- are undertaken on a voluntary basis;
- are random in terms of participation and content in relation to the needs of individual schools;
- have limited impact on practice, with little or no dissemination or follow–up;
- disrupt the teaching timetable;
- are open to possible conflict between participant teachers as theorists and as deliverers;

- attempt to cater for people who are at different starting-points and therefore are unable to satisfy all participants.
  (Craft, 1996, p. 8)

Effective professional development, where change occurs in teachers' practice, is more likely if it is embedded within the organization in which the teacher works (Carnell, 1997). Professional development needs to encompass actions for change within the teacher's own work context to make a significant impact. Our Transformatory Approach demonstrates how understanding teachers as learners, understanding action learning and action research, and understanding the learning context, can bring about effective professional development.

THE TRANSFORMATORY APPROACH TO LEARNING AND TEACHERS' PROFESSIONAL DEVELOPMENT

Our approach to professional development using the Transformatory Approach to Learning embodies principles which include:

- *Meta-learning.* An explicit focus on learning about learning, using action learning cycles, meta-learning processes, and action research techniques (see Chapter 5). This implies 'deep' rather than 'surface' learning (see Chapter 2). The goal is to increase understanding of the complexities of the learning process, the learner and the learning context, and to develop frameworks for planning.
- *Holistic learning.* The affective, social and cognitive domains are explored and integrated with personal and professional learning. Concepts of personal and professional development are explored at a theoretical and practical change level. The goal is to understand the interrelationships between all aspects of learning and their importance in bringing about change.
- *Self-actualization.* This is an empowering process, providing necessary conditions where individual learning can be most effective, encouraging risk-taking and identifying actions for change. There is work at a personal level (an exploration of subjective experiences), in relation to the teacher's own self. The goal is to increase understanding, and a change in perception of self as teacher in action.
- *Collaborative learning contexts.* Participatory learning processes and group work activities are used to analyse collaboration in groups and change in the workplace. The goal is to increase understanding of learning contexts and the dynamic relationship that exists: the effect of learner on context and context on learner.

The focus is understanding on three levels: the personal, the theoretical, and one of practical change. We suggest that it is the interconnection of these levels, in relation to the principles of meta-learning, holistic learning, self-actualization, and collaborative learning contexts, that creates a powerful base for teachers' professional development.

PRINCIPLES FOR BRINGING ABOUT TEACHERS' ACTIONS FOR CHANGE

Meta-learning

Our research with teachers indicates that learning cannot be assumed. There needs to be a specific focus on learning about learning, what is learned, how learning takes place, and how that learning can be used in future:

> It is a common belief that learning is automatic and without effort, and that it is continuous and cumulative over life. Yet we have reason and some evidence, to doubt this belief. Learning has been confused with development, and the biological metaphor of autonomous development growth is so powerful that it permeates our thinking. (Novak and Gowin, 1984, p. 10)

Professional development is structured using the 'Do, Review, Learn, Apply' cycle (Dennison and Kirk, 1990) (see Chapter 5). Participants operate as action learners and action researchers, engaging with subjective experiences, and then apply their learning more widely in professional contexts. Meta-learning, 'learning how to learn' (Nisbet and Shucksmith, 1986), is a step in the process towards self-actualization. By engaging in and analysing 'meta-learning techniques' (Novak and Gowin, 1984), teachers develop their understanding of the processes necessary to become effective learners. Reflection on application of learning is crucial. One teacher explains:

> The context has been supportive, striving, enthusiastic, comfortable and effective for learning, but the learner needs to be open and emotionally ready to learn. Experiential learning creates a type of process which creates a particular type of learner. Therefore the learning process is not value-free. The learner is part of the process and the learner also helps to create the context. They all impact on each other. The learning and teaching process has become united. We are all resources for each other. It has been non-hierarchical and everyone's experience has been valued.

This observation reveals the complexity of the relationship between learner and teaching characteristics, contexts and processes. Watkins *et al.* (1996) provide a model of elements in effective learning (Figure 10.1), developed from Biggs and Moore (1993), which encapsulates these complexities.

We see that the outcomes of this model include 'positive emotions', and 'enhanced self', identifying the way in which learning contributes to self-actualization (discussed later in this chapter).

To be effective in the future, Fullan (1993) argues that teachers must deepen their knowledge of pedagogy, and develop a much more sophisticated understanding of teaching and learning. People need to be effective learners who can 'enhance and transfer learning' and 'learn in an increasing range of contexts' (Watkins *et al.*, 1996). They must acquire learning and thinking skills, including learning to manage change and diversity, as well as developing the skills to be self-directed learners. Developing

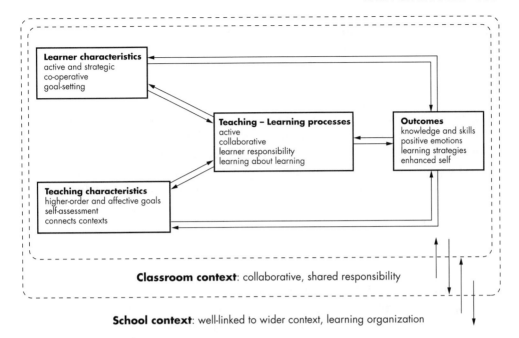

Figure 10.1 A model of elements in effective learning

the meta–cognitive processes of planning, monitoring and reflecting (Biggs and Moore, 1993) are central elements of professional development.

This explicit focus on learning helps teachers:

> It changed my approach to how adults learn, and it has radically affected team meetings. I now get the teachers to do the work, and get them to think and make conclusions. Before I felt responsible for what happened and controlled things. There is an air of open-endedness.
>
> Another important thing for me was that the school is doing a visual representation of the mission statement. This was a direct result of my action research. I got back more information and positive feedback than I ever got before. It is involving the whole school community.
>
> This would not have happened before. It came about because on the course, we did so much about visual representation of learning and about the importance of collaboration.

Learning is also made explicit in the action research process, described in Chapter 9. Action research can be used at two levels. Firstly, to develop understanding of the action research process and its value for professional development. Secondly, to reflect on learning and develop understanding of organizations by carrying out research within a particular context. Insights gained through self-reflection provide a greater understanding of change processes that affect individuals and organizations.

As we described in Chapter 9, action research is 'a form of research carried out by practitioners into their own practices' (Kemmis, 1993, p. 177). Our experience of using action research to observe, reflect, plan, and act convinces us of its value 'to improve the rationality, understanding and situation of educational practice' (Lewin, 1946). It is a powerful source of learning for teachers. Knowing it to be most empowering when undertaken collaboratively, we encourage teachers to work with others.

One teacher discussed the result of using action research with her team:

> I always thought that change was rather technical. I focused on systems rather than people. I now realize the importance of working with teachers in a very personal way. As a team leader, for example, the way I relate to my team is very much based on thinking about how they are feeling, getting reports back from them on an almost daily basis. This seems to have increased their openness and confidence. It has altered the way I operate on a day-to-day basis. There hasn't been a huge change, but the small shifts are really important.

and the result of involving young people in her action research:

> We have discovered that our students respond very seriously and have made very observant, analytical and constructive contributions. They most definitely helped us by sharing their feelings about their achievement and learning.

Interestingly, this teacher described the changes in her team, and subsequent openness and confidence, as 'a small shift'. We argue that this is a fundamental shift. In carrying out action research teachers engage in 'second-order changes' (Fullan, 1991), seeking fundamentally to 'alter structures and the way in which they perform their roles' (Cuban, 1988, p. 342), rather than improving the efficiency and effectiveness of what is already happening.

Teachers engage in action research 'tailor made for individual environments' (Thiessen, 1992). Action research embeds teacher development in the workplace. It facilitates wider change in schools, when carried out collaboratively. As Fullan states, 'The individual educator is a critical starting point because the leverage for change can be greater through the efforts of individuals' (Fullan, 1993, p. 12). Initiation at school level normally happens when an individual or small groups become enthusiastic to try out new ideas, highlighting the importance of developing a collaborative context (see Chapter 9).

Altrichter *et al.* (1993) suggest that action research, as an approach to teacher development, is in line with the concept of professionality, suggesting new types of communication among teachers:

> dynamic networks of relationships to assist them in taking responsible action in the face of complexity and uncertainty. This kind of collaboration implies exchange processes among teachers or between teachers and other groups in which there is a symmetry, rather than a hierarchy of power; it is often teacher initiated and not bound to any prespecified procedures. (Altrichter *et al.*, 1993, pp. 202–3)

Action research is best carried out in collaboration; action research itself develops collaborative cultures and supportive networks within organizations (see Chapter 9).

Most importantly, it provides a structure for reflecting, observing and discussing learning; it is a meta-learning process.

Holistic learning

When we use the term holistic learning, we include all aspects of learning, the affective, social, and cognitive dimensions. In teachers' learning, 'holistic' also includes the integration of personal and professional learning.

> Human experience involves not only thinking and acting but also feeling, and it is only when all three are considered together that individuals can be empowered to enrich the meaning of their experience. (Novak and Gowin, 1984, p. xi)

One way for teachers to focus on themselves as learners, and reflect on all the dimensions of learning, is through autobiography. When writing autobiographies, which forms a central part of our work, teachers engage in the process of reflection and evaluation at an emotional level, as a way of understanding the influences on them, their learning, their motivation, their relationships with others and their changes. This is followed by an analysis of the literature that relates to autobiography, assessing the value of autobiography for learning. Through autobiography, teachers explore how their learning can be applied and used to bring about actions for change.

One of the teachers engaged in our research into the use of autobiography writes:

> The processes have led me through numerous stages of uncertainty, to an understanding of who I am, and the reasons that underpin my views and beliefs. . . . I never dared to analyse the effect of a difficult professional period. My denial of the past was kept unchecked until I was required to write an autobiography. The impact made me realize just why my beliefs about equality and racism are so powerful and why I am doing the work I am. I am aware that teacher development is a process of personal development. . . . I have been able to 'lay the ghost to rest' on some painful experiences in my development.
>
> Now my focus must be to look at how my own learning can be put to use by looking at the transition for beginning teachers: a time of uncertainty and vulnerability.

The use of the reflective journal is another way of reflecting holistically, facilitating learning and bringing about actions for change. It can help 'challenge the thinking about events, circumstances and philosophies which constitute and value the status quo' (Knowles, 1993, p. 82). We use the journal to record our thoughts, feelings, and experiences during the week and at the end of sessions. One teacher explains:

> Highlighting things that happened during the week made me aware of what was significant. The questions you introduced to trigger our reflections were thought-provoking.

Within the Transformatory Approach to Learning the relationship between the learner, processes of learning, and the context are seen as valid discourse (see Chapter

5). The subjective experiences of teachers and their beliefs about themselves as learners, their fears and their frustrations are important to articulate. Salzberger-Wittenberg *et al.* (1983) maintain that the dread of helplessness and of being lost is harboured by all adults, no matter how capable and mature. The more unfamiliar and unstructured the situation the more disoriented people feel. Professional development needs to encompass a developmental planning process, providing structure at the beginning, giving teachers opportunities to discuss their emotions, encouraging risk-taking, giving teachers responsibility for their learning, and encouraging actions for change.

Self-actualization

Maslow's (1970) work in relation to hierarchies of need is most frequently associated with the term self-actualization (see Chapter 1). Growth towards that goal is determined by the relationship of two sets of forces operating within each individual. This is similar to what Joyce describes as the discomfort of learning:

> The need to grow is built into the fibre of our being. . . Paradoxically, however, we have an ingrained tendency to conserve our beings as they are or were. (Joyce, 1984, p. 33)

Real growth requires disequilibrium instead of comfort; problems and diverse opinions challenge fixed attitudes (Joyce, 1984). In applying the principles of self-actualization or self-renewal, it appears then that the processes of change with its associated fears and anxieties need to be balanced with stability and safety. Growing maturity is represented by moving from the unknown, accepting change and not being overwhelmed by new experiences. As part of this we need to understand ourselves. Knowles (1993) argues that we need to recognize reasons for our behaviour. Holly and Walley concur:

> Knowledge of human development – child and adult – is essential, not only for understanding ourselves and the students we teach, but as a basis for building the personal relationships that are an integral part of teaching – with colleagues, parents, administrators and community members. (Holly and Walley, 1989, p. 286)

Professional development needs to empower teachers, provide the necessary conditions where learning can be most effective, encourage risk-taking (see Chapter 2) and actions for change, while excluding experiences which are too uncomfortable. For such empowerment, the facilitator's role is important in sharing in the processes of personal, emotional, social, spiritual and intellectual growth, an antithesis of the exercise of power and authority.

This approach to teachers' learning is associated with two claims. Firstly, that the quality of teachers' class work is closely related to their growth as people as well as professionals (Fullan and Hargreaves, 1992). Secondly, their 'moral purpose' (Fullan, 1991), that is, their ability to connect, care and differentiate, is as essential to good teaching as subject knowledge and skills.

The use of autobiography, discussed in the previous section, is important in the process of understanding ourselves and moving towards self-actualization. One teacher observed:

> There was a personal shift triggered by the time line and autobiography. These exercises were very painful for some and they articulated the pain very well. They were able to see how it influenced their life and the career choices they made. They were able to come to terms with the past which they were not able to face before. It made them realize too, in particular, that they thought that by completely avoiding thinking about painful issues the pain would go away. With the aid of everyone around them, they were able to articulate it, and move on. Some associated their pain with feelings of failure, which once they started talking about it, they realized it was not. So they were able to let go of that association and realize that they are in control of their lives.

This powerfully underlines the importance of a growth environment for teachers if they are to provide for pupils' growth (Eisner, 1985).

The concept of self-renewal (Gardner, 1981) is closely linked with self-actualization. 'Self-renewing individuals' will show evidence of a system for continuous renewal, complex decision-making, self-knowledge, the courage to risk failure, fruitful relationships, critical thinking, and involvement about which they care deeply.

One teacher said:

> I got a sense of achievement through talking with others, and the processes of looking at positive and negative learning experiences. I realized that I had moved considerably. This has made me think about what I had achieved and how much success I have had as a teacher and as a head teacher. I also feel relaxed with the staff, and I sit with staff and get them to talk about how we are going to solve problems together. I am not worried about getting the right answers anymore.

Examining subjective experiences can be significant, but alone may not be helpful in achieving change. There is value in personal explorations which challenge teaching approaches, priorities and assumptions. This is an important aspect of self-actualization and bringing about change. However, we suggest that this needs to be done in relation to the other principles, to provide support for actions for change: meta-learning, holistic approaches to learning and collaborative contexts.

Collaborative learning contexts

Effective teacher development takes place within collaborative learning contexts. Rosenholtz (1989) observes that collaboration is the norm in effective schools. It assumes that improvement in teaching is a collective rather than individual enterprise, and that analysis, evaluation and experimentation in concert with colleagues are conditions under which teachers improve. North American and British research implies that collaboration among teachers is a key factor linked with effective pupil learning (Smith and Scott, 1990; Reynolds, 1992). Sarason (1990) asserts that within a school context you cannot have students as continuous learners and effective collaborators, without teachers having these same characteristics. Hilt suggests:

> Teachers must model teamwork and innovation behaviour . . . adopting a focus of teaching thinking through team learning, requires a commitment by the school staff to group problem solving, and self-development, at the very same time it encourages these activities for students . . . Some schools and teachers already understand this concept: restructuring at a school wide level parallels restructuring at the classroom level . . . As teachers invest time and effort to develop further their own collaborative skills, they will enhance their ability to teach thinking through co-operative learning. What teachers do outside the classroom will benefit them in the classroom and vice versa. (Hilt, 1992, p. 263)

Collaborative cultures are highly sophisticated (Fullan and Hargreaves, 1992), and are created over time and in combination with strong individual development.

> We have seen the debilitating effect on the tradition of individualism in teaching. All successful change processes are carried out by collaboration. (Fullan, 1991, p. 349)

In the Transformatory Approach to Learning, professional development is based on collaboration at two levels: the experience of working in collaborative groups with peers (see Chapter 3), and the experiences of working collaboratively within an organization (see Chapter 8).

At the group level, a collaborative culture develops through sharing personal and professional experiences. At the organization level, concepts of power are explored, for example, as factors which enhance or inhibit actions for change. Concrete experiences are built in to explore the concepts of personal safety, challenge and risk-taking. The cycle of learning, described earlier, helps this process.

The teachers involved in our research report on the importance of the collaborative group culture:

> I am more ready to take risks, although I had before, perhaps unconsciously. I am now more aware that risk-taking is easier in a safe situation, when working with others, when it is expected and there isn't a fear of failure.

The value of sharing professional experiences is well documented (Fullan and Connelly, 1990; Grimmett and Erickson, 1988). Working in pairs or small groups, teachers can take on the role of critical friend (Day, 1994), to explore risk-taking, change and problem-solving. These processes are effective in changing practice (Cooper and McIntyre, 1996), and within a collaborative context the process is enhanced.

When the self is central to learning, the learning processes contribute towards self-actualization. Collaborative learning processes open up possibilities for change within the teachers' own contexts. It is the interconnection of these principles that is important for change.

However, some of the teachers' concerns about change, within their contexts, need to be addressed. One teacher said:

I have become much more tolerant of the differences in other people's professional development. I believe that everybody can move forward. However, professional development is closely related to power, one's own power and the power authority figures have over one. Working alone means that there are not enough people to discuss thoughts with. I am becoming more interested in listening to understand the emotional response of why people do and do not take things on board. The school climate can work in favour of collaboration, but there is not enough time to share reflections about what happens in classrooms.

Another observed:

One of the teachers did not really understand what you were trying to achieve. It is because his school is not a happy school, it is autocratic and into accountability. He could not see a better way. Our school philosophy is empowering, and gives a sense of worth and achievement. His school system has a different culture. He had difficulty relaxing into the philosophy. He is stuck in the culture of his own school and it may not be what he wants to hear.

These comments highlight some possible conflicts in relation to organizing collaborative learning in teachers' professional development. Teachers find it harder to learn, take risks, and bring about actions for change, if they are working in a 'stuck' school (Rosenholtz, 1989), where there is no structure to support collaboration.

Processes and strategies

Table 10.1 outlines examples of processes and strategies used to incorporate the principles of meta-learning, holistic learning, self-actualization and collaborative group contexts.

REFLECTIONS ON PROFESSIONAL DEVELOPMENT AND THE TRANSFORMATORY APPROACH TO LEARNING

Interestingly, from our research it emerges that teachers become more aware of the complexity of professional development as a realization of (a) their own complexities: the complexities of their own behaviour, motives, relationships, emotional reactions and blocks, and (b) the complex contexts in which they are working. Professional development is neither simple nor clear. The data show some teachers moving from the intuitive to the explicit. Instead of working on hunches, teachers are informed. Instead of thinking they are 'lucky' to be where they are, they are aware of the work and effort which has led to success. Instead of thinking they have a 'good' class, they are aware of the important work of building relationships. Instead of thinking that the group works well together, they are aware of the processes that encourage collaboration. It is this

Table 10.1 Processes and strategies to incorporate the principles of meta-learning, holistic learning, self-actualization and collaborative contexts

Meta-learning	Holistic learning
cycles of learning used to reflect, analyse, make connections and apply learning	work at a personal level, e.g. conversations about non-work aspects of the person
participants engaged in own action research	an interaction of professional learning and personal learning
concepts of meta-cognition and meta-learning introduced: for example, concept-mapping	hindrances to change discussed; risk-taking encouraged
learning made explicit, e.g. application of learning discussed and acknowledged	exploring cognitive and affective domains and their interrelationship in learning: for example, exploring ways in which learning is helped and hindered by feelings
previous learning examined to pinpoint successful and unsuccessful strategies	
reflective journals used to record thoughts, feelings and experiences of change	professional and personal experiences used as triggers for the study of specific foci

Self-actualization	Collaborative contexts
engagement of participants in personal learning through the use of autobiography, time lines, appreciations	group contract and course agreement to make commitment to learning and joint endeavour explicit
relating concepts of professional development to teachers' own personal lives	variety of individual, small-group and whole-group tasks
valuing teachers' experiences, using their experiences as a starting-point	concepts of trust, challenge and risk explored
a shift in responsibility of facilitator to individuals and group over time: for example, participants make presentations to the group, dictated by their own interests	linking work with own contexts, and with external contexts
personal successes both within and outside the course celebrated	collaborative action for change: for example, the exploration of the concept of collaboration, working collaboratively in the group and exploring group dynamics, whilst exploring the possibilities and limitations of school settings as collaborative workplaces

overt and recognizable understanding that helps teachers feel more confident of the sorts of changes they wish to make and can plan accordingly. They are able to make choices. Insights are built from reflective processes and articulated within the group. Once made public, they are made self-aware. Keiny's explanation seems most pertinent:

> The social interaction within the group, the exchange of ideas that stem from the teachers' practice, leads to the decontextualization of personal experience, and construction of knowledge of a more abstract nature. Reflection of ideas within the reflective group . . . turns strategies into meaningful pedagogic knowledge. (Keiny, 1994, p. 165)

The teachers' accounts show an apparent shift of perspective from intuitive to overt, from personal to professional. Buckman (1983) describes two categories of experienced teachers – self-oriented and role-oriented. In her categorization, self-oriented teachers focus on personal beliefs, feelings and experiences, and those with role-oriented responses indicate awareness of common experiences, dispositions, and duties within the profession of teaching. We conclude that the learning cycle (see Chapter 5) encourages self-oriented and role-oriented reflection. Both are important in making learning explicit, in the process of making professional judgements and in bringing about actions for change.

One criticism levelled at this kind of approach to teachers' professional development is the over-emphasis on individual personal change. A focus on the person and not the context over-emphasizes personal responsibility for change. It avoids controversial questions about the ways in which contexts enhance or inhibit professional development. Little (1982) highlights the importance of the school context by arguing that teachers can be helped in their professional development simply by moving to another school. For example, a teacher working in a 'stuck' school will have few opportunities for collaboration. Whereas in another school where collaboration is the norm, professional development will take a very different form.

One teacher explained:

> It is easier to be objective with hindsight. We have become more aware of how we have been driven by a sense of inadequacy into further professional development. However, in reflecting we have become aware that we are not inadequate. The process has built self-esteem and raised confidence. The school context in which I work has been frustrating. I get excited about ideas, but somehow things go on as they always do.

This highlights the assertion that teachers may find it difficult to bring about actions for change if the internal conditions of the school are not conducive (Rosenholtz, 1989), and if teachers are not involved in goal-setting and decision-making and the collegiality of group learning (Bell and Day, 1991).

Principles relating to the teacher's learning have been identified: meta-learning, holistic learning, self-actualization and collaborative contexts. The combined principles suggest a wider perspective than on individual development alone. We conclude that the study of teacher development needs to be combined with wider social and political influences on teachers and schools, as discussed in Chapters 4 and 8.

Summary of Part 3

In this Part we explore teachers' professional development

- We identify ways in which the Transformatory Approach to Learning is applied to teachers' professional development
- We make key distinctions between action learning and action research
- We consider action research as a vehicle for teachers' professional development
- We propose that action research is a more effective way for teachers to bring about changes to their practice, organizational practice, and in informing wider educational change
- We use the concepts of meta-learning, holistic learning, self-actualization and collaborative contexts, in mapping a professional route for teachers' learning

Conclusion

Transforming Learning: Individual and Global Change outlines our vision of education as a process of transformation, for the individual, the group, the organization, and for society. The Transformatory Approach to Learning applies to everyone throughout their lives, not only learning within formal educational organizations. Barber suggests that learning involves everyone having a role in creating a learning society and that learning must have a higher priority in society.

> So in order to help create the learning society what should we ask? Isn't it obvious. The question has to be: 'What did you learn today?'. . . each time someone asks the question they play a small part in raising the priority society gives to learning, in pushing education up the cultural agenda, in building the social and political momentum, which will assist in the creation of a learning community. In this creative process, it is clear that both government and those involved in providing education – teachers and others – have roles of daunting significance to play . . . ultimately, though, the transformation depends on everyone playing their part. (Barber, 1996, pp. 304–5)

The key values which underpin our approach are equality and justice. We have presented the ideas in this book as a step towards the ideal. It is important to identify the initial steps, and to offer concrete examples of the approach, that teachers and learning organizations could take to enable people to achieve real change.

We have written this book because we believe that learning can be more effective. We illustrate how learning can be maximized for the whole person, and that this in turn brings about change in the whole organization.

Transformatory learning is about participating in the whole experience of learning. It does not stress how facts and 'objective' knowledge are learned in substantive areas of the curriculum, but focuses on the learner, the learning context and the learning process. We illustrate how the emotional, social, spiritual and cognitive aspects of learning interrelate; the importance of the group and social context on learning and how people and organizations are transformed through engaging with the learning process.

Transforming Learning espouses the nature of learning within a radical approach, and highlights key social values such as equality, respect and justice. It takes a positive, humanistic view of individuals as wanting to learn, and develop throughout their lives. Relationships with others, and the interrelationships of the learner, learning context, and learning process, are outlined as crucial in relation to potential for learning. We provide examples of the ways in which the Transformatory Approach can be put into practice.

We criticize the dominant model of education as individualistic, authoritarian, hierarchical, competitive and focused on *what* is learned. We argue that a different approach is needed, across all phases of education, which is collaborative, non-hierarchical, and which focuses on the learning experiences and processes in the social context. This approach sees everyone as proactive learners who can use intellectual and emotional skills to initiate, negotiate, evaluate their experiences and bring about actions for change. We argue that if the affective, social and spiritual aspects of learning are not taken into account, then learning may not take place, no matter how good the teaching. Teachers are taught how to teach. The assumption behind this is that if teachers know how to teach, then learning will automatically occur. We refute this.

With a stress on learning, rather than teaching, individuals take more responsibility for their learning, and gain skills which enable them to learn more effectively, thus enhancing achievement. We conclude that collaboration is a key factor in the way transformatory learning is organized. Collaboration results in the power for decision-making and evaluation being shared amongst all in the learning society. Collaboration in its true sense means that individual achievement is not at the expense of others; nobody loses, but everyone has a chance to win.

Transforming Learning demonstrates how a dynamic relationship exists between individual learners and the learning context, and it is argued that this must be made an explicit focus for work with people in the classroom. We develop this argument by outlining how this focus must also be made explicit in the whole learning organization.

The approach in the classroom is only meaningful if there is congruence between the values and goals for learning in the classroom, and the ways in which the learning community is organized and structured. For example, work on developing negotiation and respect for others' opinions at the classroom level will have more impact if positive interaction is mirrored in the way people relate in the whole learning organization.

The approach outlined in *Transforming Learning* is radical because it questions accepted notions about effective learning experiences; developmental theories about the intellectual and emotional maturity of people; the existing nature of the relationship between learners and teachers; divisions of power and responsibility within the learning environment; and the boundaries that exist within learning organizations.

The approach is democratic in that the principles of equality, justice and fairness are congruent with the experience of learning. Transforming learning takes courage and may be undermined in a variety of ways. Teachers who are attracted to this way of working are at the cutting-edge of change. They are contributing to a vision of individual and global change based on cooperation, power-sharing, justice and learning.

Appendix

Assumption of the Transformatory Approach to Learning	Model of education			
	Functionalist	Client-centred	Liberatory	Social Justice
The learner				
the self is central in the learning process		√	√	
learners are striving towards self-actualization		√	√	
everyone wants to learn			√	
learners have an equal potential for learning			√	
learners have control over what they are learning			√	
learners progress through stages of either dependence or independence towards interdependence			√	
learners are prepared to take risks			√	

Assumption of the Transformatory Approach to Learning	Model of education			
	Functionalist	Client-centred	Liberatory	Social Justice
the whole person, including emotional, social, spiritual, physical and cognitive dimensions, is involved in learning		√	√√	
the emotional state of the learner affects the capacity to learn		√	√	
capacity for learning is not fixed and can be increased		√	√	
capacity for learning increases as learning increases		√	√	
capacity for learning increases when learners understand themselves as learners			√	
learners' past experiences influence their learning in the present		√	√√	
learners experience situations differently and therefore learn different things from the same situation			√	
learners make decisions about whether to learn or not in particular contexts			√	
only the learner is in the position to identify and tell others what they have learned			√	

Assumption of the Transformatory Approach to Learning	Model of education			
	Functionalist	Client-centred	Liberatory	Social Justice
only the learners can evaluate what they have learned			√	
learners may approach the same task differently		√	√	
learners of the same social group may approach learning differently from learners of another social group			√	√
The group context				
groups are more effective in bringing about change than individuals			√√	√
individual change is facilitated by the support of the group			√√	
learning is more effective in a collaborative group			√√	
in a social situation, the group is a catalyst for learning as well as a source of learning			√√	
feedback from others is a valuable part of the learning process		√	√	
different points of view, perspectives and experiences enrich learning		√	√√	√

Assumption of the Transformatory Approach to Learning	Model of education			
	Functionalist	Client-centred	Liberatory	Social Justice
learners have support and encouragement to take risks and make changes; be dependent, independent and interdependent		√	√√	
learners learn about relationships by being in relationships		√	√	
conflict and controversy are essential aspects of learning		√	√	
learning in a group leads to a feeling of social identity and belonging		√	√	
the facilitator is instrumental in establishing the group culture			√√	
the group takes responsibility for ensuring that structures are in place to facilitate learning			√	
individuals need to learn how to learn in a group in order for learning in the group to be effective			√	
in order for learning in a group to be effective, the group needs to address the different roles taken by different individuals at different times			√	

Assumption of the Transformatory Approach to Learning	Model of education			
	Functionalist	Client-centred	Liberatory	Social Justice
the group is affected by individuals and also develops independently of individuals in the group			√	
The social context				
effective change encompasses change at both the individual and social levels			√√	√
social change follows from learning and change at the individual level			√√	
expectations and stereotypes about people affect learning			√√	√√
learning is affected by sex, ethnicity and socio-economic position			√√	√√
learning roles and styles are gendered			√	√√
our individual identity is socially constructed			√	√√
through the learning process of self-reflection, reflection on experiences, abstraction and generalization we are capable of deconstructing our identity			√√	√√

Assumption of the Transformatory Approach to Learning	Model of education			
	Functionalist	Client-centred	Liberatory	Social Justice
the learning discourse affects what we understand and value			√√	√√
the dominant learning discourse is determined by powerful groups in society			√√	√√
there are conflicting learning discourses in society			√√	√√
discussion of inequality in education and society must be part of the learning process			√√	√√
discussion about how the social context affects learning must be part of the learning process			√√	√
the interrelationship between personal and social is valid discourse in the classroom			√√	
diversity needs to be recognized within social groups			√√	√√
The learning process				
the action learning process transforms individuals and groups	√		√√	
action learning changes the meaning of experience	√		√	

Assumption of the Transformatory Approach to Learning	Model of education			
	Functionalist	Client-centred	Liberatory	Social Justice
the process involves understanding, constructing knowledge, making connections, taking control and taking action		✓	✓✓	
learning never stops; all experiences contribute to learning throughout life		✓	✓✓	
reflection on experience is an essential part of action learning		✓	✓✓	
reflection on self as learner and context of learning is essential in the action learning process			✓✓	
making the learning explicit is an essential part of action learning			✓	
action is an essential stage in learning			✓	✓✓
applying the learning is an essential stage of action learning			✓✓	✓
feedback is an important aspect of reviewing, learning and taking action		✓	✓	
learning about learning is essential for effective learning			✓	
the effect of the emotions on learning is valid discourse			✓	

Assumption of the Transformatory Approach to Learning	Model of education			
	Functionalist	Client-centred	Liberatory	Social Justice
the effect of the learning context, and the interconnection of the context, learner and process, is valid discourse		√√		

References

Abbott, J. (1994) *Learning Makes Sense: Re-creating Education for a Changing Future*. Letchworth: Education 2000.

Abbs, P. (1974) *Autobiography in Education*. London: Heinemann Educational.

Abercrombie, M. L. J. (1979) *Aims and Techniques of Group Teaching*, 4th edn. Guildford, Surrey: Society for Research into Higher Education.

Altrichter, H. and Posch, P. (1989) 'Does the "Grounded Theory" approach offer a guiding paradigm for teacher research?', *Cambridge Journal of Education*, **19**, 1, pp. 21–32.

Altrichter, H., Posch, P. and Somekh, B. (1993) *Teachers Investigate Their Work: An Introduction to the Methods of Action Research*. London: Routledge.

Argyris, C. (1990) *Overcoming Organizational Defences*. New York: Prentice Hall.

Arnot, M. (1989) 'Crisis of challenge: equal opportunities and the National Curriculum', *NUT Education Review*, 3, 2, pp. 7–13.

Arnot, M. (1992a) 'Feminism, education and the New Right', in Arnot, M. and Barton, L. (eds) *Voicing Concerns: Sociological Perspectives on Contemporary Education Reforms*. Oxford: Triangle Books.

Arnot, M. (1992b) 'Feminist perspectives on education for citizenship'. Paper presented at the International Sociology of Education conference, *Citizenship, Democracy and the Role of the Teacher*, Westhill College, Birmingham, England.

Arnot, M. (1993) 'British feminist educational politics and state regulation of gender', in Arnot, M. and Weiler, K. (eds) *Feminism and Social Justice in Education*. London: Falmer Press.

Askew, S. and Carnell, E. (1995) *Developing the Personal-Social Curricula*. Bristol: Avec Designs Ltd.

Askew, S. M. and Ross, C. (1989) *Boys Don't Cry*. Milton Keynes: Open University Press.

Ball, S. J. (1990a) *Markets, Morality and Equality in Education*, Hillcole Group Paper 5. London: Tufnell Press.

Ball, S. J. (1990b) *Politics and Policy Making in Education*, Explorations in Policy Sociology. London: Routledge.

Barber, M. (1996) *The Learning Game: Arguments for an Education Revolution*. London: Cassell.

Beez, W. V. (1970) 'Influence of biased psychological reports on teacher behaviour and pupil performance', in Miles, M. and Charters, W. W. (eds) *Learning in Social Settings*. Boston, MA: Allyn and Bacon.

Bell, L. and Day, C. (1991) *Managing the Professional Development of Teachers*. Milton Keynes: Open University Press.

Bernstein, B. (1967) 'Open schools, open society', *New Society*, 14 September, pp. 351–3.

Biggs, J. B. (1966) *Mathematics and the Conditions of Learning*. London: National Foundation for Educational Research.

Biggs, J. B. (1988) 'The role of meta-cognition in enhancing learning', *Australian Journal of Education*, **32**, 2, pp. 127–38.

Biggs, J. B. and Moore, P. J. (1993) *The Process of Learning*, 3rd edn. Englewood Cliffs, NJ: Prentice-Hall.

Blackman, C. (1989) 'Issues in professional development: the continuing agenda', in Holly, M. and McLoughlin, C. (eds) *Perspectives on Teacher Professional Development*. London: Falmer Press.

Bligh, D. (ed.) (1986) *Teach Thinking by Discussion*. Guildford: Society for Research into Higher Education and NFER Nelson.

Bloom, B. S. (ed.) (1956) *Taxonomy of Educational Objectives*. New York: David McKay.

Bolam, R. (1986) 'Conceptualising in-service', in Hopkins, D. (ed.) *In-service Training and Educational Development: An Institutional Survey*. London: Croom Helm.

Botkin, J., Elmandjea, M. and Malitza, M. (1979) *No Limits to Learning*. Oxford: Pergamon Press.

Boud, D., Cohen, R. and Walker, D. (eds) (1993) *Using Experience for Learning*. Milton Keynes: Society for Research into Higher Education & Open University Press.

Boud, D. J., Keogh, R. and Walker, D. (1985) *Reflection: Turning Experience into Learning*. London: Kogan Page.

Boud, D., Keogh, R. and Walker, D. (1996) 'Promoting reflection in learning', in Edwards, R., Hanson, A. and Raggatt, P. (eds) (1996) *Boundaries of Adult Learning*. London: Routledge.

Brown, J. S., Collins, A. and Duguid, P. (1989) 'Situated cognition and the culture of learning', *Education Researcher*, **32**, (Jan.–Feb.), pp. 32–42.

Buckman, M. (1983) *Justification in Teacher Thinking: An Analysis of Interview Data* (Research Series No. 124). Michigan State University: Institute for Research on Teaching.

Bush, T. (1995) *Theories of Educational Management*. London: Paul Chapman Publishing.

Campbell, L. and Ryder, J. (1989) 'When work in groups does not add up to groupwork', *Pastoral Care in Education* (March).

Candy, P. C. (1991) *Self-Direction for Lifelong Learning: A Comprehensive Guide to Theory and Practice*. San Francisco: Jossey-Bass.

Capra, F. (1983) *The Turning Point*. London: Flamingo.

Carey, P. (1993) 'Dealing with pupils' life crises: a model for action', *Pastoral Care in Education*, **11**, 3 (September), pp. 12–18.

Carr, W. and Kemmis, S. (1983) *Becoming Critical: Knowing Through Action Research*. Victoria: Deakin University Press.

Carraher, T., Carraher, D. and Schliemann, A. (1985) 'Mathematics in the streets and in schools', *British Journal of Developmental Psychology*, **3**, pp. 21–9.

Cheney, L. V. (1987) *American Memory*. Washington, DC: National Endowment for the Humanities.

Combs, A. W. (1982) *A Personal Approach to Teaching*. Boston: Allyn and Bacon.

Connell, R. W. (1990) 'The state, gender and sexual politics', *Theory and Society* **19**, pp. 507–44.

Connell, R. W. (1994) (Unpublished) 'Knowing about masculinity, teaching the boys'. Essay developed from paper to 1994 conference of the Pacific Sociological Association, San Diego, CA.

Cooper, P. and McIntyre, D. (1993) 'Commonality in teachers' and pupils' perceptions of effective classroom learning', *British Journal of Educational Psychology*, **63**, 3, pp. 381–99.

Cooper, P. and McIntyre, D. (1996) *Effective Teaching and Learning: Teachers' and Students' Perspectives*. Buckingham: Open University Press.

Costa, A. L. (ed.) (1991) *Developing Minds: A Resource Book for Teaching Thinking*, rev. edn vol. 1. Alexandria, VA: Association of Supervision and Curriculum Development.

Costa, A. L. and O'Leary, P. W. (1992) 'Co-cogniton: the cooperative development of the intellect', in Davidson, N. and Worsham, T. (eds) *Enhancing Thinking Through Cooperative Learning*. New York and London: Teachers' College Press.

Covington, M. V. (1983) 'Motivated cognitions', in Paris, S. G., Olson, G. M. and Stevenson, H. W. (eds) *Learning and Motivation in the Classroom*. Hillsdale, NJ: Erlbaum, pp. 139–64.

Cowie, H. and Rudduck, J. (1990) *Co-operative Group Work in the Multi-ethnic Classroom*. London: BP Educational Services.

Craft, A. (1996) *Continuing Professional Development*. London: Routledge.

Criticos, C. (1993) 'Experiential learning and social transformation', in Boud, D. and Walker, D. (eds) *Using Experience for Learning*. Milton Keynes: Society for Research into Higher Education and Open University Press.

Cuban, L. (1988) 'Why do some reforms persist?', *Educational Administrative Quarterly*, **24**, 3, pp. 329–35.

Cunningham, P. M. (1983) 'Helping students extract meaning from experience', *New Directions for Continuing Education*, **19**, pp. 57–69.

Das, J. P., Kirby, J. and Jarman, R. F. (1979) *Simultaneous and Successive Cognitive Processes*. New York: Academic Press.

Davidson, N. and Worsham, T. (eds) (1992) *Enhancing Thinking Through Cooperative Learning*. New York and London: Teachers' College Press.

Day, C. (1994) 'Professional development planning; a different kind of competency', *British Journal of In-Service Education*, **20**, 3.

Day, M. C. (1981) 'Thinking at Piaget's stage of formal operations', *Educational Leadership* (October), pp. 44–7.

Delors, J. (1996) 'Education: the necessary Utopia', in *Learning: The Treasure Within*, Report to UNESCO of the International Commission on Education for the twenty-first century. Paris: UNESCO.

Dennison, B. and Kirk, R. (1990) *Do, Review, Learn, Apply: A Simple Guide to Experiential Learning*. Oxford: Blackwell.

Donaldson, M. (1978) *Children's Minds*. London: Fontana Press.

Dreyfus, S. E. (1981) 'Formal models vs. human situational understanding: inherent limitations on the modelling of business enterprise', Mimeo. Schloss Laxenburg, Austria: International Institute for Applied Systems Analysis.

Driver, R. and Oldham, V. (1986) 'A constructionist approach to curriculum development in science', *Studies in Science Education*, **13**, pp. 105–22.

Dubin, R. (1968) *Human Relations in Administration*, 3rd edn. New York: Prentice Hall.

Dubin, R. (Ascribed to Robert Dubin: exact reference unknown.) Cited in Watkins, C., Carnell, E., Lodge, C. and Whalley, C. (1996) *Effective Learning*, SIN Research Matters No. 5, Summer 1996. London: Institute of Education.

Edwards, D. and Mercer, N. (1989) *Common Knowledge: The Development of Understanding in the Classroom*. London: Routledge (first published in 1987 by Methuen).

Eisner, E. W. (1985) *The Educational Imagination: On the Design and Evaluation of School Programs*. New York: Macmillan.

Elliott, J. (1976) 'Developing hypotheses about classrooms from teachers' practical constructs: an account of the work of the Ford Teaching Project', *Interchange*, **7**, 2, pp. 2–22.

Elliott, J. (1988) 'Educational research and outsider–insider relations', *Qualitative Studies in Education*, **1**, 2, pp. 155–66.

Elliott, J. (1991) *Action Research for Educational Change*. Buckingham: Open University Press.

Elliott, J. (1993a) *Reconstructing Teacher Education*. London and Washington: Falmer Press.

Elliott, J. (1993b) 'What have we learned from action research in school-based evaluation?', *Educational Action Research*, **1**, 1, pp. 175–86.

Entwistle, N. (1987) *Understanding Classroom Learning*. London: Hodder and Stoughton.

Entwistle, N. and Ramsden, P. (1983) *Understanding Student Learning*. London: Croom Helm.

Epstein, D. (1993) *Changing Classroom Cultures: Anti-racism, Politics and Schools*. Stoke on Trent: Trentham.

Epstein, D. and Sealey, A. (1990) *Where It Really Matters: Developing Anti-racist*

Education in Predominantly White Primary Schools. Birmingham: Development Education Centre.

Everard, K. B. and Morris, G. (1990) *Effective School Management*. London: Paul Chapman Publishing.

Ferguson, M. (1982) *The Aquarian Conspiracy*. London: Granada.

Finn, J. D. (1972) 'Expectations and the educational environment', *Review of Educational Research*, **42**, pp. 387–410.

Finn, E. E., Jr. and Ravitch, D. (1987) 'Opportunity can be made', *Los Angeles Times*, 25 October, p. 24.

Freire, P. (1970) *Pedagogy of the Oppressed*. New York: Herder and Herder.

Fullan, M. (1991) *The New Meaning of Educational Change*. London: Cassell.

Fullan, M. (1992) *Successful School Improvement*. Buckingham: Open University Press.

Fullan, M. (1993) *Change Forces: Probing the Depths of Educational Reform*. London: Falmer Press.

Fullan, M. and Connelly, M. (1990) *Teacher Education in Ontario: Current Practice and Options for the Future*. Toronto: Ministry of Colleges and Universities.

Fullan, M. and Hargreaves, A. (1992) *What's Worth Fighting for in Your School?* Buckingham: Open University Press.

Gage, N. L. (1972) *Teacher Effectiveness and Teacher Education: The Search for a Scientific Basis*. Palo Alto, CA: Pacific Books.

Galton, M., Simon, B. and Croll, P. (1980) *Inside the Primary Classroom*. London: Routledge and Kegan Paul.

Gardner, H. (1993) *The Unschooled Mind: How Children Think and How Schools Should Teach*. London: HarperCollins.

Gardner, J. W. (1981) *Self-renewal: The Individual and the Innovative Society*. New York: W. W. Norton & Company.

Garratt, B. (1987) *The Learning Organisation*. Glasgow: William Collins.

Garvey, T. (1994) 'Streaming as a masculinizing practice in the 1950s and 1960s'. Paper to the annual Conference of the Australian and New Zealand History of Education Society.

Gibbs, G. (1992) *Improving the Quality of Student Learning*. Bristol: Technical and Educational Services.

Gibbs, G., Morgan, A. and Taylor, E. (1982) 'A review of the research of Ference Marton and the Goteborg Group: a phenomenological research perspective on learning', *Higher Education*, **11**, pp. 123–45.

Gipps, C. (1992) 'What we know about effective primary teaching', The London File, Papers from the Institute of Education. London: Tufnell Press.

Glaser, R. (1991) 'Intelligence as an expression of acquired knowledge', in H. Rowe (ed.) *Intelligence: Reconceptualization and Measurement*. Hawthorn: ACER; Hillsdale: Erlbaum, pp. 47–56.

Goffman, E. (1959) *The Presentation of Self in Everyday Life*. London: Penguin.

Goldenberg, S. (1986) 'Race, sex and the missing link', *Teaching London Kids*, **23**, p. 22.

Goleman, D. (1996) *Emotional Intelligence: Why It Can Matter More Than IQ*. London: Bloomsbury.

Good, T. L. and Marshall, S. (1984) 'Do students learn more in heterogeneous or homogeneous groups?', in Peterson, P., Wickinson, L. C. and Hallinam, M. (eds) *The Social Context of Instruction: Group Organisation and Group Processes*. Orlando, Fla: Academic Press.

Goodlad, J. (1983) *A Place Called School*. New York: McGraw-Hill.

Griffin, V. (1987) 'Naming the processes', in Boud, D. J. and Griffin, V. (eds) *Appreciating Adults Learning: From the Learner's Perspective*. London: Kogan Page.

Grimmett, P. and Erickson, G. (1988) *Reflection in Teacher Education*. New York: Teachers' College Press.

Grugeon, E. and Woods, P. (1990) *Educating All: Multicultural Perspectives in the Primary School*. London: Routledge.

Grundy, S. (1987) *Curriculum: Product or Praxis?* London: Falmer Press.

Habermas, J. (1974) *Theory and Practice*. London: Heinemann.

Hall, V. and Oldroyd, D. (1991) *Managing Staff Development*. London: Paul Chapman Publishing.

Hall, V. and Oldroyd, D. (1992) *Development Activities for Managers of Collaboration*. University of Bristol: NDCEMP.

Hall, V. and Wallace, M. (1993) 'Collaboration as subversive activity: a professional response to externally imposed competition between schools?', *School Organisation*, **13**, 2, pp. 101–17.

Hammersley, M. (1993) 'On the teacher as researcher', in Hammersley, M. *Educational Research: Current Issues*, vol. I. London: The Open University in association with Paul Chapman Publishing.

Handy, C. (1991) *The Age of Unreason*. London: Arrow.

Hansen, S., Walker, J. and Flom, B. (1995) *Growing Smart: What's Working for Girls in School*. Washington: American Asociation of University Women (AAUW).

Harding, J. (1996) 'Girls' achievements in science and technology: implications for pedagogy', in Murphy, P. and Gipps, C. (eds) *Equity in the Classroom: Towards Effective Pedagogy for Girls and Boys*. London: Falmer Press and UNESCO.

Hargreaves, A. (1994) *Changing Teachers, Changing Times: Teachers' Work and Culture in the Post-modern Age*. London: Cassell.

Hawkins, P. (1991) 'The spiritual dimension of the learning organization', *Management Education and Development*, **22**, 3, pp. 172–87.

Hayes, C., Fonda, N. and Hillman, J. (1995) 'Learning in the new millennium', *National Commission on Education NCE Briefing*, New Series 5, May 1995.

Hayes, R., Wheelwright, S. and Clark, K. (1988) *Dynamic Manufacturing: Creating the Learning Organisation*. New York: The Free Press.

Head, J. (1996) 'Gender identity and cognitive style', in Murphy, P. and Gipps, C.

(eds) *Equity in the Classroom: Towards Effective Pedagogy for Girls and Boys*. London: Falmer Press and UNESCO.

Hearn, J. (1987) *The Gender of Oppression: Men, Masculinity and the Critique of Marxism*. Brighton: Harvester/Wheatsheaf.

Henriques, J., Hollway, W., Urwin, C., Venn, C. and Walkerdine, V. (1984) *Changing the Subject: Psychology, Social Regulation and Subjectivity*. London: Methuen.

Henson, G. (1991) 'Towards a spiritual perspective on behaviour at work', *Management Education and Development*, **22**, 3, pp. 201–7.

Hill, W. F. (1977) *Learning Thru Discussion*. London: Sage.

Hilt, P. (1992) 'Enhancing thinking through cooperative learning: the world-of-work connection', in Davidson, N. and Worsham, T. (eds) *Enhancing Thinking Through Cooperative Learning*. New York and London: Teachers' College Press.

Hirch, E. D. (1987) 'The essential elements of literacy', *Education Week*, **6** (April), p. 27.

Hirst, P. H. (1974) *Knowledge and the Curriculum: A Collection of Philosophical Papers*. London: Routledge and Kegan Paul.

HMSO (1988) *Records of Achievement: Report of the National Evaluation of Pilot Schemes*. A Report submitted to the DES and the Welsh Office by the Pilot Records of Achievement in Schools Evaluation (PRAISE) team. London: HMSO.

Hochschild, A. R. (1983) *The Managed Heart*. Berkeley: University of California Press.

Holland, J. L. (1959) 'Some limitations of teacher ratings as predictors of creativity', *Journal of Educational Psychology*, **50**, pp. 219–23.

Holly, M. L. and Walley, C. (1989) 'Teachers as Professionals' in Holly, M. L. and McLoughlin, C. (eds) *Perspectives on Teacher Professional Development*. London: Falmer Press.

Holt, J. (1971) *The Underachieving School*. London: Penguin.

Honey, P. and Mumford, A. (1986) *The Manual of Learning Styles*, 2nd edn. Maidenhead: P. Honey.

Hopkins, D., Ainscow, M. and West, M. (1994) *School Improvement in an Era of Change*. London: Cassell.

Hoy, W. K. and Woolfolk, A. E. (1993) 'Teachers' sense of efficacy and the organisational health of schools', *Elementary School Journal*, **93**, pp. 355–72.

Hoyle, E. (1986a) *The Politics of School Management*. Sevenoaks: Hodder and Stoughton.

Hoyle, E. (1986b) 'Professionalisation and de-professionalisation in education', in Hoyle, E. and Megarry, J. (eds) *World Year Book of Education*. London: Kogan Page.

Hunsley, J. (1987) 'Internal dialogue during academic examinations', *Cognitive Therapy and Research* (December).

Jaques, D. (1995) *Learning in Groups*, 2nd edn. London: Kogan Page.

James, M. and Ebbutt, D. (1980) 'Problems of engaging in research in one's own school', in Nixon, J. (ed.) *A Teachers' Guide to Action Research*. London: Grant McIntyre.

Jantsch, E. (1980) *The Self Organizing Universe*. New York: Pergamon.

Johnson, D. W. and Johnson, R. T. (1989) *Cooperation and Competition: Theory and Research*. Edina, MN: Interaction Book Company.

Johnson, D. W. and Johnson, R. T. (1992) 'Encouraging thinking through constructive controversy', in Davidson, N. and Worsham, T. (eds) (1992) *Enhancing Thinking Through Cooperative Learning*. New York and London: Teachers' College Press.

Johnson, D. W., Johnson, R. T., Roy, P. and Holubec, E. J. (1984) *Circles of Learning: Cooperation in the Classroom*. Alexandria, VA: Association for Supervision and Curriculum Development.

Jones, A. and Hendry, C. (1992) *The Learning Organisation: A Review of Literature and Practice*. CCSC London: Human Resource Development Partnership.

Jones, J. (1990) 'Action research in facilitating change in institutional practice', in Zuber-Skerritt, O. (ed.) *Action Research for Change and Development*. Brisbane: Centre for the Advancement of Learning and Teaching, pp. 251–70.

Jones, K. (1989) *Right Turn: The Conservative Revolution in Education*. London: Hutchinson Radius.

Jones, R. M. (1968) *Fantasy and Feeling in Education*. New York: New York University Press.

Joyce, B. (1984) 'Dynamic disequilibrium: the intelligence of growth', *Theory into Practice*, **23**, 1, pp. 26–34.

Jung, C. (1971) *Psychological Types*. Princeton: Princeton University Press.

Kasl, E., Dechant, K. and Marsick, V. (1993) 'Living the learning: internalizing our model of group learning', in Boud, D., Cohen, R. and Walker, D. (eds) (1993) *Using Experience for Learning*. Buckingham: The Society for Research into Higher Education and the Open University Press.

Keane, R. (1987) 'The doubting journey: a learning process of self-transformation', in Boud, D. and Griffin, V. *Appreciating Adults Learning: From the Learners' Perspective*. London: Kogan Page.

Keefe, J. W. and Ferrell, B. G. (1990) 'Developing a defensible learning styles paradigm', *Educational Leadership*, **48**, 2, pp. 57–61.

Keiny, S. (1994) 'Constructivism and teachers' professional development', *Teaching and Teacher Education*, **10**, 2, pp. 157–67.

Kellerman, S. (1995) *Your Body Speaks Its Mind*. Berkeley, CA: Center Press.

Kelly, A. (1985) 'Action research: what is it and what can it do?', in Burgess, R. G. (ed.) *Issues in Educational Research: Qualitative Methods*. Lewes: Falmer Press.

Kelly, G. A. (1955) *The Psychology of Personal Constructs*, 1 and 2. New York: Norton.

Kemmis, S. (1993) 'Action research', in Hammersley, M. (ed.) *Educational Research: Current Issues*. Milton Keynes: Open University Press.

Kingsland, K. (1986) *The Personality Spectrum*, self-published.

Knowles, J. G. (1993) 'Life-history accounts as mirrors: a practical avenue for the conceptualization of reflection in teacher education', in Calderhead, J. and Gates, P. (eds) *Conceptualization Reflection in Teacher Development*. London: Falmer Press.

Knowles, M. S. (1980) *The Modern Practice of Adult Education*, rev. edn. Chicago: Follet.

Kolb, D. A. (1971) *Experiential Learning: Experience as a Source of Learning and Development*, 2nd edn. Englewood Cliffs, NJ: Prentice Hall.

Kolb, D. A. (1976) *Learning Style Inventory: Technical Manual.* Boston: McBer & Co.

Kolb, D. A. *et al.* (1984) *Organisational Psychology.* Englewood Cliffs, NJ: Prentice Hall.

Larson, R. L. (1992) *Changing Schools from the Inside Out.* Lancaster, PA: Technomic.

Lee, V. and Lee, J. with Pearson, M. (1987) 'Stories children tell', in Pollard, A. (ed.) *Children and Their Primary Schools: A New Perspective.* Lewes: Falmer Press.

Lee, V. E., Dedrick, R. and Smith, J. B. (1991) 'The effect of the social organisation of schools on teachers' efficacy and satisfaction', *Sociology of Education*, **64**, pp. 190–208.

Lessem, R. (1990) *Developmental Management: Principles of Holistic Business.* Oxford: Blackwell.

Lessem, R. (1991) *Total Quality Learning: Building a Learning Organisation.* Oxford: Blackwell.

Lewin, K. (1946) 'Action research and minority problems', *Journal of Sociological Issues*, **2**, 4, pp. 34–46.

Lewin, K. (1951) *Field Theory in Social Science.* New York: Harper and Row.

Lewin, K. (1952) 'Group decision and social change', in Swanson, G. E.. Newcomb, T. M. and Hartley, E. L. (eds) *Readings in Social Psychology.* New York: Holt.

Lippett, R., Watson, J. and Westley, B. (1958) *The Dynamics of Planned Change.* New York: Harcourt Brace.

Little, J. (1982) 'Norms of collegiality and experimentation: workplace conditions for school success', *American Educational Research Journal*, **19**, 3, pp. 325–40.

Little, J. and McLaughlin, M. (eds) (1993) *Teachers' Work: Individuals, Colleagues and Contexts.* New York: Teachers' College Press.

Lorde, A. (1984) *Sister Outsider.* Trumansburg, NY: Crossing Press.

Louis, K. S. and Kruse, S. D. (1995) *Professionalism and Community: Perspectives on Reforming Urban Schools.* Thousand Oaks, CA: Sage Publications.

Lovelock, J. (1988) *The Ages of Gaia.* New York: Norton.

Markus, H. R. and Kitayama, S. (1994) 'The cultural shaping of emotion: A conceptual framework', in *Emotion and Culture.* Washington DC: American Psychological Association.

Marton, F. (1975) 'On non-verbatim learning – 1: level of processing and level of outcome', *Scandinavian Journal of Psychology*, **16**, pp. 273–9.

Marton, F. and Säljö, R. (1976) 'On qualitative differences in learning – 1: outcome and process', *British Journal of Educational Psychology*, **46**, pp. 4–11.

Marzano, R. J. (1992) 'The many faces of cooperation across the dimensions of learning', in Davidson, N. and Worsham, T. (eds), *Enhancing Thinking Through Cooperative Learning.* New York and London: Teachers' College Press.

Maslow, A. (1970) *Motivation and Personality*. New York: Harper and Row.

Maslow, A. (1972) 'Defence and growth', in Silberman, M. L. (ed.) *The Psychology of Open Teaching and Learning*. Boston: Little, Brown, pp. 44–5.

Maturana, H. R. and Varela, S. (1988)*The Tree of Knowledge*. Boston: Shambhala.

McLaughlin, M. W. and March, D. D. (1990) 'Staff development and school change', in Lieberman, A. (ed.) *Schools as Collaborative Cultures: Creating the Future Now*. London: Falmer Press.

Meichenbaum, D., Bowers, K. and Ross, R. (1969) 'A behavioural analysis of the teacher expectancy effect', *Journal of Personality and Social Psychology*, **13**, pp. 306–16.

Mezirow, J. (1978) *Education for Perspective Transformation: Womens' Re-entry Program in Community Colleges*. New York: Centre for Adult Education, Columbia University.

Mezirow, J. (1981) 'A critical theory of adult learning and education', *Adult Education*, **32**, 1, pp. 13–24.

Mezirow, J. (1983) 'A critical theory of adult learning and education', in Tight, M. (ed.) *Adult Learning in Education*. London: Croom Helm.

Mezirow, J. (1991) *Transformative Dimensions of Adult Learning*. San Francisco, CA: Jossey-Bass.

Morgan, G. (1986) *Images of Organisation*. Newbury Park, CA: Sage.

Murphy, P. (1995) 'Assessment practices and gender in science', in Parker, L. H., Rennie, L. J. and Fraser, B. J. (eds) *Gender, Science and Mathematics*. London: Kluwer Academic Publishers, pp. 105–17.

Murphy, P. (1996) 'Definining pedagogy', in Murphy, P. and Gipps, C. (eds) *Equity in the Classroom: Towards Effective Pedagogy for Girls and Boys*. London: Falmer Press and UNESCO.

Nevard, L. (1991) 'Management – a "spiritual" foundation?', *Management Education and Development*, **22**, 3, pp. 188–96.

Nisbet, J. and Shucksmith, J. (1984) *The Seventh Sense*. SCERE & SERA Annual Lecture.

Nisbet, J. and Shucksmith, J. (1986) *Learning Strategies*. London: Routledge.

Nixon, J. (ed.) (1981) *A Teacher's Guide to Action Research*. London: Grant McIntyre, p. 9.

Novak, J. D. and Gowin, D. B. (1984) *Learning How to Learn*. Cambridge: Cambridge University Press.

O'Hanlon, C. (1994) 'Reflection and action research: is there a moral responsibility to act?', *Educational Action Research*, **2**, pp. 281–9.

Open University (undated) *Learning How To Learn*, Open Teaching Toolkit. Compiled by Maggie Coates.

Papert, S. (1980) *Mindstorms: Children, Computers and Powerful Ideas*. London: Harvester Press.

Pedler, M., Boydell, T. and Burgoyne, J. (1988) *Learning Company Project: A Report on Work Undertaken October 1987 to April 1988*. Sheffield: Training Agency.

Perkins, D. (1991) 'What creative thinking is', in Costa, A. (ed.) *Developing Minds: A Resource Book for Teaching Thinking*. Alexandria, VA: Association for Supervision and Curriculum Development, pp. 85–8.

Plowden Report (1967) *Children and Their Primary Schools*. London: HMSO.

Pollard, A. (ed.) (1987) *Children and Their Primary Schools: A New Perspective*. Lewes: Falmer Press.

Prawat, R. A. (1991) 'The value of ideas: the immersion approach to the development of thinking', *Educational Researcher*, **20**, 2, pp. 3–10.

Presselsen, B. Z. (1992) 'A perspective on the evolution of cooperative thinking', in Davidson, N. and Worsham, T. (eds) *Enhancing Thinking Through Cooperative Learning*. New York and London: Teachers' College Press.

Ramsden, P. (1988) *Improving Learning: New Perspectives*. London: Kogan Page.

Reagon, B. (1983) 'Coalition politics: turning the century', in Smith, B. (ed.) *Home Girls: A Black Feminist Anthology*. New York: Kitchen Table – Women of Colour Press.

Reed, D. (1981) *Education for a People's Movement*. Boston: Southend Press.

Reese, H. W. and Overton, W. F. (1970) 'Models of development and theories of development', in Goulet, L. R. and Baltes, P. B. (eds) *Life-Span Developmental Psychology*. New York: Academic Press, pp. 115–45.

Resnick, L. B. (1987) *Education and Learning to Think*. Washington, DC: National Academy Press.

Reynolds, D. (ed.) (1992) *School Effectiveness: Research, Policy and Practice*. London: Cassell.

Rogers, C. R. (1967) *On Becoming a Person*. London: Constable.

Rogers, C. R. (1969) *Freedom to Learn: A View of What Education Might Become*. Columbia, Ohio: Charles Merrill.

Rosenbaum, J. E. (1976) 'Making inequality: the hidden curriculum of high school tracking', *Review of Research in Education*.

Rosenbaum, J. E. (1980) 'Social implications of educational grouping', *Review of Research in Education*, **8**, pp. 361–401.

Rosenholtz, S. J. (1989) *Teachers' Workplace: The Social Organization of Schools*. New York: Teachers' College Press.

Rosenthal, R. and Jacobson, L. (1968) *Pygmalion in the Classroom*. New York: Holt, Rinehart and Winston.

Roszak, T. (1981) *Person/Planet*. London: Routledge.

Rudduck, J. (1987) 'Teacher research, action research, teacher inquiry: what's in a name?', in Rudduck, J., Hopkins, J., Sanger, J. and Lincoln, P. *Collaborative Inquiry and Information Skills*, British Library research paper 16. Boston Spa: British Library.

Rudduck, J., Chaplain, R. and Wallace, G. (eds) (1996) *School Improvement: What Can Pupils Tell Us?* London: David Fulton.

Säljö, R. (1981) 'Learning approaches and outcome: some empirical observations', *Instructional Science*, **10**, pp. 47–65.

Salzberger-Wittenberg, I., Henry, G. and Osborne, E. (1983) *The Emotional Experience of Learning and Teaching*. London: Routledge and Kegan Paul.

Samples, R. (1992) 'Cooperation: worldview as methodology', in Davidson, N. and Worsham, T. (eds) *Enhancing Thinking Through Cooperative Learning*. New York and London: Teachers' College Press.

Sarason, S. (1990) *The Predictable Failure of Educational Reform*. San Francisco, CA: Jossey-Bass.

Seipp, B. (1991) 'Anxiety and academic performance: a meta-analysis', *Anxiety Research*, **4**, 1.

Selmes, I. (1987) *Improving Study Skills*. London: Hodder and Stoughton.

Senge, P. (1990a) 'The leader's new work: building learning organisations', *Sloan Management Review* (Fall), pp. 7–23.

Senge, P. M. (1990b). *The Fifth Discipline: The Art and Practice of the Learning Organization*. London: Century Business.

Sharan, S. (1980) 'Cooperative learning in small groups: recent methods and effects on achievement, attitudes, and ethnic relations', *Review of Educational Research*, **50**, pp. 241–71.

Sharan, S. (1990) *Cooperative Learning: Theory and Research*. New York: Praeger.

Sheldrake, R. (1991) *The Rebirth of Nature*. New York: Bantam.

Singh, K. (1996) 'Education for the global society', in *Learning: The Treasure Within*, Report to UNESCO of the International Commission on Education for the Twenty-first Century. Paris: UNESCO Publishing.

Slavin, R. (1990) *Cooperative Learning: Theory, Research, and Practice*. Englewood Cliffs, NJ: Prentice-Hall.

Smith, R. M. (1983) *Learning How to Learn: Applied Theory for Adults*. Milton Keynes: Open University Press.

Smith, S. and Scott, J. (1990) *The Collaborative School*. Oregon: ERIC Clearinghouse on Educational Management; National Association of Secondary School Principals.

Smythe, J., Dorward, E. and Lambert, M. (1991) *The Power of the Open Company: A Consultancy Survey of Chief Executives' Views on the Bottom-line Impact of Managing Corporate Change*. London.

Somekh, B. (1995) 'The contribution of action research to development in social endeavours: a position paper on action research methodology', *British Educational Research Journal*, **21**, pp. 339–55.

Stacey, R. D. (1992) *Managing Chaos: Dynamic Business Strategies in an Unpredictable World*. London: Kogan Page.

Stanton, T. (1986) (unpublished) quoted by Criticos, C. 'Experiential learning and social transformation', in Boud, D., Cohen, R. and Walker, D. (eds) (1993) *Using Experience for Learning*. Milton Keynes: SRHE and Open University Press.

Stenhouse, L. (1975) *An Introduction to Curriculum Research and Development*. London: Heinemann.

Sternberg, R. J. (1985) *Beyond IQ*. New York: Cambridge University Press.

Sternberg, R. J. (1991) 'Theory-based testing of intellectual abilities: rationale for the triarchic abilities test', in Rowe, H. (ed.) *Intelligence: Reconceptualization and Measurement*. Hawthorn:ACER; Hillsdale: Erlbaum, pp. 183–202.

Sternberg, R. J. and Wagner, R. (1986) *Practical Intelligence*. Cambridge: Cambridge University Press.

Stoll, L. and Fink, D. (1996) *Changing Our Schools*. Buckingham: Open University Press.

Thiessen, D. (1992) 'Classroom-based teacher development', in Fullan, M. and Hargreaves, A. (eds) *Understanding Teachers' Development*. London: Cassell.

Tizard, B., Blatchford, P., Burke, J., Farquhar, C. and Plewis, I. (1988) *Young Children and School in the Inner City*. London: Erlbaum.

UNESCO (1996) *Learning: The Treasure Within*. Report to UNESCO of the International Commission on Education for the Twenty-first Century. Paris: UNESCO.

UTMU (1978) *Improving Teaching in Higher Education*. University Teaching Methods Unit; now, Centre for Higher Education Studies, 59 Gordon Square, London WC1H 0NU.

Vygotsky, L. S. (1962) *Thought and Language*. New York: Wiley.

Walkerdine, V. (1984) 'Developmental psychology and the child-centred pedagogy: the insertion of Piaget into early education', in Henriques, J., Hollway, W., Urwin, C., Venn, C. and Walkerdine, V. (eds) (1984) *Changing the Subject: Psychology, Social Regulation and Subjectivity*. London: Methuen.

Walkerdine, V. (1990) *Schoolgirl Fictions*. London: Verso.

Watkins, C. (1995) MA course handout (unpublished) developed from Schmuck, R. A., Runkel, P. J., Arends, J. H. and Arends, R. (1977) *The Second Handbook of Organisational Development in School*. Mountain View, CA: Mayfield Publications Co. Third edition (1988) Prospect Heights, IL: Waveland Press.

Watkins, C. and Butcher, J. (1995) *Action Planning Skills: Individual Action Planning*. London East Training and Enterprise Council.

Watkins, C., Carnell, E., Lodge, C. and Whalley, C. (1996) 'Effective learning', *SIN Research Matters*, **5** (Summer). Institute of Education, University of London.

Watson, S. (1990) 'The state of play: An introduction', in Watson, S. (ed.) *Playing the State: Australian Feminist Interventions*. London: Verso.

Weiler, K. (1991) 'Freire and a feminist pedagogy of difference', *Harvard Educational Review*, **61**, 4 reprinted in Edwards, R., Hanson, A. and Raggatt, P. (eds) (1996) *Boundaries of Adult Learning*. London: Routledge, pp. 128–51.

Whitaker, P. (1995a) *Managing to Learn: Aspects of Reflective and Experiential Learning in Schools*. London: Cassell.

Whitaker, P. (1995b) *The Primary Head*. London: Heinemann Educational Books.

Wise, A. E., Darling-Hammond, L., McLaughlin, M. W. and Bernstein, H. (1984) *Teacher Evaluation: A Study of Effective Practices*. Santa Monica: Rand Corporation.

Wittrock, M. C. (1977) 'The generative processes of memory', in Wittrock, M. C. (ed.) *The Human Brain*. Englewood Cliffs, NJ: Prentice Hall.

Wood, D. (1993) *The Classroom of 2015*, Briefings for the National Commission on Education. Oxford: Heinemann.

Worsham, T. (1988) 'From cultural literacy to cultural thoughtfulness', *Educational Leadership* (September), pp. 20–1.

Zelderman, H., Comber, G. and Malstrellis, N. (1992) 'The Touchstones Project: learning to think cooperatively', in Davidson, N. and Worsham, T. (eds) (1992) *Enhancing Thinking Through Cooperative Learning*. New York and London: Teachers' College Press.

Zinker, J. (1977) *Creative Processes in Gestalt Therapy*. New York: Vintage Books.

NAME INDEX

SUBJECT INDEX